'In an age of social isolation and spir[...]
testament to the growing landscape of[...]
justice leaders who are re-imagining o[...]
and clarity, the profiled leaders speak [...]
this emerging moment in our collective story. They are unbundling
ancient wisdom and practices and remixing them with contemporary
culture in ways that speak to a generation so often absent from
traditional congregations. In our work at Harvard Divinity School
and at On Being, we've had the pleasure of thinking about the future
of our human longing for connection and formation – and Huxley's
work is the perfect place to understand what that will look like.'

— *Casper ter Kuile, Ministry Innovation Fellow, Harvard Divinity School*

'If modernity's conceit is the presumption that we humans can
categorise, index, and stabilise nature in a final knowable way, then
today's troubling global upheavals (yes, climate change included)
are a stunning rebuke of that rather rude idea. Nature is not dumb,
mute, dead or merely instrumental to our fashions. Nature is
sacred – which, for me, means that nature does something perverse;
she *moves*. She strays away from the calculability of our algorithms
and asserts her ineffability. She will not be coaxed into closure. This
book is about how a young generation of humans are awakening
to the mystery of it all, re-threading old paths, alchemising new
values, and constructing hope in a time of hopelessness. How they
are rethinking identity, working with the sensuous in recalibrating
responsiveness in a time of crisis, struggling with orthodoxy, and
co-inventing new spaces of leadership. I am fortunately a member of
the generation (Y) this book highlights, born in a time of crumbling
walls and still young enough to witness the fascist threats to build new
ones. It falls on us, many of us suspicious of modernity's discipline,
to come to the edges and linger there – long enough to be approached
by the more-than-human our parents were taught to deny.

   To read this book is to leap from one immersive youthful narrative
of struggle, feeling and playful experimentation to another, in a
constellation of voices that shimmers with promise. It is to become

intimate with a movement bigger than its name or categorisation; it is to be part of a lingering. One gets the sense that "God", whatever you might think of the nature of creation or the divine, is back at the loom, weaving new embroideries of possibility that will reconfigure the fabric of our lives. I cannot help but believe that this story of amazing grace is true.'

— *Bayo Akomolafe, PhD, author of* These Wilds Beyond Our Fences: Letters to My Daughter on Humanity's Search for Home

'*Generation Y, Spirituality and Social Change* by Justine Huxley looks to not only bridge the gap between generations, giving insight on how younger generations gather, think, and most importantly, believe. It acts both to support youth to get further organised and act against the threats to humanity, as well as being a call to older generations to listen. Generation Y are, yes, the future but also very much the present, and our existing structures and hierarchies, be they national, religious, political, etc. may not be fit for purpose for this value-driven generation and the Digital Age. Standing on shoulders of previous generations, Generation Y can teach us how to live and thrive in a diverse world, which is increasingly more complex. We had best learn quickly, for all our sake.'

— *Stephen Shashoua, Founder of Plan C: Culture and Cohesion and Co-Director at The Caravanserai Collective*

'Mark Fisher once claimed that "capitalism seamlessly occupies the horizon of the thinkable". But in this collection, we hear the power of a radical imagination that challenges old delimitations of the possible. The voices gathered here express an emerging vision, both spiritual and political. They articulate efforts to honour the inseparability of transforming the self and the world. They reject the reductive, atomising and disempowering narratives of recent decades. And, amidst the twilight of neoliberalism, they illuminate new spaces for committed inquiry and courageous action.'

— *Guhyapati, Founder of Eco-Dharma Centre, Spain*

'The inspiring stories of the millennial generation collected in this book present us with new dreams, visions and ventures that can help to heal the wounds of our world. These multiple voices from different cultures and faiths belong to actively engaged trailblazers who are exploring spiritualities that are daring and challenging. Theirs are voices of protest, innovation and experiment with transformative spiritualities of action and peace-making, speaking to all ages, not only the young. Here we can meet people full of great hope and deep love for the whole Earth community of life.

Their words are spoken from the heart; their activities grounded in the power of collaboration, in their visions of what they can give to nurture a more collaborative and peaceful world. In Teilhard de Chardin's words they are "following the road of fire" that will set the world alight. May their examples inspire many others.'

— *Ursula King, Professor Emerita of Theology and Religious Studies, University of Bristol, author of* The Search for Spirituality: Our Global Quest for Meaning and Fulfilment

'A rising generation of spiritual leaders are unbundling the jobs of traditional religion and remixing them in juicy new ways, sparking our imagination and at the same time refreshing our understanding of the ancient human longing for meaning. Justine Huxley brings open-hearted, generous curiosity to these remarkable conversations with people who reflect the leading edge of all that wants to emerge. Anyone who fears that our collective spiritual future is at risk will take heart from these deeply soulful, creative leaders!'

— *Revd. Dr Sue Phillips, Director of Strategy, Impact Lab, On Being Project*

'Based on her rich experience working with activists from different faiths, Justine Huxley profiles a remarkable group of young people attuned to the needs of the soul as well as the planet and adept at creating new forms of leadership and collaboration. This is a book of hope and inspiration which challenges us all to change ourselves and help change the world.'

— *Rabbi Jonathan Wittenberg, New North London Synagogue and Senior Rabbi of Masorti Judaism*

'We need this book. The voices of young people do not get the attention they deserve, it really is time to do things differently. For faith institutions it's time to start enjoying, and looking after, both old and new wine, as Jesus told us all those years ago. God isn't some stale bearded old bloke, but is within us all constantly pressing the renew and refresh button, jamming down a Divine Finger and waiting for us to pick up the task! Are we brave enough to embrace those who are telling us that the old ways don't work and that traditional structures are as off-putting when they are focused on themselves? Generation Y is waking us up to the fact that traditional religion is clunky. Now read on.'

— Julian Bond, Methodist and Interfaith Activist

GENERATION Y, SPIRITUALITY AND SOCIAL CHANGE

of related interest

Fortress Britain
Ethical Approaches to Immigration
Policy for a Post-Brexit Britain
Edited by Ben Ryan
ISBN 978 1 78592 309 8
eISBN 978 1 78450 620 9

The Moral Heart of Public Service
Edited by Claire Foster-Gilbert
Foreword by the Dean of Westminster
Afterword by Stephen Lamport
ISBN 978 1 78592 255 8
eISBN 978 1 78450 540 0

Towards Better Disagreement
Religion and Atheism in Dialogue
Paul Hedges
ISBN 978 1 78592 057 8
eISBN 978 1 78450 316 1

God-Curious
Exploring Eternal Questions
Stephen Cherry
ISBN 978 1 78592 199 5
eISBN 978 1 78450 473 1

GENERATION **Y**, SPIRITUALITY AND SOCIAL CHANGE

EDITED BY
JUSTINE AFRA HUXLEY

Forewords by
His Holiness, the 17th Karmapa, **Ogyen Trinley Dorje**
and The Most Reverend and Right Honourable
Dr John Sentamu, Archbishop of York

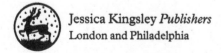

Jessica Kingsley *Publishers*
London and Philadelphia

First published in 2019
by Jessica Kingsley Publishers
73 Collier Street
London N1 9BE, UK
and
400 Market Street, Suite 400
Philadelphia, PA 19106, USA

www.jkp.com

Library of Congress Cataloging in Publication Data
A CIP catalog record for this book is available from the Library of Congress

British Library Cataloguing in Publication Data
A CIP catalogue record for this book is available from the British Library

ISBN 978 1 78592 305 0
eISBN 978 1 78450 616 2

Printed and bound in Great Britain

This book is dedicated to the next generation, to the courageous pioneers, young trailblazers, heartful leaders and spiritual activists who show us what it means to walk the talk in times of great change.

CONTENTS

FOREWORD

HIS HOLINESS, THE 17TH KARMAPA, OGYEN TRINLEY DORJE

His Holiness the 17th Gyalwang Karmapa, Ogyen Trinley Dorje, is the head of the 900-year-old Karma Kagyu Lineage and guide to millions of Buddhists around the world. Currently 33 years old, the Karmapa resides in his temporary home at Gyuto Monastery in India after making a dramatic escape from Tibet in the year 2000. Travelling the world, the Karmapa teaches traditional Tibetan Buddhist dharma while also speaking on themes such as environmental conservation, feminism and digitisation of the dharma.

We live in a time when human actions are the cause of great suffering, a source for unimaginable destructive power, and the reason for irreversible environmental damage. And yet, we also live in a time of hope. A time when young people are engaged more than ever in cultivating their minds, their compassionate hearts and mindful action.

As the Karmapa, I am visited by hundreds of young people every year – some who travel from various parts of the world to Dharmasala, India where I live, and some who live a few kilometres away. While they may come from very different backgrounds and have very different life experiences, I often see how much they have in common as individuals. What is revealed in our private conversations is their deep desire to be of benefit to the world, to make a positive difference for their communities and loved ones, and to rise above whatever circumstance or difficulties they face. This combination of pure motivation, altruism and courage is the essence of Buddha nature – the seed of enlightenment – to me.

As a young person who is getting older every day, I want to say to other young people: the moment is now. Find your purpose, hone your compassion, plan your strategy, because your actions can end suffering, can bring peace and non-violence to this hurting world and restore environmental balance to the planet.

At the same time, young people have a great deal of pressure on them. We feel pressured to do well in school, to get a good job, to be successful in life, and the pressure bears on us from all sides since the world today is so much smaller. Things seem to progress at an unimaginable rate, and we find ourselves unable to rest mentally in our effort to keep up. We are more aware than previous generations of how difficult things are around the world and how hard it is to achieve social change. It is not easy to be young today.

And yet. Only humans can solve the problems made by humans. So, what I say to you is this: just as you will take on this work, so will I, and together we will find the wisdom and courage needed to do so.

FOREWORD

THE MOST REVEREND AND RIGHT HONOURABLE DR JOHN SENTAMU, ARCHBISHOP OF YORK

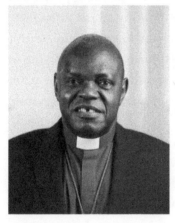

Credit: The Office of the Archbishop of York

John Tucker Mugabi Sentamu was born into Uganda's Buffalo clan in 1949, the sixth of 13 children. He studied and practised law before coming to the UK to complete a PhD in theology at Cambridge and then training for ordination. After serving as a priest in a number of London churches, he was appointed Bishop of Stepney in 1996, Bishop of Birmingham in 2002 and Archbishop of York in 2005. One of the Archbishop's key areas of focus is supporting and encouraging young people in England.

The Archbishop has often spoken about the leadership potential of young people and is proactive in encouraging them to take an active role in society and decision-making processes, as well as in the running of the Church. In 2009 the Archbishop launched his own Youth Trust, helping young leaders across the North of England in the work they are doing within local communities. Throughout his life in England the Archbishop has been outspoken on issues of gun and knife crime, gangs and the damaging effect of celebrity culture on self-esteem.

This collection of stories provides an inspirational insight into the tenacity and determination of young people to make a difference. What they need more than anything else is people to believe in them, to walk alongside them and to give them responsibility to be leaders in their homes, schools, in their local and global community.

One of my most frequent and most favourite duties as an Archbishop is talking to students. Young people ask questions that really matter on subjects that they care deeply about – from consumerism and social media, to religious or political extremist views, the refugee crisis, or care for the environment. In reading the chapters in this book, you will sense just how eager and ready they are to stand up for what they believe in, to express freely who they are and to be welcoming of others. This is so energising and life-giving!

I like to describe it this way: God calls young people to act as his representatives in their friendship groups, communities, colleges and universities, workplaces and on the street – yes, young people can be God's hands and feet in those places, making all the difference. This is a challenge, but it is one for which God longs to equip us with everything we need. Young people are exploring every day trying to find out what they are *called to be*, not what others around them are saying they should be or what the world around them is suggesting that they ought to be.

In my experience, and as we find in their interviews and stories here, young people love diversity in a way that no other generation before has done. They explore difference in a way that seeks to build relationships and to celebrate what they see around them. They don't let other worldviews take over without forming their own view first – seeking to be good neighbours, exposing the limitations and definitions that separate groups from each other, and encouraging a deep listening to understand others. We are called to love God with all of our being and to love our neighbour as ourselves – young people have this ability to love God radically and to show this radical transforming love to others.

It is this radical love and passion for life that enables them to overcome overwhelming odds. They have an insatiable appetite to live extraordinary lives. When we get older, our dreams for who we are and our zest for life may become dulled; but young people, they dream big and aim high. They have a passion for life – they have dreams and ambitions. Their faith makes the impossible possible, and living their spirituality and their deepest values means that nothing is beyond the reach of God's transforming love.

ACKNOWLEDGEMENTS

I treasure the moments in life where I get to pause, to share a pot of coffee with a fellow wayfarer and dive into a long conversation about spirituality and how it is lived in these times of transition. So firstly, a massive thank-you to all of the contributors – for your generosity in sharing your stories and your passion, for your honesty and also your patience. I enjoyed every interview immensely and learned a great deal from you all. I hope this book will in some way support your work and your journey, making visible the contribution you are making, and also helping others to find you and their own place within this emerging movement.

Particular thanks go to Adam Bucko whose book *Occupy Spirituality: A Radical Vision for a New Generation* was a foundational influence for me, and to Amrita Bhohi whose arrival at St Ethelburga's Centre for Reconciliation and Peace helped to shape the direction of our work. Appreciation also for the work of Harvard Divinity School, to Casper ter Kuile, Angie Thurston and Rev. Sue Phillips, whose work is such a great contribution in this field.

Deep gratitude also to Llewellyn Vaughan-Lee and Emmanuel Vaughan-Lee for their guidance, commitment to the spiritual development of the next generation and interest in St Ethelburga's work with young adults.

I had a fantastic team of interview transcribers, without whom I would have surely drowned. So thank you Qaisra Khan for your awesome and painstaking commitment, to Hina Khalid and Hirra Khan Adeogun. I was lucky to have you! Thank you to those who introduced me to contributors – to Sir Tony Baldry and Rev. Sue Phillips among others. I'm also indebted to Clare Martin for her astute editing skills, invaluable feedback and for helping me get the final manuscript into shape when my motivation was flagging.

A big shout out to Hawkwood College and to the Francis W Reckitt Arts Trust for funding an artist's residency in the summer before publication. The time out, space and beautiful environment were a truly wonderful gift that played an important part in bringing it all together.

St Ethelburga's also owes a debt of gratitude to the Kalliopeia Foundation, the Methodist Church, Shinnyo-en, Full Circle Foundation, the Kitchen Trust, Bhai Sahibji Mohinder Singh of Guru Nanak Nishkam Sewak Jatha and others for funding different strands of St Ethelburga's young leadership work and enabling us to meet so many amazing millennials.

Thank you to Andrew for his endless patience and for putting up with so many truncated working weekends. I couldn't have done it without you.

And last, but by no means least, a deep bow to Natalie Watson and Simeon Hance at Jessica Kingsley Publishers. Natalie, thank you so much for your interest in St Ethelburga's work and for reaching out. It was a real joy getting to know you and working alongside you. Thank you for recognising the spark of the future in the lives of these young people and for being willing to give them a platform for their important message. And thank you to Simeon for seeing the book through its final stages. I hope this collection will encourage other publishers also to recognise the wealth of wisdom emerging through this generation and help to strengthen their voice.

INTRODUCTION

'When young people with vision come together, a spark ignites, a spark that is to do with people coming together for the sake of the whole, for the sake of life, for the sake of the survival of the planet.'

LLEWELLYN VAUGHAN-LEE

It has been a tremendous privilege to get to know so many dedicated young leaders through the work of St Ethelburga's Centre for Reconciliation and Peace over the last five years. I've been both inspired and challenged by millennial thinking. Through their eyes, I've seen a piece of the future. What has moved me more than anything else has been witnessing the very particular spark that some young people carry within them – a regenerative quality Llewellyn Vaughan-Lee described to me as 'life re-creating itself'. This book is a testament to that spark – to those who are putting spiritual values into action, reuniting the sacred and the mundane, and evolving new ways of doing and being.

My intention was to provide a platform for young adults to speak about how spirituality is being lived in their lives, and to mirror back the themes and threads that, woven together, make visible the emergence of a much bigger movement or evolutionary impulse.

The conversations also reflect some of the immense challenges the younger generation face, growing into adulthood in a world that is splintering apart. Faith is being redefined by the urgent need to respond to global crises. I hope younger readers will feel strengthened by hearing how others are meeting that challenge, and I hope elders will see more clearly what is needed and how they can participate.

The contributors

In this book you'll meet young people from different backgrounds who are practising their spirituality in many different ways – within traditions, between them, outside them, and all three at the same time.

They are a mix of accomplished leaders who are already making a difference and regular young people (if such a thing exists) who are responding in their own ways to the call of the times. Some have been chosen for what they bring to the table as activists and change-makers, some for their honesty about their struggles or the failings of their elders, and some for the reflections they offer on new emerging identities – how they see themselves and their relationship with the whole.

Their social contributions are in many different fields – ecology, peace, social justice, humanitarian aid, activism, community organising, black and LGBTQ rights, the arts, media, education, spiritual teaching and new forms of ministry. Many are crossing over disciplines and boundaries, forging flexible portfolio careers and mixing social entrepreneurship with regular employment, volunteering, travel or retreat.

The contributors are arranged in seven themed sections, but each could easily have sat in multiple sections. For that reason, each chapter has markers to reflect which additional motifs show up, either in their words, or in their wider lives and work.

This collection is not intended to be a thorough representative survey, rather a snapshot of the trends we see in the spiritual lives of young adults associated with St Ethelburga's work or connected to it via a network of global relationships.

Intergenerational solidarity

This is not a book purely about millennials.[1] It includes Xennials, born on the cusp of Generations X and Y, such as Adam Bucko and Dekila Chungyalpa (who themselves act as committed mentors to younger people and recognise their critical role). It also includes spiritual elders with messages of support and intergenerational solidarity.

The new ways of thinking and acting Generation Y are bringing have the potential to make a vital contribution to change. However, it is their elders who have the resources and power. As Parker J. Palmer puts it in Chapter 19, if 'the generations can dance together', much more will be accomplished than if hostility and frustration develop on both sides. Our future is looking decidedly fragile, and we simply can't afford to take the risk of that fissure – which most definitely exists – widening. There is a need for deep listening, particularly on the part of elders – a need to recognise that something has gone wrong on our watch and we are all involved. Something is required of us as a result. And there is much we can do.

The key messages in this book
This is evolution!

Generation Y are showing us the future. The way they are engaging with spirituality reflects an exciting evolution in the way we relate to the sacred. As the author and new economic thinker Charles Eisenstein said at a talk he gave at St Ethelburga's in 2014, 'Young people are standing much more firmly in the story of interbeing.' They are making a worldview of interconnectedness into a lived reality. They are dissolving the binary opposition of heaven and earth, spirit and matter. They are bringing the sacred and the everyday together. Through the words of these young people, I hope all of us – no matter what age – will catch a glimpse of our evolving

---

1   Millennials (or Generation Y) are those born between 1981 and 1996, Generation X between 1965 and 1980.

relationship with the Divine, our aspirations, rituals and practices, reinventing themselves for a new era.

Faith is inseparable from action

The core message of the contributors is that no one can afford to see religion or spirituality as a private, individual matter any more. Whatever our age, we are all called to integrate our deepest values with practical action. For many young adults, it is not so much that they are 'putting faith into action' but rather that social action rooted in this new worldview is a spiritual path in itself. Action based in connectedness is the journey. Reading their words is an opportunity to ask ourselves, ever more deeply, 'What's mine to do?'

Bringing the inner and the outer together

Young people are experimenting with many ways of making the link between their outer and inner worlds. For some it's about knowing we cannot go beyond extractive economics unless we change our relationship with ourselves and how we define work and play. For some it's to do with recognising that our physical Earth and our bodies have a sacred, inner dimension. Others are recognising the need for disciplined work on the shadow so activism is not simply a projection of one's inner victim and persecutor or other psychological dynamics. Some are experiencing how spiritual practice can help us transform the ego patterns of selfishness and greed that keep us stuck in the problem. Or for many it's in the simple knowledge that we cannot sustain commitment to a path of action unless it is balanced with regular quiet time and a striving for inner depth. Our spirituality is needed to resource us for the long haul, and operating from a shallow place inside ourselves will just replicate the same patterns.

The stories of activism in this book are tightly woven together with a commitment to inner life, and to congruence between what is within and without. This is an exciting metamorphosis in how we approach spirituality, religion and social change-making.

Protecting what is sacred

Alongside the emergence of new ways, we are also in danger of losing much that is precious. We need open minds to taste the new. We also need rigorous discernment to separate genuine spirituality, which takes us beyond ourselves, from the dangerous distortions of spiritual materialism. Whatever our age, we need a passionate commitment to keeping real depth alive and selfless service fully in focus – no matter what its container or tradition or lack thereof. We need to nurture those flames wherever we find them, lest they be drowned out by the ubiquitous distractions that risk hollowing out our inner lives.

As one contributor (Jesse Israel, Chapter 1) described very eloquently, the stress, anxiety and scatteredness of modern life make us blocked, and then it's hard to discriminate our path through life. Spiritual practices are essential to, as he put it, 'create a clear channel between the gut, the heart and the brain'. Protecting our relationship with space, solitude and silence is important lest something essential to living a life of meaning is eroded whilst we are caught up in the ever-increasing onslaught of everyday busyness.

Earth calling

While many remain in denial, young people are facing up to the obvious: that nothing is more important than our relationship with Earth. If any of us are to survive the environmental holocaust looming on our collective horizon and establish a more sustainable way of life in the longer term, that surely has to be our biggest priority. Although regularly battling with grief, burnout, hopelessness and the magnitude of the task ahead, young people are much more likely than their elders to care about what we so reductively call 'the environment'. Many are also turning to nature as their primary source of connection with a sense of the sacred. Their spiritual nourishment comes from nature and they are putting themselves on the line for the sake of the natural world.

One contributor told me privately that he thought this movement represented the younger generation laying down the foundations for a new global Earth-based spirituality that is informed by the teachings of different faiths but not limited to them. It is perhaps too soon to know if that is true, but in many ways this may be what is needed. As Vandana Shiva says, to turn this around 'we have to create the cultural mechanisms to protect life. And that cultural mechanism is the category of the sacred.'[2] If humanity can return once again to seeing nature as worthy of reverence, then perhaps the destruction can end.

Earth can unite us

Earth also has the potential to unite us. On St Ethelburga's spiritual ecology retreats we see how passion for protecting Earth can be a powerful reconciling force across faiths and cultures. Faith institutions that make the commitment to properly link their core teachings with actively protecting the environment also seem to have an aliveness about them that speaks to the younger generation. That commitment also makes it easier to collaborate across traditions, since the urgency of the task overrides other differences. Many people without faith identities are also experiencing meaning and nourishment from nature, and science is confirming its power to change our inner state. If we rethink our language, re-establishing the centrality of our relationship with the natural world can also build bridges across the religious, spiritual and secular worlds.

---

2   In an online book trailer for *Spiritual Ecology: The Cry of the Earth* (2013) edited by Llewellyn Vaughan-Lee at www.youtube.com/watch?v=xIo2qzG2L6o

Institutions: Can we listen deeply?

Much has been written about the rise of the 'spiritual but not religious' identity among millennials. Many religious institutions are in panic, desperately trying to engage the missing generation and avoid their own demise. But what if Generations Y and Z are not coming back? Are faith leaders brave enough to examine this sea-change objectively? Where are we protecting traditions and practices that keep us in a living relationship with the Divine, and where are we simply propping up dying infrastructure that no longer serves a true purpose? Can faith institutions work side by side across traditions, relinquish the goal of conversion and find new ways to deploy their resources, land, leadership, messaging and prayers for the common good? What are religious institutions really called to offer in this new landscape? We need imagination, courage and a willingness to go beyond self-interested attachments in asking these questions.

Ministry is being reinvented

Religious and spiritual ministry – the act of supporting and caring for individual and societal spiritual needs in all their complexity – is being reinvented outside hierarchies and institutions in a million different forms. The young people in this collection are almost all influencing, teaching and supporting each other spiritually, and their stories could be read as stories about ministry. Currently there is little infrastructure to support young people in that role. How can youth-led and wider communities better recognise the importance of these roles? How can we evolve new ways of supporting and training each other, and holding ourselves accountable? Perhaps our first step is to recognise there is something radically different going on.

Cutting-edge thinkers at Harvard Divinity School see millennials as separating out the different elements historically found in a faith tradition, and recombining them in a bespoke manner, according to individual need.[3] They identify seven contemporary roles

---

3   *Care of Souls*, Casper ter Kuile, Angie Thurston and Rev. Sue Phillips (Harvard Divinity School, 2018).

via which the younger generation are fulfilling the functions spiritual ministry. These roles include: Gatherer (who constella communities of meaning), Seer (who helps us approach the sacred), Maker (who uses imagination and art to offer new rituals and cultural expressions of spirit), Healer (who helps us move through pain and break cycles of violence), Venturer (who invests resources in new expressions of human flourishing), Steward (who creates new infrastructure for spiritual life) and Elder (who connects us to lineage and tradition).

Many of the young people in this book are Gatherers, using their leadership to bring people together and create spaces for spiritual nourishment (e.g. Jesse Israel and Ruth Moir). Others are Makers, using the arts or reinventing rituals for a contemporary age (such as Abbas Zahedi or Samson Hart). Our Seers are committed to honouring the sacred in how we live, work and organise – such as through spiritual ecology or sacred activism (Amrita Bhohi, Adam Bucko) – and our Healers give us new tools for personal and societal reconciliation (Camille Barton, Orion Stephanie Johnstone).

Ceremony and ritual

Young people have a hunger for ritual and ceremony. Traditional religious rituals are no longer authentic for many people (of all ages), hence the rapid expansion in the availability of trained celebrants for non-religious or interfaith marriages and funerals. Millennials are inventing their own ceremonies – to mark transitions, build community and access the dimension of the sacred. For many young people in the spiritual but not religious space and beyond it, co-creating ritual and ceremony is rapidly becoming a key spiritual practice.

The rise of the feminine

Within many millennial-led communities, the participation and leadership of women is coming to the fore. At St Ethelburga's Centre, in groups where there is a faith or social change focus, young women frequently outnumber young men. Their more relational nature and instinctive understanding of holism is having a big impact on leadership styles. One young man in our networks described the role of women movingly:

> My path so far has taken me on many journeys through inner worlds and outer. The resounding song is one of a return, a return to what is true, to what is real, a return to ourselves. I have seen this within myself and most of all I have seen this in my sisters – strong women, paving the way, sowing seeds of growth, through song and sound, through ritual and ceremony, celebrating life and what is true. This to me is the start of what is to come.

Let's celebrate this and welcome it!

Language

In these chapters, you will rarely see the word 'God'. As the younger generation dismantle hierarchies and binaries of all kinds, many aspects of our religious language start to feel clunky or problematic. When it comes to describing the world through the lens of connection rather than separation, our spiritual vocabulary is definitely lagging behind our perception of reality. There are inspiring new wordsmiths in the activist world making delicious experiments (such as Paul Kingsnorth, David Abram, Drew Dellinger), and we can learn a lot from non-dualistic indigenous languages such as Lakota, but it is clear we are in an in-between place where we have not yet evolved a language that can describe our experience very reliably or one that can reflect and embed the new worldview in our thinking and writing.

I was acutely aware of this in interviewing the contributors to this collection. Some of my questions began to feel out of date, and there was the danger that filtering responses through my Generation X consciousness could easily kill the more subtle nuances of the new.

Language is tremendously important. It has the power to unite or divide, to liberate or oppress, to include or exclude. Personally, I feel a wild joy in the opening up of language and am energised by all the experimentation, but, working in a peace centre, I'm also aware of the necessity for immense sensitivity. We cannot assume the words we use make sense to others, and the potential to alienate is very real. Our communities will be stronger if we build in tools and approaches that make space for diversity in our language, that resist too much definition, that adopt multiple options and maintain a dialogue and sharing about the words we each resonate with.

The role of faith in resilience

The young people I interviewed seemed more outspoken and realistic than many of their elders about the future we may be facing. Though some struggle with regular bouts of hopelessness, overall they share tremendous determination and moral courage. I was often left wondering how well we are preparing ourselves for the social, ecological and economic upheavals of the next 50 years. We will need great resilience – and our spirituality and our resilience are closely connected. Religious and spiritual leaders who are proactively preparing their communities are in the minority. Surely leaders of all kinds need to be fearless in facing what lies ahead? We need inspiration to make meaning from the mess. We need stories and myths, teachings, practices and prayers powerful enough to sustain us through these times.

We also need to be reminded of the spiritual opportunities hiding within the crisis – the potential for great need to elicit great tenacity, sharper discipline and more sincere selflessness. In our individual lives, times of crisis are also times of growth and inner change. Chaplains, ministers and wise friends who walk beside us can help us make conscious what life is teaching us in those times.

In this global transition, there is space for much stronger narratives to emerge from our leaders.

Part of something bigger

All the young adults in this collection share a sense of being in service to something beyond themselves – their life is a fragment of a much bigger story of change. This is a profoundly important understanding. Being part of something bigger than the individual self gives infinite meaning and plugs us into a source of limitless nourishment. It gives solid ground to stand on in a landscape of shifting sands and uncertainty. Identified with ourselves, in times such as this, we might easily drown in despair, loneliness or superficiality. To be identified with a planetary or cosmic Whole makes possible the impossible. It gives energy and courage, turns us into spiritual warriors and adventurers, enables us to 'walk through the valley of the shadow of death'[4] and hold fast in the face of turmoil.

Through the words of these young people, may we all be called to live the ways of love in the world, as the world, not just in our private prayers and worship, but also in making whatever contribution we can to global change. May we know ourselves to belong, to be deeply connected with each other and with Earth in ways we are only just beginning to understand. May we see how desperately every one of us is needed. May we taste what we can achieve – together – when we recognise the greater reality of which we are a part.

---

4   Psalm 23.

PART 1

NATURAL LEADERSHIP

The world is in dire need of leadership with transformative power to free us from the global gridlock we are trapped in. We need leaders prepared to build the foundations for a society where the sovereignty of economic growth is replaced with a vision of equality, justice, sustainability and compassion.

How are young adults rising to that challenge? How does their leadership differ from their elders'? Is this leadership found within faith communities or outside them?

Those we meet through St Ethelburga's are often leaders of micro-communities – they come together with like-minded peers, dream, innovate, set up new spaces, projects and social enterprises, and network with others doing the same, creating connections that reach into a wider global movement. Their leadership is often characterised by an ability to rip up old templates, experiment, bypass limiting structures, and scale up rapidly. We have seen many times how action begets action – the willingness to jump in and try something out has a galvanising effect on others. Young people's dynamic energy, coupled with the power of social media, creates a powerful multiplier effect.

Authenticity, transparency and vulnerability are big themes. Leaders from Generation Y do not present themselves as infallible. Nor do they separate out their private and public selves. They line them up in integrity, bringing their whole selves into every endeavour. They often look more readily to each other for mentoring than to their elders, not wanting to replicate the tired models of previous generations that ultimately haven't worked. They are pulling things apart and putting them together in new ways.

In this collection, only four contributors have a position of religious authority within an established community (and three of these four are at the older end of the spectrum). The rest are developing and testing their spiritual wisdom within a purely *applied* setting, and sharing it with others as they go. We know that young people are far less likely to be affiliated to a faith institution, and that a calling to teaching or ministry demands maturity. But as Bruna reminds us in Chapter 9, 'faith without works is dead'.[1] Young people are drawn to live their beliefs through action.

It is clear that spiritual leadership is changing. For young people whose own spiritual journey is bound up with social change-making rather than religious institutions, they naturally seek spiritual guidance from within that sphere. They are hungry for spiritually sophisticated mentorship, but are seeking it in new places. As their inner and outer experience deepens, they also offer it to others within that space. Through this lens, spiritual leadership is beginning to look very different!

All the young people in this book are leaders. They are all initiating projects, inspiring others and driving change – on a large or small scale. There are of course many ways to lead – directive or facilitative, visible or invisible, masculine or feminine – and those different kinds show up in their diversity throughout this book. The leaders in this first part are of the 'just do it' variety. They share an ability to sense what is possible, gather others around them, and turn ideas into reality. Fuelled by faith, they get their hands dirty and they make stuff happen!

---

1   James 2:14–26.

Chapter 1

JESSE ISRAEL

LEADERSHIP AND VULNERABILITY

Credit: Kelly Marshall

'Bringing people together, using our collective voice to do good, has real power.'

Jesse Israel is 33 years old and was raised a Reform Jew in Los Angeles, California. Whilst studying film at New York University in 2005, Jesse co-founded a record label with his dorm mates and signed an up and coming college band called MGMT. Cantora Records became a successful business operating from a Manhattan office, which Jesse ran with his business partners. He also started the Cyclones, a bike club that grew into more than a thousand riders and raised money for bike-share programmes in Africa. Nine years later, sensing that a life chapter was over, Jesse walked away from it all. After taking some time out to travel, Jesse set up Medi Club, a community of young New Yorkers who meet to share meditation, connect with each other, and talk about life challenges. The Big Quiet later emerged from these gatherings, meeting the same needs for quiet and connection but on a bigger scale, held in venues such as Madison Square Garden and attracting thousands of people.

Growing up in the Jewish tradition, Jesse has always valued its emphasis on gathering, family and celebration. But like Camille (Chapter 20) and Emmanuel (Chapter 6) he is also influenced by the self-development movement, and by parents involved in Eastern spiritual traditions. After moving to New York aged 18, the business of going to synagogue no longer hit the spot for Jesse, and his experience of non-institutionalised spirituality through meditation and self-help began to take precedence.

Jesse craves meaningful community, honest spaces where personal challenges can be shared, space for silence and inner nourishment, and creative ways to generate social good. He instinctively unbundles the offerings of religious community, takes the elements he most needs, and reinvents them in true Gen Y style. The combination of uninhibited leadership, clever use of social media and a keen sense of the zeitgeist mean Jesse's projects rarely stay small – they grow exponentially, tapping into the needs of a generation.

Much has been written about millennials and loneliness. Connected globally online, they find intimacy and meaningful community harder to come by. Jesse is outspoken about this predicament and the impact on mental health, bravely sharing his vulnerability and witnessing how that gives others much-needed permission to be real with each other. His gatherings hit 'the double whammy of what people are yearning for' – time out from all the over-stimulation; and a sense of belonging.

Jesse also articulates something vitally important that we should all be attending to – that the stress of modern life blocks our access to a certain inner depth, and makes it harder to navigate with wisdom and discernment. How many of us recognise this? For Jesse, meditation is his antidote, enabling him to keep 'head, heart and gut' connected. As Joanna Macy has said: 'If ever we needed spiritual practices and disciplines for staying alert and connected, it is now.'[1] But even meditation can be polluted by the culture around us. And what of those without the discipline or the opportunity to implement counter-strategies? Have we considered what the impact might be, for our young people but also for our society as a whole, after ten, twenty or fifty years?

---

1   'Spiritual Practices in Times of Crisis', 29 January 2018: www.dailygood.org/
     story/1822/spiritual-practices-for-times-of-crisis-joanna-macy

So does DIY meditation, outside the context of a tried and tested tradition, deliver the same potential for spiritual transformation? And are mass meditations a passing phenomenon or are they emerging 'new wine skins' destined to be a part of the spiritual landscape of the future? What do you think?

Motifs in this chapter:

- Natural leadership

- New spaces

JH: I'd love to hear some of your story, Jesse.
Jesse: I've been drawn to bringing people together since I was young. In 8th grade we were on a school retreat in the woods for a weekend. The boys' cabin was separate from the girls' cabin. I created a secret mission with the boys – all 80 of us – to sneak into the girls' cabin and surprise them late at night. The teachers were infuriated. When we got back to the cabin, they said if we hear a single sound or if we see a single flashlight, whoever is responsible is going to have to sleep with the teachers. So I went around with this little microphone and recorded all the students saying, 'Can you believe the teachers? They're suppressing us! They're not allowing us to express what we care about. They're keeping us from our girl students!' I used interviewing them to rally everyone, and told them, at the count of three, we're going to scream at the top of our lungs and flash our flashlights. We just went nuts. The teachers couldn't calm us down because we were all sharing in this experience of chaos. I loved this sense of shared accomplishment through breaking the rules and the camaraderie and bonding between us. Even the students who never really talked to each other were all connected.

Later, I found other ways to explore that. I started a record label with some friends when I was 20. We signed a band called MGMT, and when they took off, it really put us on the map. We were young, just graduated college, and we had this really fun ride. I loved it when we threw concerts and brought people together. Especially when I watched thousands of people singing the lyrics together, all instantly connected through music and celebration. Those were very special moments for me.

I also started a cheeseburger club. My ten best friends and I would get together every other week and eat a cheeseburger. It was permission to talk about real stuff in our lives. We'd talk about careers, dating and challenges. It was a really cool space and the first time I had a sense of community in New York.

When our burger club split up, I wanted to find other ways to have that sense of connection and support in a fun environment. So I started a bike club called the Cyclones, where a group of us went on a bike ride to a secret destination in Brooklyn. By the end of the summer, there were hundreds of us, exploring unknown parts of the city and having a unique way to get to

> "I started to see how hungry people of my age were to connect in a new way."

know one another. And after about a year of doing the Cyclones, I found that people were falling in love, getting engaged, starting businesses, forming friendships. That's when I really started to see how hungry people of my age were to connect in a new way.

I loved being in that leadership role. I loved organising those rides, talking to the group. Later we introduced a social impact element. I'd spent some time in an orphanage in Tanzania and saw many students were walking up to 20 miles daily to get to school. So we had this whole other purpose to why we would ride. It wasn't just to connect and explore the city, it was also to support this greater cause – to raise money for our bike-share programmes in Tanzania. Six hundred members of our bike club shared the campaign on their Facebook pages. We raised three times the amount of money we needed and set up bike-shares in five different schools. That's when I saw that bringing people together and using our collective voice to do good has real power.

JH: And how did you get into meditation?

Jesse: My dad had introduced me to spirituality and meditation as a child, but in my twenties I took it up more seriously and got into self-development. Being in the music industry while still so young was really intense. I started experiencing panic attacks and debilitating anxiety. So it started off as a tool for coping with stress, but what it's evolved into for me, seven years later, meditating regularly twice a day, is a tool for me to connect with my deeper truth.

When I left the music industry I didn't know what I wanted to do next. I just knew when I was in a position of community organising or community leadership – I felt fulfilled. So I started experimenting with different projects. I noticed that a lot of friends were interested in meditation, people I knew from the music industry, the tech industry, the places I was going out at night. So I decided to organise a group meditation at my buddy's apartment in Soho, where we would share 20 minutes of quiet and then have a conversation about what was going on in our lives.

So we had our first one. It felt really vulnerable to share quiet with people that I was always so busy and creative with, or partying with. And afterwards, I shared about my fear and uncertainty around my next career steps and how freaked out I was that I was about to turn 30 and didn't know what I wanted to do with my life. It was pretty nerve-racking, but it instantly created permission for other people to do the same. It was the first time I realised the power of leading with vulnerability. It creates a deeper sense of belonging, which comes from realising that we're all going through the same stuff.

> "I realised the power of leading with vulnerability. It creates a deeper sense of belonging, which comes from realising that we're all going through the same stuff."

After four or five months of doing these once-a-month gatherings called Medi Club, many people were expressing their appreciation for a space in New York City to connect with themselves and to connect with each other in this very honest way. It was very accessible, you know, we weren't wearing all white or doing things that people might think of as meditationy or self-helpy.

So we created 'The Big Quiet' as a way to share these values on a larger scale. And The Big Quiet was born at Summer Stage, Central Park, which is one of the great venues in New York. Hundreds of people came, meditated, listened to someone share about challenges, talked in small groups, and there was performance. It was a really cool moment.

The Big Quiet has happened over 15 times, at landmarks like Madison Square Garden, or the top of the new World Trade Center with a thousand people, plus 300,000 people tuned in online. It's very participatory and people really feel connected to something greater and charged up. We've also built a 'circles' programme, which is really inspired by small church groups where members of my community host their own weekly gatherings in different neighbourhoods around New York. On a Tuesday night there'd be five different circles meeting in different neighbourhoods. It was really cool to see the community self-organising, spreading these values. That was our most intimate offering, whereas The Big Quiet was a much larger version of the same ethos and values.

JH: So why do you think those gatherings are so popular? What need is it that they're really serving?
Jesse: The first is that people feel very isolated in the city. Technology feels like a way to connect, but it's so ephemeral and so surface, it's making people feel more alone. People are craving human connection. They're stressed out. So to have space for quiet and to calm down through meditation, and then to have space to connect, it hits this double whammy of what people are yearning for. It combats some of the loneliness that a lot of people experience in the city and creates that sense of validation – that we're not going through these challenges alone.

JH: Do you think mass meditation is going to be a feature of the future?

Jesse: I think meditation is going to continue to really explode. The more science supports the benefits of it, as more technologies and communities come together to support the practice – through apps, drop-in studios, social clubs like Medi Club – I think meditation is going to come into our lives in a meaningful way. When you're meditating with thousands of people, the experience you have in that quiet is really powerful. I do think we're creating an experience that may be the modern version of church or religion – without the dogma or 'this is the way it needs to be'.

> "We're creating an experience that may be the modern version of church or religion – without the dogma or 'this is the way it needs to be'."

JH: So where do you think you're going with it personally? Do you think this is your life's work?

Jesse: In the three years I've been doing this, I've experienced two extremes. There are moments of 'I can't believe I'm doing my life's work, this feels so energising, this is why I'm on this earth to be in service through using my gifts in this way', and I also feel the doubt, the uncertainty, the confusion. Most of my friends are financially successful and my situation is different. I often find this work daunting, disheartening and tough. And it sits on some of my greatest fears around being judged, public speaking and things I really feel challenged by.

JH: What's your advice to a young person who is trying to find their purpose?

Jesse: This I think is a very big topic and an important one. For me, it starts with finding a meditation practice that an individual can connect with. All the stress and anxiety that so many of us are experiencing in our daily lives makes us blocked. It becomes really hard to make sense of why we're here. What's so powerful about meditation is that it begins to create a clear channel between the gut, the heart and the brain. It's a really important tool as we start opening up to purpose and finding meaning in our lives. So that's my first suggestion – to find a meditation practice.

The second is to begin experimenting, to really look at what energises us most, what makes us feel most alive. And regardless of whether they make money or not, just be open to what can be born from that experience. I've seen a lot of people step into their purpose through experimenting in this way first. This is how my work was born. It was born from Medi Club as an experiment.

And the last thing that I'll say is find the spaces or the people where you can talk about challenge. Because an important part of connecting with deeper purpose has to do with communicating and expressing our blocks. There's something about talking about what's holding us back and what's freaking us out, that when we share it out loud, and when it's communicated and heard and received by others, it starts to melt. Through that process of release, we get more opening around what excites us and why we're here. So those are the three things that I suggest.

Chapter 2

JAMES ADAMS

A LIFE OF MEANING

'I have a **responsibility** to use my privilege to support those who are not so lucky.'

James is 24 years old and was born in Stoke-on-Trent to a family of Christians. Currently training as a doctor in Manchester, his real passion is social enterprise. A few weeks before leaving for university, James was diagnosed with a brain tumour. This brush with his own mortality led him to a moment of epiphany, a call to rethink everything, drop down into his faith, and reorient his life towards making a difference. Soon after, he founded his first charity, CATS (Cancer Awareness in Teenagers and Young People Society), after realising how poor awareness of common cancer symptoms was among young people. Later, he co-founded Pregnancy Twinning, whose purpose was to reduce maternal mortality rates in Malawi. His most recent start-up, Number 11, is a community centre in the heart of Stoke-on-Trent, providing holistic and relationship-based support to vulnerable groups such as the long-term unemployed or those struggling with addiction. James speaks regularly at conferences, events and churches around the UK. As reflected in his TEDx talk 'Kick-starting your dreams', he loves to support both individuals and groups, helping them craft their vision and turn ideas into reality.

James has the instinctive ability to make things happen. The digital age gives us the means to build a website in an afternoon, generate social media connections across the world, to manifest creative ideas in a way we've never been able to do in the past. With someone like James, that means an idea born from a conversation with a mate in a pub can become a functioning social enterprise remarkably fast!

I loved interviewing James. His personal story has real power. Commitment and drive just roll off him in waves. But he is also humble and accessible, his seeming ordinariness giving out the message that, whoever we are, we have the means to follow in his footsteps and live a life of impact. The apathy Generation Y is sometimes accused of stands no chance here!

Unlike those deserting institutions and heading down the spiritual but not religious route, for James, church is still at the heart of his faith. Like many Generation Y Christians, he wants to see Christ's teachings lived fully and completely in the world, fully engaged with the critical issues of the day. He rejects church that is about a big stone building, that is 'hypocritical' or 'pretends to be holier than thou', in favour of a dynamic, growing, relational church that walks its talk.

Another big theme here is experimentation. We are in an era of looming catastrophe. The old no longer works. As Einstein said, 'a new type of thinking is essential if mankind is to survive'.[1] Getting creative, being prepared to do things differently, ignore existing templates, get it wrong, learn from our mistakes and turn on a sixpence – this quality of agility is both essential and also very refreshing. Being less conditioned by the past and less attached to doing things a certain way is a vital ability that the younger generation bring to the global table.

---

[1]   'Atomic Education Urged by Einstein', *New York Times*, 25 May 1946, p.13.

At this juncture in human history, we are facing a similar moment to the one James experienced after his cancer diagnosis. A brush with our own collective mortality. And we have the same choice. To stay with our unconscious and self-centred lives, or to realise we can give everything we have to making a difference. And far from losing something precious, we find only meaning, belonging and self-respect.

Motifs in this chapter:

- Natural leadership

- Sacred activism

JH: So, James, I'd love to start with your faith story. What influences were around when you were growing up and how has your faith changed as you've grown older?

James: I was brought up in the Church. When I was maybe 16 I started going a little bit more, it started to become more my own faith rather than my parents'. I started preaching, did a lot of speaking and had a youth group. I loved the fellowship aspect of church, loved doing holiday clubs with kids and that sort of stuff. But in my day-to-day life, it wasn't having much impact. Then when I was around 18, being quite ill prompted me to think things through a little bit more. I realised if I'm going to do this, I don't want to be on the fence, I want to be committed, and live a life that lines up with the words of the Bible and its emphasis on social justice.

JH: The themes of persistence, passion, vision come up a lot in your public speaking. That's a million miles away from the 'culture of apathy' Gen Y is sometimes accused of. So I'm wondering what motivates you?

James: It's very much been a journey. I've always been keen on doing new things, I love starting things and had always wanted my own business. I remember when I was ill there's one memory that stays crystal clear in my head. It was the day I was told I might need quite a risky operation that could have left me blind or not able to walk. Straight after being told, I was in an MRI scanner for over two hours. Quite a long time to be stuck with your thoughts! All I remember is thinking: 'I'm not scared to die, I don't think that worries me, but what really scares me is that I've always been on the fence – I've never done anything significant in my life that hasn't just been for me. It's all been very selfish.'

> "All I remember is thinking, 'I'm not scared to die, but what really scares me is that I've always been on the fence – I've never done anything significant in my life that hasn't just been for me.'"

I'd been active in church, at least with the bits of church I liked, it was all very me-centric, I chose the bits that built me up and made me happy, but I'd never lived my life for others or making any impact. I remember having a realisation that I had been given pretty much everything you could need to make a good start in life. I'm a white, middle-class male who's been given a good education and a stable home that has always loved and supported me, giving me confidence. My parents taught me important attitudes and values, they always protected my health and made sure I ate well, they never smoked around me, made sure I did my homework, and so forth. All the ingredients I needed for a successful life had been given to me on a plate. Therefore I have a responsibility to use that to support those who haven't been given that same start. That was the moment it really started for me. I was planning on doing Physics at university, and starting up my own business. But I knew that was all focused on me and what I wanted, so I switched my focus and started studying medicine in Manchester, setting up charities instead.

JH: That sounds like a life-defining moment. Where does your faith fit in with that?
James: My faith that tells me my life is not about me. It's a story that's much bigger than my own. It's not focused on what I want or

what makes me comfortable or happy. I am part of something much greater. As a follower of Christ, I am asked first to love and honour God, and second to love and serve people. Those are the most discussed topics in the

> "If I fully believe in the words of the Bible, how can I ignore that call to action?"

Bible. Therefore that is my calling. That's my instruction. If I fully believe in Jesus, if I fully believe in the words of the Bible, how can I ignore that call to action?

JH: Many millennials in the West are moving away from organised religion. What are your thoughts about leadership in the Church? And the future of church?

James: When I started studying in Manchester, I found a new church. It's a small church, based around relationship and community. We eat an awful lot of food together – which is a bonus for me, I have to say. It's all about people and relationships, and so whenever we get too big, we just plant a new church. I'm part of a team there and I absolutely love it. I think disillusionment with the Church is not necessarily because church isn't the right thing, but because perhaps the way we've been doing it is wrong. In the early Church, they would meet in each other's houses and break bread and eat together, they were very much people and community orientated. My church is full of young people. It has grown exponentially over the last five years. I think what's happened is we've become confused. When it's about the experience of church, the big building, the service on a Sunday – the religious aspects, etc. – it becomes inward focusing and people lose interest. I think that's where 'organised religion' gets its negative label from. Whereas at the heart of what church is, it's about community and about relationship, not ornaments, flashy shows or solemn candlelit services.

When churches support each other, eat together, are really stuck into loving their local communities – when church gets the heart behind what it does right, when it's genuine and it's not hypocritical, when it doesn't pretend to be 'holier than thou' or just about the superficial 'feel better factor' – that is the future of church. Community and relationships.

JH: So tell me how the social enterprise started. You've created three successful start-ups alongside doing your medical training...
James: I've always been quite an enterprising type, I love getting new things going. CATS (Cancer Awareness in Teenagers and Young People Society) was to do with my own journey. Most people don't know very much about young people's cancers, and traditional methods of putting a leaflet into someone's hands just don't work as well any more. I thought there had to be a better way to engage young people with key health messages about common cancer signs and symptoms, and help promote positive behaviours. I met with a few friends in a pub, had a chat about it and it was born from there. It was the same with Pregnancy Twinning (an enterprise that helps expectant mothers in countries, such as Malawi, with a high maternal mortality rate). I was having a conversation with a friend – she's definitely the brains behind it, I'm just the dumb face. And I was like, 'Oh, why don't we do something about this?' So we went for it. Nine months later (yes I appreciate the irony) we had a charity up and running and started making a real difference to the lives of so many women!

The Number 11 Centre for Holistic Crisis Support is a big focus at the minute. It's about getting to the heart of social change, looking at long-term solutions, not just a plaster over the problem. It's about relationship and a sustainable, holistic focus. It's pointless putting someone into a job club if you've not worked to resolve crisis in their life and develop their self-esteem, and helped them reach a stable place with their mental health. That's why a holistic approach is so important. That's the role of a doctor, not just the physical but also the psychological, spiritual and emotional – all working together. We've just got £400,000 of funding, and to be honest, it's been a hard year. I've written an awful lot of funding bids, which is not what

I enjoy, but I do it because I know the bigger story is more important. There are times when I really don't want to do it. I'm hitting one brick wall, then another brick wall. But what pushes me through is that sense of calling, knowing I'm not just here for me, instead I have responsibility to use what I've been given to make a difference.

JH: What advice would you give to young people who want to make a difference, but perhaps get overwhelmed with all the need in the world or all the different choices they need to navigate through to find their purpose?

James: Big question! First and foremost, it's find what you *can* do rather than what you can't do. Find what you *can* do and give it a crack. You will only become a good leader and be successful at making an impact if you give it a go and make mistakes. You hear about the projects I've created that worked. You haven't heard about the mistakes I've made or the ones that flopped. I think the problem nowadays is that we don't give young people enough of a chance to have a go and get it wrong. That's where you do all the learning.

> "We don't give young people enough of a chance to have a go and get it wrong. That's where you do all the learning."

In the last five years, my major journey has been learning how to work alongside and manage and inspire people. That's the key skill that young people miss out on nowadays in the world of social media. My generation is losing those people skills. Having people around me who are good mentors and can challenge my thinking is also so important.

But also, if you are someone of faith, go deeper in your faith to the point where you don't just believe it in your head but you believe it in your heart – then you will want to act, and apathy will no longer be an issue because you've really comprehended why you are doing it.

Chapter 3

SUN KAUR

BALANCING PRAYER AND ACTION

'Have faith and just do it.'

Sun Kaur is a human rights and social welfare activist. She is 33 years old and was born in Birmingham, UK into a traditional Sikh family. Now, she works for the international humanitarian charity UNITED SIKHS, a UN-affiliated NGO involved in social development, emergency disaster relief, and advocacy. UNITED SIKHS aims to eradicate poverty by empowering the less fortunate, especially disadvantaged minority communities. Over the years, Sun has taken the lead in many challenging projects around the world. Known to her friends as 'Kaur on a Mission', Sun is one of very few Sikh female activists in the UK to appear on mainstream radio debates and television productions. She was the winner of the Unsung Heroes Award in 2017.

I first met Sun through my work at St Ethelburga's. She was part of a group of young adults from different faith backgrounds who volunteered with us at a refugee camp in mainland Greece as part of a leadership programme in sacred activism. Sun's group were working with the camp residents painting murals in communal living areas, building raised beds for a tiny community garden, sorting an intimidating mountain of donated clothes in a vast warehouse, and helping teach in the very basic camp school. Sun caught my attention with her boundless energy, apparently indestructible optimism (or *chardi kala* spirit) and ability to seize the moment, whether it was organising groups of children, or instigating spontaneous football games with the young men. Sun has a quality of fearless leadership that is badly needed amid our current plethora of intersecting crises. What's needed is the ability, as she says often, to just do it, and the resilience to keep doing it even when the complexity or the impossibility of it all seem overwhelming.

At the refugee camp, Sun, along with three fellow Sikhs in her group, showed us in countless ways the essence of the Sikh way of life: prayer, devotion and selfless service. It was humbling to see that lived out through the attitude they each brought to volunteering in a very harsh and challenging environment. Sun's faith is clearly a tremendous source of strength and courage, but also keeps her alert to the risks inherent in this kind of humanitarian work – the potential for arrogance, developing a messiah complex or becoming an adrenaline junkie. Real spiritual service breaks down the dichotomy between helper and helped. We are in this together. All of us know, in the midst of such unpredictability, that in the future we might be the ones in need. Prayer balanced with service is the map that guides Sun through the current insanity of our world.

Motifs in this chapter:

- Natural leadership
- Sacred activism

JH: So, Sun, tell me a little about your faith and how it informs your life and your activism.

Sun: The principles of the Sikh faith are my driving force. The religion is a monotheistic religion and one of the youngest major world religions; the word Sikh means learner. The Guru Granth Sahib ji, our Holy Book, which is also considered the eternal Guru and supreme spiritual authority of the Sikh religion, is where I seek my guidance. My faith teaches me to recognise the human race as one, live with compassion, truthful actions, stand up to tyranny and most importantly meditate on the Lord's name to

> "I see faith as my shield."

eradicate one's own ego. When working on challenging projects or whilst undertaking precarious aid relief, I fear no danger, as I always have a sensation of security and protection. I see my faith as my shield.

JH: So the human race being one family, what does that mean for you? How is that taught in your tradition?

Sun: The story of our ninth Guru, Guru Teg Bahadur, gave martyrdom; as a champion of human rights, Guru ji gave the supreme sacrifice for the protection of others, for people to be given their basic human rights and to freely practise his or her religion without interference. I feel this was a moment in history that has had a great impact on many.

A fundamental concept that has been instilled within Sikhs from generations is *seva* (selfless service); my parents have always taught me to give to others and put others before myself. In many of our aid missions our team spread the message of our first Guru, Guru Nanak Sahib ji, who started *langar* (the free community food kitchen at every Sikh temple), which is designed to uphold the principle of equality between all people regardless of their social status, age or gender. The aim of *langar* is to express the ethics of sharing and inclusiveness of all.

I recall going to Sunday class and our teacher telling us the significant story of Bhai Ghanaiya, a Sikh disciple whose mission was selfless service, and who, in the battle of Anandpur Sahib, served water to everyone on the battlefield, including the Mughal army's soldiers. This act generated criticism amongst his fellow Sikhs. When asked by the tenth master Guru Gobind Singh ji about his actions he replied, 'I was serving water to everyone, as I saw God in everyone.' This is a story that resonates with many young and old Sikhs as truly inspiring and is a great motivator when our team serves aid to disaster zones and poverty-stricken areas. To me being one big family means not to look at another's faith, gender or background but to see them as a vessel of God.

Recently I was driving back from work, and I was passing a school. A girl had been run over on the road as she was leaving school. People were sitting in their cars. I started coordinating cars and pedestrians to make space for the ambulance and ensuring the girl was breathing. Whilst doing this I felt the Sikh spirit within me. Our Gurus taught us that one Sikh can be the equivalent to 125,000. Therefore, impossible is nothing.

JH: 125,000?

Sun: Yes, this concept originated from the Battle of Chamkor,[1] where Guru Gobind Singh announced on the battlefield that one Sikh is equal to 125,000. This idea today allows Sikhs to continue to have a fearless mindset, instilling courage into our hearts. Sometimes on an aid mission you can be in the loneliest of places; I always have the *sava lakh*[2] spirit in my mind – that there are 125,000 within me. This allows me to walk without fear in a disaster zone; some will ask me, 'Are you alone?' I smile and respond, '*Sava lakh* spirit, just do it.'

---

1   The Battle of Chamkor was fought between the Khalsa led by Guru Gobind Singh and the Mughal forces led by Wazir Khan in 1704.

2   125,000 in Panjabi.

JH: Just do it. Maybe that should be your motto.

Sun: Yes! Nike should sponsor us.

JH: And how do you put those values into practice in your own life?

Sun: I would like to believe that I try my utmost to practise many Sikh values and one day be part of the *Khalsa*.[3] There is a line in our holy book, '*Hum nahi changey bura nahi koi*',[4] which translates to 'I am not good, and no one is bad'. I sometimes feel when serving humanity, we can develop a kind of arrogance; it is important to have a steady balance with prayer. It's like a bird, we have prayer as one wing and service as the other. If they are not balanced how, will you fly high? Sometimes when you are involved in a community *seva*,[5] you become deflated – tired and mentally drained. The thing that brings you back up is your *simran*[6] – your prayer. Mind, thought, action – sit and meditate. Yet, also take action to serve. You need both. Prayer gives you the strength to work in those hard places, it allows me to stay focused on this journey.

> "When serving humanity, we can develop a kind of arrogance; it is important to have a steady balance with prayer."

JH: That's beautiful. So how did you get involved with UNITED SIKHS and what it's about?

Sun: Sometimes you come to a crossroads in life, and you think, what do I do now? It was eight years ago I met my senior, Mejindarpal Kaur, from UNITED SIKHS, who was at our *Gurdwara*.[7] I remember literally running across the hall chasing her, saying I wanted to get involved! We started doing small community projects here in

---

3   *Khalsa* – a baptised or initiated Sikh who wears the five articles of faith.

4   Guru Granth Sahib ji, Ang 728.

5   Selfless service.

6   Meditating on God's name.

7   Place of worship.

the UK together. Four months later I am in Vancouver making a presentation on Sikh identity in front of a thousand people. And since that day it's been a huge rollercoaster ride. I've been from Canada to India to Africa, Europe and the United Nations in New York. Even to 10 Downing Street – having tea with David Cameron. It has been pretty full-on. I think God keeps testing my strength to see how far He can take me and I keep accepting his challenge. I've learnt so much and had so many experiences. I think I'm lucky to be able to serve in this way.

> "I've learnt so much and had so many experiences. I think I'm lucky to be able to serve in this way."

JH: What does UNITED SIKHS do?
Sun: UNITED SIKHS is involved in humanitarian aid across the world – from Haiti, after the tsunami, Africa, drought, Philippines, Nepal and recently in Bangladesh with the current Rohingya refugee crisis. We have over 20 missions across the globe, including education and empowerment and a human rights directorate fighting discrimination against Sikhs, which has had a real impact since 9/11. It's important to empower the next generation, to have that spirit, to have the strength to fight for what's right.

A project close to me is 'Rescue a Family'. There has been a surge of suicides in Panjab: farmers unable to pay off their debts, which leads them to commit suicide, and leaving families behind. It really hit me, as to how lucky we are! Whilst out in Panjab our team were giving out donations to farmers' widows in the Panjab. They receive £20 a month – what is £20? It's a lunch here in the UK. We finished the day and, getting into the car, a lady tapped me on the shoulder and gave me a hug. This is a moment I will never forget. It meant something to her – it gave her hope. When you're doing the work, you try and block all the emotion out because you just want to get it done. It's when you sit down and start talking that you realise how immensely hard it is for some people and what we are doing is making an impact in their lives.

JH: You said earlier on that your faith is like a shield for you. How do you feel about the future? And how do you bring your faith to bear on the future unfolding before us?

Sun: I could tell so many stories about how I've experienced that shield, in tough places and situations. No matter what faith you belong to, God is truly immortal, and the baton of faith will continue to warm people's hearts. When it comes to the future, I feel there is a gap bringing Generation Y on board to follow their faith, as nowadays there seems to be more scientific reasoning and lack of belief in God. I think social media can be a double-edged sword; we can become narcissistic, and hate and fear is beginning to breed between many communities. I think the Y generation is quite angry because of everything that is going on in the world. They have walked away from faith and we need to bring them back. *Sangat*[8] is crucial, the people you hang around with, the community motives we learn from one another. I think it's more important than ever to start learning about different religions and backgrounds so that we begin to understand each other.

JH: I agree! So how is it for you as a young adult facing a future that is full of so much uncertainty and challenge? With your whole life ahead of you. Do you have hope?

Sun: Yeah, I have hope. Sometimes it only takes one person to change the world – to inspire people to change. We have a duty on this planet to give back, even if only in a small way. It's important, there are people in the world less fortunate. We must start making change. Believing we can save the world. Superheroes! We're gonna do it. I don't know how yet, but we will.

JH: What do you think the role of your generation is in that change?

Sun: We're in a digital age. Before, to protest you had to go to a location with placards. Now it's a tweet on social media. Like Black

---

8   Congregation.

Lives Matter, that was a campaign that went viral and really made a difference. We need to take on board the opportunities for change and start using everything we can. Digital campaigns are great motivators; it starts moving a generation who struggle to maybe see how to contribute to make a better world.

JH: What is it you really care about when you look at the world around you?

Sun: I really enjoy bringing courage to people and uplifting their spirits, connecting with people from all walks of life. It's called the *chardi kala* spirit; it means positive spirit, a state of optimism and joy.

JH: What would be your message to young people at this point in time?

Sun: Don't ever think you can't do it. Because you can. My journey started literally coming back from a lunch break at the bank, sitting at my desk, thinking, what am I doing here? I went to my manager and said, I want to leave, I don't want to be here any more. I am not telling you to quit your jobs, but I think sometimes taking risks, going beyond our boundaries, is necessary. You should never fear because He has something planned for you. He truly does – I've witnessed it. For the next generation, I say go for it. There are so many opportunities out there – you must have faith. Have faith and just do it!

Chapter 4

RABBI LAURA JANNER-KLAUSNER

LEADERSHIP AND DISRUPTION

'Part of the identity of young people today is their willingness
to question and break down hierarchies.'

*Rabbi Laura Janner-Klausner serves as the Senior Rabbi to Reform Judaism. She grew
up in London before studying theology at the University of Cambridge and moving
to Israel in 1985. She returned to Britain in 1999 and was ordained at Leo Baeck
College, serving as Rabbi at Alyth Synagogue (North Western Reform Synagogue)
until 2011, when she became inaugural holder of her current position. As Senior
Rabbi, Janner-Klausner represents a progressive Jewish voice to British Jewry and the
wider public, speaking on affairs including Israel–Palestine, social justice, same-sex
marriage and interfaith relations. She is a regular broadcaster on the BBC, and the
Huffington Post declared her 'fast becoming the most high-profile Jewish leader in*

the country' and described her as 'wildly likeable, emphatic, intense, and outspoken'.[1]
She is currently writing a book on the theme of resilience.

Rabbi Laura Janner-Klausner writes:

Young people today have a totally different experience of life. It's not just different from the experience my generation had, it is beyond what we could have even imagined. Growing up today means being shaped by the most open and connected world that has ever existed. From an early age, they have an understanding of the world around them, not just influenced by what is happening on their doorstep, but by a knowledge of events from every country in the world. It is unsurprising when young adults today describe themselves as 'citizens of the world'. Revolutionary technological advances allow us all to get what we want and get it now, letting us engage with a diverse range of people and ideas.

"At a time where we are all able to access a multitude of ways to do things, where we are all able to take more control of our own lives, why should it be a surprise that young people today bring those expectations into the religious sphere?"

We shouldn't be surprised, then, that the radically different experience the new generation has been born into also shapes their connection with religion. At a time where we are all able to access a multitude of ways to do things, where we are all able to take more control of our own lives, why should it be a surprise that young people today bring those expectations into the religious sphere?

One of the most exciting and transformative aspects of Reform Judaism today has been the work of our youth movement, RSY (Reform Synagogue Youth). Run entirely for and by young people themselves, it has not only provided hundreds of participants with

---

1   www.huffingtonpost.co.uk/2014/10/29/beyond-belief-rabbi-laura-janner-klausner_n_6067064.html

their most engaging way to connect with Jewish identity, it is now shaping the future of Reform Judaism in Britain. Indicative of their generation, their leaders are unafraid to try new and unorthodox ways of doing prayer and Jewish learning, which are slowly filtering into adult communities across the country. Looking at them today is looking at Reform Judaism as a whole in perhaps five or ten years' time, and I can't wait for it!

It's not just a tired cliché to call our young people 'leaders of the future'. It's plain wrong. They are leaders of today. Part of the identity of young people today is their willingness to question and break down hierarchies, manifesting in religious life as wanting to take control of their own experiences. Rabbinic colleagues of mine have been worried about this challenge to their authority, that the young people are demanding what they want. I only wish even more of them would do the same. This disruption of norms is what makes our best communities as vibrant as they are. It is not a challenge to face, it is as valuable a resource as any.

> "It's not just a tired cliché to call our young people 'leaders of the future'. It's plain wrong. They are leaders of today."

I've not only seen young people shaping religious spaces, but creating them. Grassroots religious communities with a very young demographic compared to traditional congregations are creating their own experiences and breaking the mould. Other groups who realise the intrinsic connection between their religious identities and global challenges are doing their religious service not in prayer, but in action, creating projects together having a tremendous impact on the world around them and bringing religious ideals of justice and helping the needy to life.

That's enough from me, though. This book sets the example for what we need to see more of: young, religious leaders given the chance to share their experiences and what is important to them. The most important work people like me in positions of supposed authority can do is listen.

PART 2

EVOLVING TRADITIONS

Our world is changing rapidly, and our religious institutions are struggling to keep up. The disaffiliation of Generation Y from institutions is well documented, and tension around falling congregational numbers can be intense. Leaders are often skewered between the need to protect time-honoured traditions and the need to innovate to keep pace with the new.

Responses to this challenge vary. Creative leaders are turning laundromats into faith-based community hubs and setting up neighbourhood halaqas for un-mosqued Muslims to study and share together. Shabbat meals are appearing in the pop-up restaurant space, and new kinds of 'monasteries without walls' are available for those who want a deeper journey.[1] The chaplaincy movement has gone interfaith, and gained momentum taking faith to the people, rather than expecting people to come to the faith. Meanwhile, independent networked churches expand and utilise their freedom to experiment, and hip global megachurches like Hillsong continue

---

[1]   *Faithful*, Casper ter Kuile, Angie Thurston, Rev. Sue Phillips, Rev. Lisa Greenwood and Rev. Gil Rendle (Harvard Divinity School, 2018).

to thrive, drawing in a predominantly young congregation with powerful music and marketing.

There is a need both to revitalise what is offered to those who are religiously affiliated, and to think hard about what to offer those who aren't – which can bring up tensions between hierarchical and networked approaches to growing community. Institutions are by nature centralised, non-agile entities that cannot easily metamorphose into the flexible patterns the younger generation operate within.

Meanwhile, billions live in poverty because we build our lives on a model of economic growth that favours the few over the many, and our Earth is at a critical juncture because we have been treating Her as a commodity rather than an expression of the Divine.

The inability of organised religions truly to practise the values preached and to meet the needs of the moment – this was mentioned over and over again by the young people I interviewed. Can our religious leaders wake up? Can they begin making a more powerful contribution to transforming the mess we are in, offering a meaningful alternative to the consumerism that is destroying us – inspiring us to widen our circles of compassion, speaking out about injustice, honouring all creation as sacred, proclaiming the values of simplicity and sharing, generating a sense of urgency, speaking truth to power, and calling all of us – individually and collectively – to take responsibility for our way of life and to face the needs of the moment with radical moral courage? This must surely be the real motivation for reaching out and ministering to people everywhere, whatever their affiliation.

The structure of institutions limits rapid change, and yet that is where the resources, land, infrastructure, reach and influence lie that could be leveraged for the cause. Perhaps there needs to be a shift in both the perceived purpose as well as the *modus operandi* of our religions before that potential can be fully realised. If the emphasis shifted from how to sustain themselves as institutions to how to work side by side with other traditions to make a more radical and dynamic contribution to building a just and sustainable world, maybe numbers would no longer matter.

So whilst many young adults are powering change from outside religious institutions or from the fringes, what of those who are leading change from within? Where are our younger faith leaders adapting their traditions to meet the needs of the next generation? Are younger leaders changing the way institutions define their role in the wider secular landscape? In what way does their leadership differ from their elders? And what kind of support do they need?

In Part 2 we hear the perspectives and aspirations of a Christian, a Sufi and a Buddhist who are listening carefully to their own instincts as well as to the needs of their generation, and bringing ancient teachings and their own unique leadership style to bear on the challenges of the times.

Chapter 5

ADAM BUCKO

FOLLOW YOUR HEARTBREAK

'What's your gift? And are you offering it to the world in service of compassion and justice?'

Adam Bucko is a Christian contemplative, new monastic, activist and co-author of Occupy Spirituality: A Radical Vision for a New Generation. He grew up in Poland in a Catholic family during the totalitarian regime and spent his early years exploring the anarchist youth movement as a force for social and political change. His life-defining experience took place in India, where on his way to a Himalayan hermitage, he met a homeless child who lived on the streets of Delhi. This encounter led him to the Ashram of the Poor where he began working with the homeless. He co-founded The Reciprocity Foundation, an award-winning nonprofit dedicated to transforming the lives of New York City's homeless youth. Later he established HAB, an ecumenical and inter-spiritual 'new monastic' fellowship for young people which offers formation in radical spirituality and sacred activism. Adam collaborates with spiritual leaders across religious traditions and mentors young people, helping them discover a spiritual life for the 21st century and live in the service of compassion and justice. He is currently studying to become an Episcopal priest at Nashotah House, an Anglo-Catholic seminary in Wisconsin.

Adam has been a mentor on St Ethelburga's leadership programmes for young adults for a number of years and has been a huge inspiration. He is a powerful voice for his generation, articulating trends, stirring others to rise up, and offering much-needed spiritual direction to young people between or outside traditions. His own story encapsulates a central theme for the younger generation – that spirituality can no longer be lived in separation from the immense problems unfolding around us globally. When the young homeless girl Adam met in Delhi put her hand in his and walked with him, her vulnerability and need changed his world. She set off a series of experiences that would lead him to pursue a different experiment – that of marrying the intense desire for inner life with immersion in the world of activism and social justice. In *Occupy Spirituality* Adam says:

> Given today's crises the world over, we can no longer afford to hide our contemplatives in comfortable monasteries. We need to reunite contemplation and action. We need spiritual activists, and indeed, spiritual warriors on the streets and in all our professions and institutions.[1]

Adam is an important voice for the rapidly growing numbers of young people defining as spiritual but not religious. When discerning his vocation as a priest, he was encouraged to train in one of the most conservative Episcopalian institutions in the US (whether the purpose was to bring him into line or shake the institution up wasn't clear!). But from within his traditional enclave, Adam witnesses this monumental shift in our religious demography without the preconceptions that older leaders might have. He doesn't shy away

---

1   *Occupy Spirituality: A Radical Vision for a New Generation*, Adam Bucko and Matthew Fox (North Atlantic Books, 2013), p.xxii.

from full implications of this trend, but fully engages with it, asking the question, 'How do we know this change isn't the will of God?' He re-envisions ministry without conversion and asks what he as a priest can give those outside his own tradition that supports their spiritual journey regardless of their identity.

Motifs in this chapter:

- Evolving traditions

- Sacred activism

- New spaces

- Natural leadership

- Challenging orthodoxy

JH: Do you think the younger generation has a different way of being with religious identity?

Adam: I've got a story I think answers that question. Some years ago, we organised a gathering of young people and elders from different traditions and we spent a week together in upstate New York at a Buddhist monastery. At first, the elders were very focused on this idea of interfaith collaboration. They wanted to spend time on making sure we could speak to each other properly, that we could develop some kind of methodology for sharing, that we could basically feel at home and be okay with being in an interfaith setting. After a couple of days it became clear that it wasn't an issue for us younger people. Historically speaking, to get to this point, the older generation had to do a lot of work trying to ensure that our traditions can sit at one table without essentially wanting to beat each other up. But for the younger generation, everyone was like, 'Interfaith collaboration? That's so old!'

JH: Can we talk more about that?

Adam: I think the first thing that we see in young people is that their relationship with religious traditions is very different. They might identify as being part of a specific tradition, but they're not usually stuck in that tradition. Others might want to argue about whose God is the real God. For younger people, many of us, it's very clear we see God as present in all of the traditions. Our religious leaders and many media pundits might still be arguing whether Muslims and Christians worship the same God, but many young people have already moved beyond that. Not only do they believe that there is one underlying reality at the foundation of all major world religious but they are also convinced that different traditions and their unique approaches to God complement each other.

Since the 1960s we've seen a change because of the influx of teachings from the East. It's no longer a problem to be a Christian and then on the weekend, for example, go and do yoga. Young people might be rooted in one specific tradition, but at the same time they are okay with borrowing different practices from different traditions as long as those practices enrich their experience of God. They don't see a conflict there. We see examples of this even among 'religious profess-ionals'. It is not that uncommon

> "Young people might be rooted in one specific tradition, but at the same time they are okay with borrowing different practices from different traditions as long as those practices enrich their experience of God."

these days to find Christian monks or nuns who have been enriched by their Zen practice and who claim that without Buddhism they could not be a Christian. I personally know a Zen Master who is also a Catholic priest. The religious world is changing a great deal!

But it's also important to say, a lot of young people don't actually identify with a tradition any more. In *Occupy Spirituality* we quoted some research from Philip Clayton from Claremont School of Theology in the US who said that 75 per cent of Americans between the ages of 18 and 29 now consider themselves 'spiritual but not religious'. Again, many of our churches, synagogues and mosques are freaking out when they hear this, thinking that young people are no longer interested in the sacred. But to me it is clear that young people are not necessarily rejecting God, they simply feel that many religious organisations lost touch with reality and are too concerned with money, power, self-preservation, maintaining the status quo and 'having right beliefs'. As a result, they tend to view them (and often rightly so) as organisations that are spiritually bankrupt, that are no longer able to speak to and address some of the big questions of our time. And it takes deep insight and spiritual courage to see that. It is for this reason and many others that I don't think of the rise of 'spiritual but not religious' among our youth as a sign of spiritual decline but rather a new kind of spiritual awakening.

> "I don't think of the rise of 'spiritual but not religious' among our youth as a sign of spiritual decline but rather a new kind of spiritual awakening."

JH: Adam, you yourself are rooted very firmly in the Christian tradition. So do you believe spirituality can flower just as deeply if one is doing a mix of practices in that way?
Adam: Well, first of all, we have to acknowledge that when people hear about spiritual and not religious people, they often immediately think that these are people who are just shopping around and not really that committed. That they want to use many different tools to dig different holes and as a result they can't go deep. But when we look at some of the people who come from that group, we realise that actually many of them spend more time practising than regular churchgoers.

As one Hindu monastic once said to a Christian priest friend of mine, 'Well, it's possible to use many different tools to dig one hole. For most things we need to accomplish in our lives we actually use more than one tool.' So, maybe it is actually possible to use different practices to go deeper in your spiritual life too.

I think we have to be cautious about criticising this. It would be arrogant to assume all those people are just simply wrong. What if that whole movement is the Holy Spirit doing some kind of work? And a whole new generation is being called to the new way of pursuing God? Having said that, we should also be cautious in accepting this as a given and acknowledge that we need proper discernment on this.

When we look at our traditions, it's very clear that in order to go deep, we need some very specific things. We need theological frameworks that can help us see what spiritual maturity looks like and how it is lived in the context of hearing 'the cry of the poor' and 'the cry of the earth', we need practices that can allow us to 'gather the marginalised parts of our hearts' and turn them into prayers. We need mentors and spiritual guides who can help us listen to the presence of the Divine in us and in our world. We need communities where we can help each other to build courage to say yes to what is emerging in our hearts and begin to live in service of God's dream of compassion and justice in the world. And in this new space of spiritual but not religious, at least in my view, those frameworks and practices have not yet been developed.

This leads to my conviction that in this time our religious and spiritual traditions have two roles. In the past, they had one role, which was to basically make disciples and to initiate people into the experience of God in the way that the tradition offers. Perhaps in this day and age, they are also called to be present to this spiritual but not religious movement, to be helpful to them and to be in a deep relationship with them. Not to convince people to become Christians or Muslims, but to be present to them in a prayerful way, offering them the gifts of our traditions and helping them to discern their way forward, with an understanding that God might be doing something new in this new generation.

In order for this new movement to develop properly it needs to be developed in close partnership with our living spiritual traditions. Rory McEntee and I tried to begin to articulate what this new path for 'spiritual but not religious' could look like if done in partnership with the traditions in our book *The New Monasticism*. In it we offered our intellectual and spiritual reflections on what contemplative life could look like in the 21st century. We drew heavily on the work of Raimon Panikkar, St Teresa of Avila, Pierre Teilhard de Chardin,

Ewert Cousins, Fr Bede Griffiths, Thomas Merton, Brother Wayne Teasdale, St John of the Cross, and the Russian sophianic tradition. We also incorporated some popular modern-day academic, cultural and contemplative theorists, such as Ken Wilber and Fr Thomas Keating. They speak to young people about creating a more sacred and just world while providing them with sophisticated tools for psychological analysis and integrated action.

JH: Speaking of spiritual but not religious, how do you personally engage with this group in your own work?

Adam: Fr Thomas Keating, a Trappist monk and a key figure in Christianity who played a very important role in helping Christians rediscover the contemplative dimension of their faith, said that after 90 or so years on this planet he is convinced that the best way to teach spirituality is through telling each other our stories. Pir Zia Inayat Khan, a Sufi teacher, while commenting on spiritual mentorship, said: 'In my experience, spiritual mentorship means holding up a mirror in which a seeking soul is enabled to perceive the light of its own divinity.' Both of these ring true to me and reflect how I was mentored by my mentors. My mentors were less concerned about passing their tradition on to me and more concerned about sharing with me how God was present in their lives and how they responded to that presence. They shared their lives and their struggles with me. They shared their joys. They shared moments of losing and finding God. And in the process they helped me notice how God was present in my life. Their stories and ways of being present became that mirror that Pir Zia is talking about, in which I had begun to see my true life. The way in which they walked with God and lived their lives became a map for how to respond to the call that I felt in the depths of my heart. In the end, that is what enabled me to rediscover the Christian tradition that I was born into. To rediscover it not as an abstract system of beliefs, rules and regulations, but rather as this motherly presence with her arms around me loving me into who I was born to be.

I feel grateful for having such mentors in my life, and as a mentor to those who come to me I try to do the same. I try to be less about passing on the tradition and more about guiding people into the sense of God that is already there hidden in the depths of their hearts. My role as a mentor is to help them notice that presence, deepen their relationship with it, and begin to live as a response to its holy generosity and love. And each person does that differently: some experience a non-violent Jesus who calls them into the heart of the Church and others feel that their life needs to be about building this new emerging paradigm that we talked about.

God is much bigger and much more generous than we can imagine! Genuine spirituality should help us see that. As the great African American mystic Howard Thurman said:

> There is something in every one of you that waits and listens for the sound of the genuine in yourself. It is the only true guide you will ever have. And if you cannot hear it, you will all of your life spend your days on the ends of strings that somebody else pulls.[2]

May we all live listening to that sound of the genuine in us. May our traditions help us do that. And, may the 21st-century spirituality be about that. God knows our world needs it!

JH: Do you think our faith in institutions is still making sense to young people? What do you think the main challenges are for institutions in relation to younger people?
Adam: For me, the main question is: Are religious spaces capable of initiating us into an experience of God that can empower us to go into the world and become instruments of peace, justice and compassion? If we are honest about that, my sense is very few of our religious spaces are actually capable of doing so. And if our faith spaces and traditions can't do that, then what's the point?

---

2   Quoted by Kathryn McElveen in 'To Hear the Sound of the Genuine within Us', 2 January 2015: www.couragerenewal.org/sound-of-the-genuine-within-us

JH: Maybe the problems now are so much more challenging than in the past…? And we are failing to meet them?

Adam: I think that failing to meet the challenges is not the problem. The problem is, can we acknowledge that we are failing? Our religious institutions are failing to acknowledge that they are failing. As the 12-step programme[3] makes clear, confessing our powerlessness and helplessness is the first prerequisite for true prayer (and therefore healing action).

> "Are religious spaces capable of initiating us into an experience of God that can empower us to go into the world and become instruments of peace, justice and compassion?"

JH: And what would be your message to people who head some of those institutions about what is happening?

Adam: The message to the older religious leaders is that maybe it is time that you stopped caring so much about preserving your institutions and actually begin to listen to the new generation, not so that you can coerce them into your way of doing things, but rather begin to listen for the presence of God that might already be present there, in their actions, in their questions and in their lives. That would be a good starting point.

JH: How would you express your main message for a young person who is seeking?

Adam: My message to young people is always the same and it's very simple. What's your gift? And are you offering it to the world in service of compassion and justice? Religion and spirituality are the tools that take you into your gift, and being in your gift is your experience of God. Use that gift so you can be with those who suffer, and with the suffering of the Earth. That is your experience of God.

---

3   12-step programmes are fellowship groups for recovering alcoholics and addicts based on a set of guiding principles.

Chapter 6

EMMANUEL VAUGHAN-LEE

REAL-WORLD SOLUTIONS, NOT JUST SPIRITUAL IDEAS

'Young people today are drawn to engaged spirituality that has a practical outer dimension.'

Emmanuel is a teacher for a small group of committed Sufi[1] students in their twenties and thirties. A lineage holder in the Golden Sufi tradition,[2] Emmanuel's father, Llewellyn Vaughan-Lee, is also a Sufi teacher and author. Emmanuel grew up in London and his family home included the residence of Irina Tweedie, who brought this lineage from India to the West. He grew up surrounded by spiritual seekers and students who came

---

[1] Sufism is often described as the inner mystical path of Islam.

[2] Golden Sufi is the name given to a Western branch of the Naqshbandiyya Mujaddidiyya Sufi lineage.

to see Irina Tweedie and attended meditation groups in his house. When he was 11 his family moved to California. Emmanuel initially pursued a successful career as a jazz musician. He later became a documentary filmmaker and founded the Global Oneness Project, an online multimedia educational platform and library of stories exploring cultural, environmental and social issues. He directs the Spiritual Ecology Fellowship, supporting young leaders in the development of innovative projects that unite spiritual values with environmental and social change. He is also the Executive Editor of Emergence Magazine, a publication exploring the threads connecting ecology, culture and spirituality. The interview below took place at a retreat Emmanuel was leading in a country house in County Durham. Some of his students' questions are included in the dialogue.

In the 20th century there were a number of Sufi teachers who came from the East to the West to establish lineages and communities based on the inner principles and teachings, without the outer form of Islam and Shariah law. Emmanuel belongs to one of these traditions. Western Sufism emphasises disciplined meditation and other inner practices, the relationship with the teacher, and being of service in the world.

In his work with people in their twenties and thirties, Emmanuel is evolving his own distinct approach that is practical and fully engages with the multiple crises of the 21st century. He is outspoken about the realities of the future he and his students are likely to see, saying, 'It's not going to be easy. It's going to be tough!' Emmanuel models an embodied approach to spirituality, a groundedness that brings spirit and matter together consciously, that treats the physical world as sacred, and looks to the underlying causes of the devastating ecocide sweeping the planet. It also offers young people much-needed tools for developing spiritual resilience, for withstanding the corrosive effect of consumerism and the constant online distractions that can be so detrimental to inner life. When he draws a comparison between our time and the era of the Mongol invasions, Emmanuel invites us to orient towards a potentially desolate future as a spiritual challenge, as an opportunity to live in the moment, to be agile, and to practise non-attachment in a very immediate and practical way. My sense is rather than evoking fear, this combination of frankness and pragmatism is much needed by young people and generates trust. There is often a relief that comes with naming that which we fear to face.

Emmanuel's style of leadership reflects many generational changes – a different relationship with hierarchy, the ability to be vulnerable and authentic, and a marked feeling that he is fully with his students, among them, as one of them.

For me, there is much in Emmanuel's dialogue that speaks of the need for young people to prepare spiritually for what is to come. This is surely a vitally important function that many more faith leaders could be offering – the inner strength to be realistic about the future scenarios that may unfold, practices that grow our resilience, and principles that help us live through dark times and make sense of it all. Faith can be a tremendous source of courage, and we may need it!

Motifs in this chapter:

- Evolving traditions
- Natural leadership
- Protecting Earth
- New spaces
- Sacred activism

JH: So, Emmanuel, you grew up in a Sufi household surrounded by seekers and spiritual students of all ages, from 18 to 80. You saw two older generations in your Sufi community come and grow up in the tradition, and now you are just beginning your work as a teacher to a generation of students currently in their twenties and thirties. What do you see as different about spirituality for the younger generation?

Emmanuel: I think there was a real hunger for spirituality that came out of the generation in the 1960s and 70s. They were searching for meaning, and I think that was representative of the culture as a whole back then. But since the 80s that yearning somehow hasn't been as alive in the younger generations in the same way. But more recently, in the last ten years, and the last five years especially, I've seen many young people express a sincere interest in spiritual life. They are a generation growing up in world that is falling apart – environmentally, socially, economically, politically. The future they are inheriting is so uncertain – all the truths their parents believed in, and lived and worked for, have changed. Many young people are searching for meaning, for something that feels authentic, for community, for answers – how to deal with grief and pain and the challenge of the future we're facing.

The Naqshbandi Sufi's spiritual practice has always been integrated with outer life. 'Outwardly to be with people, inwardly to be with God' is one of our lineage's primary principles. Yes, outer life has changed, become more busy, more disconnected and harder to deal with, but the practice remains the same. It just requires a lot more attention to be able to do it than it did in the previous generation.

When I was young my own experience of spirituality was coloured by the unusual experience of growing up in a house that was in some ways a modern-day ashram, an ashram that just happened to be in North London. Sufi teacher Irina Tweedie lived in the ground floor apartment and opened her doors to people each afternoon to come and meditate. She was in her eighties then, and following in the Indian *satsang* tradition of her teacher, people would come and sit with her in the afternoons. In the summer when I came back from school, I would find many people appearing to just hang out in my back garden. So unlike many other spiritual communities at that time, there wasn't much outer engagement. No communal gardens, or work weekends building rock walls like they did at the Mt. Madonna yoga community where I lived for two years when I was in high school. People mostly meditated and had spiritual discussion, shared dreams and spoke about their lives. There was little talk of what was happening on the environmental or social level, or how this connected to our own spiritual path. Although there was always the teaching that we need outwardly to live what we are inwardly striving to achieve spiritually, it wasn't in response to outer collective challenges – the environmental crisis was still only on the horizon. Now the questions about the role of spiritual life and spiritual values in understanding and responding to the environmental and social crisis are the questions at the core of this younger generation. Those are the questions we need to ask.

JH: What do you think are the main challenges for young adults wanting to pursue a spiritual life at this time? And how are you adapting the teachings to meet those challenges?
Emmanuel: I don't know if the younger generation is as drawn to having people from an older generation impart teachings in the same way. They want to relate to people who are going through similar things to them, but perhaps this is always the case in each generational shift. But I do think that young people today are searching for real-world solutions, not just spiritual ideas, and this is a bit different from the previous generation. While there are traditions of engaged spirituality – the engaged Buddhism that Thich Nhat Hanh, Joanna Macy and others practise – many traditions have focused on individual self-development, and the teaching that the outer world is a world of illusion. I think many younger people today are more drawn to engaged spirituality that has a practical outer dimension. Their parents' generation's spiritual traditions and teachings had tremendous value and wisdom but didn't focus on applying those teachings to address outer challenges in the same way the younger generation is asking for. And the question young people are asking is: 'How are we going to deal with what's happening with the world now?' I think that's a piece of it.

How am I adapting the teachings? In some ways the teachings will always remain the same, and in some ways it's like a blank piece of paper. In our tradition it is said that the form can change and respond to the needs and the time and the place and the people. It can adapt. There's so much uncertainty about what's going to be happening in the future. It would feel very naive to think I can use everything that worked in the past. Things are changing so fast. There are big questions before us in these uncertain times – how will we be able to function spiritually in a world ruled by materialism and greed that has mostly forgotten the sacred? And on a very practical level the issues of where am I going to get my food, my water, my shelter and energy are ones we will be facing in the next 50 years. What's it going to be like watching one empire crumble while we wait for the new world we want to see emerge? We don't know how long this will take.

In some ways we have to create something together, because it requires new ingredients. Ours is not the only tradition that is saying this. The Dalai Lama said you can't expect a spiritual tradition from one place and one time to work in a different place, in a different time, with a different set of challenges. It has to adapt, it has to change. But the most important thing is the essence, the inner essence. That must remain alive. If you're a mystic, you're always living on the edge. You never know what's going to happen. You live in a state of uncertainty. You accept that God is a mystery you want to journey towards, that you are leaving the security of your ego, leaving the security of your identity behind, letting go of that. You're saying, I want to give all of that up in search of something. And I don't even know what that something is. However people describe it to you, it won't be that because it is a mystery. So if you go back to the core, the essence of what mysticism is, it can provide you with a way to handle the uncertainty of the times. Mysticism teaches you to not be attached to the past, to not be attached to the future, just to live day by day by day by day.

My Father and I like reading books on Genghis Khan. Genghis Khan was a really interesting individual, especially his relationship to religion and spirituality – he accepted all religions even as he was guided by his shaman. So much happened as a result of the incredible destruction he brought across Asia. There is a Sufi story about some students who came to their teacher and shouted, 'The Mongols are coming! The Mongols are coming! We have to run!' And the teacher said, 'I've been teaching you to be ducks, now swim!' That really makes sense to me because today in some ways the Mongols *are* coming, just disguised. There is destruction coming all around us. So let's swim! Let's be a duck! Let's actually learn how to respond to the challenges we are facing. Not just to the *idea* of detachment, the willingness to go from here to here in a heartbeat. Let's actually use the opportunity, the challenge it presents us with to live from this place and swim!

The challenges of the world today really do present us with opportunities to deepen and strengthen our practice. Because if I don't focus, really focus on my practices, I could get thrown to the Mongols! There's so much uncertainty. It's not going to be easy. It's going to be tough. Then the other thing is, what can we give? How can we contribute? If you are really committed to being in a state of spiritual awareness, remembrance, that alone is a contribution. If you're in a state of remembering the sacred, that actually helps keep the sacred alive.

So much has been destroyed in the past hundred years that used to hold the sacred. In Tibet alone, there were six thousand monasteries that were destroyed by the Chinese in 12 years. So few of the monasteries that were once there remain. That's one place in the world that used to hold spiritual truth and wisdom. Were they just praying and chanting? No, they were also holding a sense of the sacred for the whole world. Many of the world's indigenous traditions and communities also did that – and so many have now been destroyed or displaced. And the spiritual traditions that have spread far and wide in the last 50 years have too often been commercialised, and many are about creating a happy life or just making you feel better. All those things, you put them together and it's like a certain light in the world is going out.

We're just a small group of people, but maybe by remembering God, we can make a contribution inwardly. That's a given, it's something we all have to do. But then what do we do outwardly? That varies from individual to individual. But we have to have environmental and social responsibility in how we live our lives.

We need to live simply. We need to treat the Earth with reverence. We need to integrate the sacred into our daily life and actions.

Student: That leads me to a question I have about freedom. I struggle with that a lot. It's hard to make a decision about what you want to do with your life. In the past you did what your father did. But these days it's not like that. It paralyses me somehow that I have so many choices. There are so many things I could do that are meaningful, I end up not doing any of them. Is it important what I do?

Emmanuel: I think it is totally important, I think it matters a great deal. And yes, the multiple options can be paralysing. You know there is a phrase people say, 'Follow your bliss, follow your dreams', which in our individualistic and celebrity-driven culture tends to glamorise certain professions over others. But you can also find meaning doing things people view as mundane. Is it mundane to be a nurse? I don't think so. If you are called to be of service as a nurse, you can do incredible work. You can do incredible things when you cook food for people and nourish them, when you're a carpenter and build houses for people. Sometimes you don't have a choice – circumstances mean you have to make a living doing something that does not appear to fulfil you at a soul level. But you can use this as an opportunity. To become more mature, be kinder, more patient, more compassionate. It can be the sandpaper that rubs away at your ego. But if you do pursue a spiritual life you learn to connect to your higher self a little bit, to have a certain intuition. You start to be a little bit more guided in your decisions that can help you find something that feels more authentic to your real nature. Maybe it's not what your mum and dad wanted you to do, it may not be very glamorous, maybe you're not going to make a lot of money, maybe it's not what you studied in school – but you feel drawn there. It has a spark in it, it feels right. Maybe you feel drawn to working in service to the Earth and the tremendous ecological needs at this time. There are many different contributions we can make.

JH: This theme of bringing spiritual values into action is an important strand in your work. You've already made changes in the tradition by bringing in a more embodied focus. Can you say more about that?

Emmanuel: There is always the danger of mystical or spiritual practice making you ungrounded. Traditionally in some Sufi lineages mystics were often crazy dervishes, like the *sanyasi* in India, only owning one blanket, travelling from town to town, half naked. Seriously! In the older generations I saw growing up around me, there were a lot of people who were a bit ungrounded and perhaps a bit too immersed in the inner dimension of spiritual life. This never really appealed to me. It was also a luxury that was more possible in the past – the luxury of being able to fully immerse oneself in spiritual life – but it doesn't work in the same way any more. The world is so much denser, and I don't think you can escape the world in the same way you could before. We live in a world that is so disconnected, noisy, filled with *stuff* everywhere, virtual and physical. There are so many challenges outwardly and inwardly. So you can't access a certain inner dimension as easily as you could before – because you're hit by all these dense thought forms that throw you off balance. I think we have to be as firmly rooted as possible. The practice of walking with the *dhikr*[3] is about physical embodiment. The *dhikr* is a spiritual practice that we have had for hundreds of years – using each and every breath to remember God. I teach walking with the *dhikr* because it is important to embody this physically in your relationship to the Earth – it both helps ground you and also is a prayer for the Earth.

Physical exercise helps one become more embodied, more connected. People who work with their hands have to be more embodied. If you work with the Earth, you become more embodied. These things can help. But it's also something that can be embodied through many of the simple things we do in everyday life, we just need to put our attention there. That's what we have been trying to do with some of our spiritual ecology work. Bring spiritual teachings

---

3   A mantra, Divine word or phrase repeated on the breath.

and values into relationship to the Earth through simple practices, practices that can be embodied and are easily accessible.

In some ways it was a luxury to be able fully to devote oneself to an inner spiritual practice. But we don't have that luxury any more. We need to be outwardly and inwardly engaged in our spiritual practice, and this requires a certain attention it didn't before. We also need practical skills. Learn how to cook, learn how to grow your own food, learn the basic things we need to do just to meet our basic human needs. I'm not talking about starting your own fish farms, although that isn't that hard to do either these days! And each of these simple things we can learn is an opportunity to bring our spiritual practice into everyday life.

JH: That brings me into another question. There is a simplicity and directness about you that's really compelling...
Emmanuel: That's a nice polite way of saying it! You want me to explain why?

JH: My question was really whether that is just who you are as a person, or whether you've chosen to be that way because you see a need for it in these times?
Emmanuel: How honest do you want me to be?

JH: Completely honest!
Emmanuel: Well...part of it was growing up and seeing a lot of people misunderstand the simple essence at the core of spiritual life. People always think it's something different than it is. They love to talk endlessly about themselves and their own spiritual journey. That's not to say there weren't really sincere spiritual seekers around when I was growing up – there were. But I grew up around so much of it, and witnessed so much being misunderstood. Imagine you're a young boy and every day a hundred people come to your house,[4]

---

4   Spiritual seekers who came to be with Emmanuel's father Llewellyn Vaughan-Lee and Irina Tweedie.

all sorts of people, all wanting to learn about spiritual life, or experience spiritual life. People asking questions, wanting answers to their life problems. When you grow up with so much talk, after a while you just start to hear a lot of noise. I think I just got tired of that. So partly, it's a reaction to that experience and wanting to cut through that noise.

But also I just think it's in my nature to be direct. And it's funny because in Sufism there is a tradition of never being direct, of teaching through hints. You talk to the walls so the door will listen. Or you drop hints. But I'm not sure that really works in Western cultures, not the way it does in the East where there was more understanding of subtlety and a cultural context for spiritual life. And you can't be subtle with Americans at all! So from a practical perspective, that part does not work. So that is something I consciously don't do very often.

JH: Also in your work with the Global Oneness Project, you use very simple, direct language. You don't use spiritual language. You make it very ordinary, very real.

Emmanuel: The goal of that work is to make certain stories and ideas accessible to a mainstream audience. Using rarified or spiritual language can create a barrier to connecting to those stories or ideas. As a storyteller, I'm interested in reaching as many people as possible. Language is a big part of making those stories accessible. But also I think an authentic spiritual experience transcends language. If you're hung up on language, that's a limitation. In storytelling you try to show, not tell.

JH: You're also talking about the need to bring ordinary life and spiritual life closer together. Of course, that has always been present in Sufism in some ways. But in your work and teachings you seem to be demonstrating a new way to do that. Can you talk about that?

Emmanuel: I grew up in a household where ordinary life *was* spiritual life. It was ingrained in me, that there was no difference.

Just watching my parents, there was no difference between their meditation practice and cleaning and taking out the trash, dealing with people and their problems, it was just all one. But I think historically spirituality for a long time was in places where it was less integrated with everyday normal life. It was in monasteries and nunneries, away from the world. But now it has come to the world. But even for traditions like ours that was always integrated into everyday life – as you said, Sufis aren't monks or nuns – the times have changed so much in the last hundred years that how it worked in the past no longer applies in the same way. The world is so busy, noisy, complicated, fast-paced and out of control that the only way to stay sane in my opinion is to integrate spiritual life into every aspect of our lives – inwardly and outwardly.

> "The world is so busy, noisy, complicated, fast-paced and out of control that the only way to stay sane is to integrate spiritual life into every aspect of our lives."

I don't know if I am demonstrating a new way to bring ordinary life and spiritual life together, I'm just emphasising the need to find simple and practical ways to bring these worlds together. It's all very simple, but requires a great deal of attention to integrate in our modern world of distractions.

JH: Earlier on you talked about the need for new ingredients, and for creating something new together. The younger generation have many ways of co-creating, of coming together in non-hierarchical spaces and creating together. But you are part of a lineage that has a certain hierarchy. Can you say how you relate to hierarchy?

Emmanuel: That's a really great question. The very traditional formal teacher–disciple relationship has always been present in Sufism. It was an intimate relationship between teacher and disciple, held within a chain of energy and transmission. That can only really happen on an individual level. The nature of a teacher–disciple relationship is in some ways hierarchical, but it doesn't have to be a negative hierarchical relationship. We've seen hierarchy misused and abused, but it isn't about that. When I think about what it means to be a Sufi teacher in a hierarchical context, it means you take responsibility for the wellbeing of that person's spiritual destiny, for their journey. That's the way I was trained. You never take it lightly. You commit yourself fully to responding to everybody's needs – be they spiritual or not. It isn't just that you sit in a chair and impart wisdom. Not at all. It's that you're there for somebody as they go through all the inner and outer challenges of life, its ups and downs – when their partner leaves them, or their child dies, or their business fails, or they lose everything in a fire, or they have a psychological breakdown, you have to be there for them. Not to hold their hand or be a shoulder to cry on, but to help support them as is best needed on their spiritual journey, which includes their human needs as well. And you also share in their joys, like the birth of a child, and all the moments of wonder that are sprinkled along the journey.

I will be here to guide you from this place to that place – not because I'm better than you, not because I have power over you – but because I love you. That's very different from the kind of hierarchy that I see misusing power and creating so many problems in the world. That's when people say I know better than anyone else here so I'm going to decide. The teacher doesn't gain something from their role – it doesn't work like that – you put yourself in a complete state of service. And sometimes you have to tell people no, don't do this, I don't think that's a good idea. And sometimes you have to be stern – because you're taking responsibility for this person and it's your duty to be stern. But you never say I'm going to convince you to do something, or convince you to be a student, it doesn't work like that. People must be left completely free.

That traditional relationship between teacher and student will continue on within our Sufi tradition. But I also believe we can co-create certain things together. Yesterday, my students were talking about their own lives and challenges. I learn from them, I ask myself how can I best serve and understand the challenges they are going through. And if the traditional way of doing things is an obstacle, then let's shift it slightly. As long as it doesn't compromise the essence, then things can be shifted. And the essence can't be compromised. The essence is love.

People have this idea that being a teacher means you've arrived somewhere. But you've not arrived anywhere, you just *are*. If you think you are something because you're a teacher, you shouldn't be a teacher. There are a lot of false teachers out there who think they are something. They create lots of problems. There shouldn't be any ego identification in being a teacher. You have to have surrendered somewhere and not be attached.

When I was younger I learned to play music by going up on the stage to play, even when I didn't know the song, in front of a lot of people. That's how I live my life, that's how I do everything, with commitment and vulnerability. For me they go hand in hand. I just want to be as present as I can for my students and as real to myself as I can be. Even if that makes me vulnerable. Because my students are vulnerable – so why shouldn't I be vulnerable?

> "I just want to be as present as I can for my students and as real to myself as I can be. Even if that makes me vulnerable."

JH: This is a bit of an impossible question really, but how do you see the future of spirituality? There's going to be so much change in the coming years – technological leaps as well as ecological collapse and migration – huge changes. Do you have any conception of how your tradition will look, when your daughter grows up, say in 50 years' time? How do you think spirituality is going to function on the planet then?

Emmanuel: You know, I used to think about that a lot. Now I just think how can I hold what I have been given, for the future. That's my job, and that's all I want to do. I just want to hold it the best that I can, keep what's essential to this tradition alive in whatever way I can, be of service in whatever way I can and not think too big. Ten years ago it was a different story. I remember in 2008 when we were watching the stock market crashing, and thought the whole thing was going to go, finally. We were so excited! But clearly the empire is going to take a little longer to crumble. So I don't think too much about that now.

Spiritual ecology is going to be my work for a long time. That is not about some big plan for the future, in many ways it's about going back to the basics and a simple way of being. First we need to remember the world is sacred. Then we can begin to plant some seeds. When and where those seeds are going to sprout, we don't know. Some might sprout in our lifetime. Some might in my children's lifetime. I'm not going to break the concrete that has paved over our world, or even try to figure out the concrete any more.[5] I just want to plant the seeds, nurture them as best I can and see what they can do by their own power over time.

One of my students was in Scotland last week, where she saw trees that over the last few years have been planted in a denuded landscape. But after several years the trees are still only a foot tall. It's going to take a long time to revitalise the land and bring back what has been lost. Seeds grow from small beginnings and can sometimes take time to take root and grow. I don't think about what's going to happen in my lifetime so much any more. I think things will take longer than that to really change. And I also want to enjoy things as they are now while nurturing those seeds. Do my best to contribute to what might happen in the future. Try to have some fun sometimes. Eat good food while we can get it. Drink good coffee while we still can.

> "I don't think about what's going to happen in my lifetime so much any more. I think things will take longer than that to really change."

---

5   Used as a metaphor to mean structural change.

Chapter 7

DUNGSE JAMPAL NORBU

HANGING OUT WITH A FRIEND

Credit: Michael Velasco

'In all this mess, we're trying to understand who we are and how we fit in the larger world.'

Dungse Jampal Norbu was born into a dharma family in 1988, as the son of Dzigar Kongtrul Rinpoche and Elizabeth Mattis Namgyel. Under his father's wing he received many teachings and transmissions. He spent five years studying Tibetan language and traditional buddhadharma in India, and now spends 100 days a year in meditation retreat in order to deepen his experience of the practices of his lineage. He explores the Buddhist teachings in a natural and relaxed way, and is particularly interested in the challenges of establishing a practical worldview for young people, one that is based on compassion and self-reflection. He has taught on Basic Buddhism, Buddhism and ecology, and Buddhism as a response to tragedy. He travels and teaches in the United States and Asia.

Dungse, like many of his generation, is of mixed heritage – bringing East and West together in his bloodline. His father was one of a wave of tulkus (recognised reincarnations of Tibetan lamas) who fled Tibet in the 1950s and 60s and helped to seed Buddhism in America. Dungse grew up steeped in spiritual teachings just as Buddhism was beginning to make its mark on the religious landscape of the US, alongside a host of other spiritualities arriving from the East. (Dungse and his father spent time in Crestone, Colorado, for example, which is a minor Mecca of retreat centres, ashrams and temples from dozens of different traditions.)

Dungse was trained as a lineage holder from a very young age. Despite that, like many of his generation, he refused to take his family tradition on blind faith (which would be difficult to rationalise with so many religious alternatives in the neighbourhood) but instead tested it thoroughly against the needs and challenges of his life. Dungse's chapter references many of the difficulties the millennial generation have grown up with – the constant onslaught of online distractions, the awareness of conflict around the world, environmental depletion – and woven through that experience is the central question of how to live a life of meaning.

For Dungse, Buddhism is a tested system, consciously chosen, giving him not just inner strength, but a means to avoid the pitfalls of self-centredness and the seduction of materialism. What touches me about his chosen path is the sense of simplicity – he has clearly found a reliable inner compass with which to navigate the chaos and complexity of the world around him. He takes the ancient teachings (which he is now responsible for continuing) and successfully applies them to everyday 21st-century life. I love that Dungse is a teacher with some status, but who retains a very relaxed relationship with that role, and doesn't use his status to separate himself from others.

Motifs in this chapter:

- Evolving traditions

- Natural leadership

Dungse Jampal Norbu writes:

It's just another day, and morning meditation has ended. My phone plays a text tone from a friend, 'Dude, you want hang out?' I certainly do.

I've known this friend since I was three. We grew up in different Buddhist communities, but we've remained close. We've known each other so long, in fact, that I just call him 'Dude'. When I arrive at his place, we have some pizza and beer, take a walk, sometimes play a video game and, inevitably, end up talking about dharma and spiritual practice. Sometimes it's about meditation; sometimes it's about activism; and sometimes it's about working with the mind in difficult situations. There is always plenty to talk about. Engaging with the world. Understanding ourselves. There is so much conflict, it's hard to process – on the drive over, the radio plays yet more stories about conflict in Syria, political corruption and millions of people in need of help. In all this mess, we're trying to understand who we are and how we fit in the larger world. That's where a spiritual life comes in.

I was born in Bangkok, Thailand, to a Tibetan-American family. I grew up in the United States, but spent long, scattered periods of time in Northern India, studying Tibetan Buddhism. Both my parents are spiritual teachers. My father, Dzigar Kongtrul Rinpoche, is the latest in a long lineage of important Buddhist teachers coming out of Tibet. Aside from his monastery in Tibet, he has been establishing centres throughout the world, particularly in the United States. My mother, Elizabeth Mattis Namgyel, grew up in the West, but came from a family with ties to Buddhism. Since meeting my father, when she was 23, she became a practitioner and, later, a spiritual teacher and author. Like many people born into spiritual families, I always carried parts of my family tradition with me. But my decision to become a spiritual practitioner came while I was in high school.

That time was a major crux in my life: it was time to decide what I wanted to do with my future. I didn't feel connected with mainstream work. My friends and I would talk about breaking the status quo, living alternative lifestyles. We would watch *Fight Club* or *V for Vendetta* and talk about the futility of living in a cyclical system of working and spending money with no fulfilment. Sometimes I felt like an existentialist philosopher, like Friedrich Nietzsche or Jean-Paul Sartre.

I came to see that, while I wasn't sure what kind of lifestyle I wanted, it was clear that no matter what I chose, I would need some kind of internal support and means of self-discovery. No path of life offers guaranteed happiness or success. I wanted to find a meaningful way to live that didn't depend on my position in society or how much money I had. Something that would always be with me.

> "I wanted to find a meaningful way to live that didn't depend on my position in society or how much money I had."

Although I was born as the son of a Buddhist lineage holder, teaching didn't occur to me. I didn't really like public speaking. I just wanted to have confidence in what I was doing with my life. So I decided to go to India to study dharma (Buddhist philosophy) as part of my higher education after high school. I trusted the dharma, not because I grew up with it, but because I spent so many years trying to disprove it in the context of my own experience. I wasn't a super-rebellious kid; I just didn't like accepting anything on blind faith – and the beautiful thing is, I was never asked to.

In high school I spent a lot of time clumsily trying to explain Buddhist philosophy to my friends. I had many good experiences from the little meditation I had done, and I wanted to share that. I ended up realising how little I knew and could therefore share. I had to study more, mostly for my own clarity. Since making that choice, I haven't looked back.

> "In high school I spent a lot of time clumsily trying to explain Buddhist philosophy to my friends."

Now, Dude and I talk about spiritual life every time we see each other. When you've known someone for 25 years, small talk is basically non-existent, and everything becomes an existential discussion – of YouTube videos, an inside joke or some way of making a positive difference in the world. Mostly, we talk about what it means to live a meaningful life. Dude brings up the main issue, that while no one truly wants to live in a rat-race society and only focus on personal issues, the question is: How do we bring our actions and our intention together? I agree with him, and the point we constantly return to is that happiness is not found in the outside world, in objects, or in experiences that depend on outer circumstances. I recall that the great Buddhist sage Shantideva said that 'to walk without cutting your feet, you can either cover the whole world in leather, or put leather on your soles'. We both take this to mean that by working with our own minds, we empower ourselves to live a good life no matter where we go, and in that way, we develop a good relationship with the world, too.

But this attitude doesn't come easily. Yes, it's easy to claim that happiness comes from within, but we live in a time when advertisements suggest that we can't be happy without certain products, or idealised body images make us feel self-conscious, and money seems to make the world turn, so it's quite easy to fall into the habit of looking for some external thing to give us happiness, and it's exactly that habit which pisses us off.

So how do we live by the insight that genuine happiness comes from within? On the Buddhist path, it is said, 'All the joy the world contains comes from wishing happiness for others. All the suffering the world contains comes from wishing happiness only for oneself.' This phrase isn't about totally sacrificing one's own wellbeing. The phrase refers to attachment to ourselves, and how that attachment stirs up neurotic emotions, which in turn prevent us from relaxing and being happy.

As an example, when Dude and I hang out, and I'm stressed out about something, my mind gets reactive because I'm solely focused on 'my problems' or on how everything is getting in 'my' way. It's hard to hang out that way. My habit is naturally to focus on myself, but this approach doesn't help me much when I'm with a friend or part of a larger situation. The way to let go of that attachment is to think beyond my own ego concerns to consider others as well.

By including someone like Dude in my concern, I can let go of some of my issues and chill out. Once the attachment to the ego fades, then there is more natural joy to life.

When I follow this process of relaxing the attachment I have to myself, confidence slowly builds in the Buddhist path. Dude and I both understand this, otherwise we wouldn't be on this path. Confidence isn't something we can fabricate. Any genuine spiritual development comes from experience, patience, and lots of self-reflection. Otherwise it is no more than blind faith, which can fall apart as soon as the shit hits the fan.

These days I'm so used to getting things I want within three or four business days, I need to practise patience, and be consistent in my spiritual path. Without the hard work, I can't develop any depth. A writer can easily make a point in 140 characters, but it won't have the depth of understanding that a novel would.

In these circumstances, I realise that I cannot be a part-time practitioner. For some of my friends this sounds too hardcore; but I feel that dharma practice is something that supports living well, and so it shouldn't be just a hobby. Spiritual practice is a way of living. For this reason I take 100 days out of the year for meditation retreat. It's not to run away from anything, but to face my mind and internal challenges directly. Through repeated deep contemplation and reflection I've developed further confidence in my dharma path, and in my ability to change my attitude about the true source of happiness. And that shows up no matter where I am. I see more and more how dharma is practical in everyday life.

When we talk, Dude usually doesn't play the devil's advocate, so I play it instead. 'How does an attitude-change help anyone besides oneself?' I ask. 'Isn't one of the main practices in Buddhism compassion for others?'

This is a question we've both heard a lot, growing up in Buddhist communities. We both believe that changing our attitude about the true source of happiness supports us to be compassionate towards others. Because if we're wrapped up in our self-concerns, what good are we going to be to anyone else? If we don't have the strength of inner support, how can we continue to care for others without burnout? Active compassion and kindness need support, and that support can only be constantly generated from within through patience and confidence. The point of a spiritual life is precisely to find happiness in our own lives *without* disconnecting from everything around us; and we don't. Dude and I are always talking about new ways to be involved in the world, supporting sustainable communities, helping friends going through hard times, volunteering, and so on.

For us the Buddhist path is essentially a guide for how to meet life head on. Whenever there is negative media... Who am I kidding? Every day, when we see negative news posts about how we live under some kind of threat, or how we are not matching up to an ideal body image, or how an animal from an endangered species was shot, we don't seek to soothe or distract ourselves with videos of kittens, or by suddenly jumping onto a cushion to visualise how everything is 'all good'. We know life is too dynamic to 'fix' in any controlled way, so we don't waste our time worrying too much about how permanent our impact is. Through compassion, and clear intention, we can always find a way to help, or reach beyond ourselves to make a difference. I always feel happier when I can go beyond myself, with confidence and the tool of self-reflection. I do feel like I am living a meaningful life.

> "Through compassion, and clear intention, we can always find a way to help, or reach beyond ourselves to make a difference."

PART 3

SACRED ACTIVISM

Working with the younger generation at St Ethelburga's has been about shifting from talking to doing. For me this is the most important and refreshing quality of Generation Y and at the heart of this collection – an uncomplicated readiness to walk the talk, out there in the messy, complex, screwed-up world.

St Ethelburga's, and the interfaith initiatives that sprang up everywhere after 9/11 and 7/7, focused on forming relationships across traditions, being with our differences, shifting from debate to participatory dialogue. We sat in circles, listening to each other's stories, slowly, often painfully, forging a path from competition to collaboration, from separation to co-creation. When the millennials showed up, we took a leap forward into *acting together* – boldly, without inhibition.

In the summer when the refugee crisis hit Europe with a vengeance, thousands risked their lives in grim journeys across the Aegean, jammed into overflowing inflatable dinghies. While I consulted with other NGOs and faith groups, mapped responses, strategised and talked on the phone a lot, a younger member of my team, Meghan Fulton, jumped on a plane and spent the weekend hauling people out of the Aegean and wrapping them in foil blankets. A month later we were all there, learning what it means to put our values to the test in a seemingly hopeless situation. In the mud and chaos of Lesbos, our belief in a worldview of interdependence grew deeper roots. Reflected in the eyes of the desperate Afghan and Syrian families, we tried in some brief, minuscule way to serve.

Young people are coming of age in a world that is falling apart. The problems are endemic and overwhelming. Elders in positions of conventional power show little ability to solve them, often failing even to acknowledge the depth and systemic nature of the crisis we are facing. Many of those who should be role models seem wilfully blind, intent only on protecting their own interests and maintaining the status quo.

What options do the younger generation have? Even if multinationals have the world in lock-down, there is still a powerful drive for change, and to live with integrity. As Courtney Martin says:

> We must accept that we will fail and try anyway, try to fail always more exquisitely, more honestly, more effectively. We must wake up in the morning naively believing in the power of our own dreams and the potential of our own gifts, and go to bed exhausted and determined to do it all over again.[1]

We see many examples of how young people, more firmly embedded in a lived experience of interdependence, are constantly evolving new ventures and projects where compassion and connectedness are lived out in a plethora of small-scale experiments around the world. Their worldview is based not just in ecological interconnectedness or systems thinking, but also – of particular relevance to spirituality – in the relationship between inner and outer. Regenerative activism recognises that we cannot create a harmonious, connected world with aggressive, dualistic methodologies. Equally, we cannot build a sustainable world with unsustainable approaches. Standing Rock,[2]

---

[1]   *Do It Anyway: The New Generation of Activists*, Courtney Martin (Beacon Press, 2010).

[2]   The Dakota Access Pipeline protests at Standing Rock Reservation in North Dakota were part of a grassroots movement that began in early 2016 in reaction to the approved construction of an oil pipeline in the northern United States.

the women's marches that swept the world after the election of Trump, the Black Lives Matter movement – all point towards the emergence of a new form of activism that includes an inner dimension, whether through an explicit relationship with spirituality, a commitment to self-care, or an acknowledgement that our inner psychology plays out through our actions.

The theme of burnout is huge in the younger generation. Burnout is not just exhaustion but also the impact of too much heartbreak and overwhelm. We all struggle to hear each news story of more shocking injustice, another extremist attack, each new species disappearing into extinction. But it hits young people hardest. It is their future disintegrating, and they often feel tasked with 'saving the world' as no one else seems to be bothering. Unlike Generation X, who are prone to overwork, young people know there are no quick fixes. When the need for change is endless, self-care is an imperative.

Young activists live out their spiritual values in activism, and also attend to their spiritual lives in order to sustain their activism. These are change-makers intent both on 'being the change' and on resourcing themselves for the long haul. For them, action and spirituality are one.

Chapter 8

SARAH CORBETT

THE ART OF GENTLE PROTEST

'We need to slow down, not just react in anger and fight hate with hate.'

Sarah Corbett is an award-winning campaigner and one of the leading spokespersons in the global craftivism movement. Her approach to craftivism, called 'gentle protest', is about using craft as a tool for thoughtful and kind activism. Sarah worked in the charity sector for Christian Aid, the Department for International Development and Oxfam before setting up the Craftivist Collective in 2009. The collective now has thousands of members all over the world engaged in craftivism projects on their own and in group 'stitch-ins'. She has written two books, A Little Book of Craftivism and How to Be a Craftivist: The Art of Gentle Protest. The Times named Sarah one of their five 'New Tribes of 2012' and the Craftivist Collective was given the 'Innovator Award' by Care2 in 2017.

Sarah is a wonderful example of activism that integrates inner and outer. Growing up in a Christian family in the 1980s in Everton, Liverpool, the fourth most deprived ward in the UK, Sarah was brought into the world of activism from a young age, having experienced first-hand her community battling against the effects of inequality. She is a committed Christian and a regular attender at a new church plant aimed at millennials and creatives. Sarah doesn't often talk about her faith in the context of her work, but it is quietly woven through everything she does: 'Faith, for me, should be about everything,' she says. 'It's how you walk on this planet.'

Sarah's commitment to non-oppositional protest means not vilifying the power-holders she seeks to influence – but recognising their humanity, seeking to change one heart at a time.

The atmosphere in Sarah's workshops is very memorable. The peaceful hush, the embodied mindfulness, the sense of relationship and community, and the pleasure in making together – these are well known to crafters everywhere. When that is combined with shared purpose and a movement towards social justice that recognises our interbeing with each other – then that nourishment becomes richer. There is a connection and a joy present, which I've come to associate with the spirituality and activism of the younger generation. How much the world needs those qualities!

Like many others in this book, Sarah has a significant narrative about burnout. She originally sought craft as an antidote to the stress of a computer-dominated life, is painfully aware of the limitations of what one person can achieve, and the need to avoid feeling overwhelmed by the rest. Sarah walks her talk, treading a path through the overwhelming problems of our world, one day at a time, offering what she has to offer and trying to stay true to her values.

Through our conversations, I developed a great respect for Sarah. Her unassuming manner belies a wisdom beyond her years, and there is real authenticity and congruence in everything she does.

Motifs in this chapter:

- Sacred activism

- Natural leadership

JH: Why don't we start with the story of your faith? I'd love to hear what your experience of faith was when you were growing up. And what's your faith about for you now?

Sarah: I grew up in Liverpool. Dad was the local vicar, and Mum was a Bishop's daughter. My parents met in St Peter's Church, West Everton, where they lived in community with 12 other Christians doing service in a low-income area. It always felt natural that as a Christian you should be practising your faith in social change. That was just how I grew up.

Faith, for me, should be about everything. It's how you walk on this planet, how you treat people. Loving your neighbours, loving your enemies, loving people you disagree with. It's about trying to wear things that are ethical but beautiful. It's my Keep Cup, because it's beautiful and useful – made of natural resources and I use it every day rather than disposable cups. For me it's about being this strange, unique human being, knowing God knows every hair on my head. But also being part of this messy world and part of a complex community. It's a manual for living and it's about seeing how amazing the world is and can be. The more I look at things, the more I'm like, 'this is magical'.

JH: So how does that journey fit together with your journey into craftivism?

Sarah: I started doing craftivism in 2008. I was frustrated with how activism was either really transactional or demonising of people. It didn't fit my principles. Jesus never just said, 'Quick! Come and be mobilised to show that we have loads of people who care about this, and then you can piss off back home.' Activism is about making the world a better place, but we are often doing it in ugly, loud, disrespectful ways. I started thinking maybe activism can be

> "Activism can be beautiful, it can be small and powerful."

beautiful, it can be small and powerful. We need to slow down, not just react in anger and fight hate with hate. I was thinking about how gentleness is the fruit of the spirit. I kept coming up with this phrase, 'gentle protest'. The Bible and the Christian faith are totally strategic for me as an activist. I believe that Martin Luther King was the best activist there ever has been, and faith was a core part of everything he did.

JH: So what's your favourite success story? Where have you seen this method create change?

Sarah: Here's a really clear example. I was approached by ShareAction who wanted to get a large and very well-known retail company to pay the real living wage. Over three years they'd tried everything just to get one meeting with the CEO to discuss it. They'd tried all kinds of traditional activist methods, from petitions to being outside stores with placards, and nothing had worked. They came to me and said, 'We've seen your book, *A Little Book of Craftivism*. We think you could help us try something different that might work.' They told me I had five weeks before the AGM and asked what I could do in that time. So I focused on the board members of the company since they are above the CEO and can influence him. They don't often get targeted in campaigns. They're not used to it, so it could have more impact. We bought shares so we could go to the AGM in person and meet them. And I got together a team of craftivists from across the UK who either dressed like they were part of the core audience or actually were their core audience of the company – the board will listen to their loyal customers more than others. I also thought, 'Who do the board listen to? They listen to the Chief Investment Officers of their biggest shareholder companies.' So we included the CIOs of those five companies, and also five of their celebrity models, such as Annie Lennox.

So I had 24 craftivists and five weeks. They were each assigned one person to craft a gift for. We had handkerchiefs bought from the targeted company to show that we were customers and not boycotters.

I gave them craft thought questions to work on while they stitched. And instructed them to google the *bleep* out of their target person, figure out what colours they wear, where they used to work, what makes them tick. Are they loud and flamboyant or are they shy? Look on LinkedIn to see what their jobs have been, if they were trustees anywhere. And embroider them a handkerchief that *they* will really like. It's not about what you like, but about them. And each one had a message on it, encouraging them in their job, saying, 'Don't blow it, use the power you have for good.' So a bit of humour too, that works well and helps make it more memorable, if it's not laughing at them, which it wasn't. It was all very positive.

One board member, one hanky-receiver, was a trustee at Kew Gardens, so theirs had a quote about how they could flourish in their role, and the quote was surrounded by embroidered flowers. Another was linked with the Royal Opera House, so they had a quote from a musician about being the change, surrounded by musical notes, all in purples because he wore a lot of dark purple. I asked people to hand-write letters, not typed, and to write things like, 'While I was making you this gift, I was thinking about how much power you have, how much opportunity and how much hard work your job probably is. So I wanted my gift to encourage you in your role. But also I was thinking about how shocked I am that you don't pay the living wage. I love your company, I wear your stuff, but I know how difficult it is to live on the minimum wage. And also I was thinking about how it makes sense in terms of a business strategy to pay the living wage for these reasons...' So it was a robust argument but it was also very emotive.

We intentionally didn't share it on social media, we kept it very intimate and we hand-delivered the gifts in boxes with ribbon, with smiles. And they were genuinely moved. All we asked for was a meeting. And we got four meetings over the year. They started to trust us and open up, and before the next AGM they announced they were paying the real living wage to 50,000 staff.

So we went back to the AGM to thank them – not to say well done us – but to say well done you, that's a big thing that you've done, really powerful. And they all said how moved they were by their hankies. So it's a very human way to engage. Later, the chair of the board said it was so memorable all they wanted to talk about was their hankies, every time they met, and the living wage kept coming up in their meetings even if it wasn't on the agenda. Craft can be powerful. It's the words you use, the humility in saying that we believe they can do a great job as human beings, not presuming because they are in a position of power they are automatically horrible people. For me it felt like what Jesus would do – quietly challenge people in a loving way.

JH: I find that really moving. It's just so humane and deeply non-oppositional. It's also a very feminine, relational way. I'm always inspired by anything that moves us from a dualistic approach to something more connected, that avoids 'othering'. You talked about power earlier and it's clear millennials are helping to shepherd in a different relationship with power and a different relationship with hierarchy. Can you say something about how you see that?

Sarah: A lot of activism is still quite immature from people of all ages, including young people. We demand this or we want that. 'These people are awful'… Sadly a lot of the fourth-wave feminism stuff I see from millennials on Instagram tips into 'Men are all awful'. It can still be very immature messaging, not very loving. It stereotypes and demonises, which is exactly what you are fighting against. You're saying that you shouldn't treat women this way and that you've objectified us, and then you objectify the other side in the same way. I think soft power is getting more credible. There's definitely more discussion around it. Some people are saying, yeah, you've got a point you know, fighting hate with hate doesn't work. Young people are starting to see we need a different way, but sadly it's still unusual to see emotionally intelligent and loving forms of protest.

> "Fighting hate with hate doesn't work."

JH: Standing Rock was such an inspiration to so many people, and that was an example of a particular way of doing sacred activism. What you're doing is similar somehow, but the spirituality is not explicit. Maybe it has broader appeal because of that?

Sarah: My experience, living in the UK, is it's still quite difficult to say you're a Christian without people suddenly putting this wall up. In liberal leftist circles it seems to be easier to say you're a practising Muslim or Buddhist than to say you're a practising Christian. I find that quite upsetting. But it's about being strategic really – when is it helpful for me to be explicit about faith and when is it more inclusive not to be?

JH: I guess your work is one expression of the maker movement, which is about changing how we engage with the practical, physical elements in our lives, something I see the millennial generation adopting in interesting ways.

Sarah: Yeah. We were talking about how amazing the online world is for millennials. It's just part of our lifestyle – I'll Instagram this, tweet that, follow this person, it's interwoven in everything we do, but it also means we crave for something that's not tapping with our thumbs. That's the reason I picked up the cross-stitch kit that set me off down this path in 2008. It was the craving to create something with my hands. Because all I did was look at blue screens and write reports. We're online so much we need something else to balance it out. It's also about feeling we can create something. Globalisation has made us feel really tiny. We love our artisan stuff – because we know who made it, we know the skill it took.

> "It was the craving to create something with my hands. Because all I did was look at blue screens and write reports. We're online so much we need something else to balance it out."

JH: I think that also you picked up the cross-stitch kit in a time when you were feeling burnt out, is that right? And it was healing – an antidote to the overwhelm and constant technology...

Sarah: Craft is great because you can't do it fast. Immediately I noticed how I was trying to do everything quickly. I was anxious and short-tempered, really impatient. My shoulders were hunched and my breath was really shallow – completely out of pace with the action of stitching. The physicality of using craft made me aware of my chattering brain and slowed it down, it helped me think critically and use the comfort of craft to ask myself uncomfortable questions, such as 'Was I being an effective activist or just a busy one?' Noticing how I am feeling, preventing burnout, is vital and necessary. It shouldn't be seen as a luxury. It's about how to be an effective sustainable activist.

JH: Can you say more about that? I just wonder how it's been for you growing up in a disintegrating culture, responding with activism – which took you into this space of burnout. Now the world appears to be disintegrating even further – so how is it to stay true to the business of slow activism?

Sarah: It's a daily struggle. I stopped watching the news and I don't read that many newspapers, because for me at the moment it feels like a distraction. All this bad news isn't helping me, it's just making me overwhelmed and disempowered. It's a real challenge, day in, day out. It's really difficult to carry on doing activism because it's slow paced. You can go backwards before you go forward. There's all this injustice in the world and I'm *sewing* – you know, how can I justify this? Sometimes I have to re-read emails from people who've told me my work has helped them, has had some impact in an organisation or legislation.

It's that tension around where can I be of use in the world and have impact, but also knowing I'm just a little human being and at the end of the day you can't change people's hearts and minds. It's down to them. So when do you let go? When do you plant a seed and move on?

And when actually do you barricade yourself on the runway and say, in this campaign, in this current moment, you've got to get out and be much louder and say this policy has got to stop?

JH: So what would be your one main message to the younger generation?

Sarah: Just see that you've got amazing power as one piece of the jigsaw puzzle. And make your jigsaw piece as beautiful, as attractive, as thoughtful as possible, and as lovingly challenging and inspiring and powerful as possible. But know you're just one piece of the puzzle – don't try to do everything, don't try and compete with other pieces. You're part of this complex universe, but you're an important part, and if you don't show up we notice. And don't try to squeeze yourself into the wrong space, because then you may burn out or you might piss people off. So being yourself is really important.

> "You're just one piece of the puzzle – don't try to do everything, don't try and compete with other pieces."

JH: And what would you say to senior leaders, elders and power-holders?

Sarah: Be curious. Ask questions. Being curious is a scary thing because you can open a can of worms, and it means offering some of your power to others to use. But see it as an interesting journey. You don't need to know all the answers. Work with young people to find answers together.

Chapter 9

BRUNA KADLETZ

FAITH WITHOUT WORKS IS DEAD

'Life calls to us in mysterious ways.'

Thirty-five-year-old Bruna was born in Florianopolis, Brazil. She is a 'spiritual humanitarian' whose work focuses on bringing awareness to global forced displacement and the spiritual dimension of humanitarian crises. Her work has taken her to connect with displaced communities around the globe, including South Africa, Lebanon, Jordan, Palestine, Turkey, Greece, Serbia, France, the UK, Germany and Brazil. Bruna is the co-founder and director of Círculos de Hospitalidade (Circles of Hospitality), a Brazil-based NGO focused on reviving the deep meaning of hospitality and receptivity among refugee communities and host societies through the promotion of educational, cultural and social initiatives.

For many millennials in the UK, home ownership has become a distant dream. But overshadowing everyday aspirations for a stable home is the bigger spectre of mass displacement, likely to be an unavoidable part of our global future. Current forecasts predict anything between 25 million and 1 billion environment-related refugees by 2050.[1] How does the average young adult make sense of that future or prepare for it? How can one hold on to personal goals in the face of impending chaos? And how does that overwhelming uncertainty impact on faith and belief?

Bruna, like Adam Bucko in Chapter 5, originally thought her love for God would take her into a life of seclusion, until she came to see that 'the injustices of the world awaken my humanness and a sense of responsibility'. Bruna has incredible courage and inner strength that has allowed her to follow a calling into the darkest places. She observes how the Divine begins to reveal Itself to her not just through silence and peace, but also through the suffering and pain of those who have lost everything. Like Adam, Bruna recognises that, in these times, spirituality lived in retreat would be a betrayal of our world.

Bruna combines a very healing and empathetic nature, with the quality of a global visionary. Her identity is located beyond her personal nationality or religion, demonstrating a planetary consciousness that would have been incomprehensible to most of humanity 50 years ago. Bruna's sense of self is inextricably bound up with the conviction that there is 'just one cry interconnecting us all'.

On a daily basis Bruna engages with grief, insanity and devastation. Self-care is critical, and her spiritual discipline is clearly one aspect of that. Alongside the need for resilience, she poses an essential question for all young people of faith – how to sustain an open heart and remain sanely present in the midst of chaotic times.

For me, Bruna is an inspiration, a role model in how not to turn away from the harsher realities of our world, but to walk into them holding fast to an inner light, knowing that, in the end, all we have is our capacity to love each other.

---

1   'Climate Migrants Might Reach One Billion by 2050', 21 August 2017: https://reliefweb.int/report/world/climate-migrants-might-reach-one-billion-2050

If the numbers of refugees across the world does reach the proportions some are predicting, we will all need to find that capacity within us.

Motifs in this chapter:

- Sacred activism

- Complex identities

Bruna Kadletz writes:

Life calls to us in mysterious ways. In 2012, when I was attending a workshop on Spirituality and Quantum Physics, I heard someone referring to God as 'Beloved'. He had devotion in his eyes and sweetness in his speech. Something within me clicked. Suddenly, the workshop lost its magic, and all my attention turned to the beloved. It was as if an ancient call within me had awakened to the devotional nature of relating to God as the beloved one in my heart. Later, I learned about the Sufis and how their relationship with God was based on a love affair between lover and beloved. Although mysticism was a familiar ocean to me, I knew nothing about the Sufi path other than it resonated with me.

Between prayers and meditation, I then realised my path was interwoven with those in suffering. The vulnerability of others and injustices of the world awake my humanness and a sense of responsibility to contributing with life more meaningfully. I was not destined to live in seclusion, as I first imagined. Quite the opposite. In embracing Sufism, life has taken me to unexpected realms of action tuned with spiritual practice. It is in the tears of a child or in the pain of those brutally displaced from home that the refined human qualities of empathy, care and love come into being. Some people find

> "It is in the pain of broken hearts that the divine reveals itself."

God in scriptures or by chanting sacred words, others in the beauty of nature or in a joyful moment. For me, it is mostly in the silence of solitude and in the pain of broken hearts that the divine reveals itself.

Yet, the seed of being of service to the whole was planted many years before my encounter with Sufism. I was eight years old the first time I learned about being an instrument in God's hands. My mother was a volunteer doctor in a spiritual centre next to a slum in my hometown. The centre, founded on the principles of the Spiritism of Allan Kardec, cared for the physical and spiritual needs of the community. On a practical level, my mother worked mainly with dispossessed women affected by domestic violence and other malaises linked to life in the Brazilian favelas. The spiritual work consisted of public lectures, learning groups and healing touch.

On Saturday mornings, the centre opened its doors to the children as well. In the building, the kids and teens, who were subjected to structural violence and racial discrimination on a daily basis, found a safe haven. Once a week they received nutritious food, attention and care. Instead of taking me to shopping malls or parks, my mother used to bring me along with her to the centre. I remember serving the youngsters bread and then wiping the blue tables and sweeping the wooden floor. Our mornings were filled with joy, and if I finished my chores on time, I could also play with them.

Mrs Lourdes, a strong and strict woman, led the work in the centre. With her, it was tough love. Mrs Lourdes barely smiled, but she was always prompt to help anyone in need. Her presence was powerful and, as a young child, I was scared of her rigid tone. She was the incarnation of her mantra, 'Faith without works is dead' (James 2:14–26). In those early years, I was taught by example that faith and spirituality are empty of meaning if disengaged from social change.

Refugee crisis

There is a saying in my tradition, 'Sufis are children of the moment', and we believe that responding attentively to the needs of the moment is part of the practice of servanthood. There is an inner response, which involves looking within to witness what is the truth underneath the surface, and an outer response, which is acting from this place of truth and awareness.

In the wake of mass forced displacement, followed by the worst humanitarian crisis we have witnessed since WWII, I started working with displaced communities and shedding light on their predicament through public talks, writing and advocating for their rights. I soon realised we were witnessing not solely a crisis of outward mass displacement, but also a collective crisis of inner displacement. If, inwardly, we are not connected with the place where our true being resides, we are out of place, we are displaced. This story of separation, which different traditions and spiritual teachers articulate so eloquently, stratifies in ecological destruction as well as in the destruction of social fabrics and human relationships. Not surprisingly, fear and violence dominates the mainstream narrative in which refugees are met with military power and fortified borders. This dehumanising response mirrors how displaced we are from our shared humanity.

Before exploring in which ways faith and spirituality can empower our response to the refugee crisis, I will share, from a personal experience, what can happen when we ignore this dimension. When not attentive and without discipline, darkness and burnout easily put us out of balance. I had to be sucked into the darkness to understand this, and to learn the value of self-discipline.

South Africa: Descending into darkness

I landed in Johannesburg in the midst of the early 2015 xenophobic violence. The atmosphere was heavy and tense. African nationals were under attack. Foreigners' businesses were looted, livelihoods destroyed, bodies were injured and lives lost. Unceasing threats from locals stirred fear and insecurity among refugees and migrants who had sought security and stability in South Africa. Tens of thousands were uprooted during the attacks, reviving the memories of previous experiences of fleeing home. Being a foreigner in the country, I was not under threat though. The attacks were racialised and located in marginalised and underprivileged areas.

During the months I stayed in the country, I was in contact with communities affected by the attacks. I visited the edges of shantytowns and the heart of Johannesburg's inner city. The legacy of apartheid was alive in the racialised poverty and structural violence. It was difficult to navigate through areas inhabited with drug dealers, human traffickers and sex workers. It was painful to witness children growing up in inhumane conditions, playing on the streets where raw sewage ran. It was distressing to hear stories of war and torture, sexual abuse and discrimination. In spite of meeting inspirational people, and participating in peace marches and cheerful events, my heart was broken over and over again.

My experience in Africa washed away my naivety about humanitarian projects. I was disappointed to see political agendas and corporate interest co-opting the principles of humanitarian action. Corporate humanitarianism was all about serving the interests of donors and profiting from human suffering, rather than serving the needs of communities.

These realities were an invitation for me to descend into darkness. Forgetfulness took hold of me and I lost my discipline. I had forgotten how to keep myself balanced and centred in the face of hardships. Day after day, I replaced self-care and awareness for numbness and distraction. This forgetful attitude triggered older patterns of conflict, and I got completely out of balance. A dear friend said that I was on the tangent of myself. Not in alignment with my true being any more, I even lacked the energy to re-balance myself. I was in a state of inner displacement.

This experience of inner displacement made me realise how important it is to revive spiritual values and practices in the humanitarian field. The work is demanding. Pressure, frustration and anger are common for many who work in this area. It is challenging to sustain a positive and balanced attitude when rescuing endless drowning refugees from the Mediter-ranean. Working in refugee camps is draining, particularly when

> "Acting from a place of pressure, frustration and anger only feeds the cycle of violence we aim to transform."

there are violent outbreaks or when legal and political restrictions eradicate resettlement and family reunification opportunities.

Acting from a place of pressure, frustration and anger only feeds the cycle of violence we aim to transform. In trying to change the reality of those impacted by war, persecution, climate change and punitive migration politics, how do we escape from becoming the very reality we seek to change?

Spiritual humanitarianism: Weaving of inner work and outer meaningful action

Living the deepest call of our souls in a world whose meaning is fading away is a daily challenge. It is painful and heartbreaking. Especially when your inner call takes you to work in the dark geographies of dispossession, violence and despair. There is grief and uncertainty in the air the collective consciousness is breathing. In the face of so much desecration, ecological devastation and human suffering, there might be an

> "Living the deepest call of our souls in a world whose meaning is fading away is a daily challenge."

inclination to feel powerless and turn away from reality. And the question of how to sustain an open heart and remain sanely present in the midst of chaotic times is an essential one.

How to respond from a healing place when life invites you to listen to the cries of the world? Central to this response is the weaving of inner work and outer meaningful action. All great religions have provided us with the framework for such synergetic combination. When life invites us to hear the cries of the vulnerable and dispossessed, we understand there is just one cry interconnecting us all. As we respond to this one cry, we bring healing to ourselves and to the injustices of the world. As I walk the path of life hand in hand with those in suffering, I discover how my humanness is tied to recognising the sacred humanness present in others. In this path, the divine unfolds mysteriously.

KARA MOSES

FIERCE SOLIDARITY WITH ALL LIVING BEINGS

'The biggest gift I can give is myself, my life.'

Kara Moses is a Buddhist with a passion for justice, and huge energy for confronting structural violence through a path of grassroots activism. Her faith journey has taken her deeply into the principles and practices of the Triratna Western Buddhist tradition. But it has also brought her in touch with some apparent dilemmas in how Buddhism is sometimes lived in the West, as an individual interior journey, divorced from the socio-political context. As a climate activist, she has organised with UK-based Reclaim the Power and Plane Stupid, and is currently environment editor for Red Pepper magazine. Kara is also a facilitator of rewilding, leading courses on nature connection, spiritual ecology and skills for social change. She teachers regularly at EcoDharma, Schumacher College, St Ethelburga's Centre for Reconciliation and Peace, and the Centre for Alternative Technology, where she also works part-time in forest management. A graduate of St Ethelburga's spiritual ecology leadership programme, she is a prolific freelance journalist whose work has appeared in Emergence Magazine and Resurgence, among others.

Kara's story is one of a passionate and committed journey into both spirituality and activism, and a heartfelt endeavour to bring the two together. She is conscious of the capitalist illusions that intoxicate our minds, but also refuses to be put to sleep by spiritual teachings that insulate us in a comfort bubble. She chooses 'to live a life of integrity and solidarity rather than one of security and comfort'. She also can't fully sign up to a tradition that doesn't make a genuine connection with Earth or recognise its Divine nature. At the time of our interview, she defines herself as a 'nature-based Western Shamanic Buddhist', and one senses she has needed to draw from different sources to cover all her bases.

Like Dekila in Chapter 26 and Vero and Zoë in Chapter 13, her identity is not just global but ecological. She draws 'great power, energy and resilience from connecting to the wider web of life', and urges us to 'not shy away from the pain and damage being inflicted upon the Earth and its inhabitants'.

For me, Kara is a spiritual leader in the making, but one who will break the traditional mould. Her discipline, depth and uncompromising adherence to her own truth offer a rallying call to other young people, and a wake-up call to some of our religious elders who could usefully re-examine the gap between religious teachings and how they are lived in response to a world in great need.

Motifs in this chapter:

- Sacred activism

- Natural leadership

- Protecting Earth

- Challenging orthodoxy

Kara Moses writes:
'When you see violence, greed and narrow-mindedness in the fullness of its power, walk straight into the heart of it, remaining open to the sky and in touch with the earth.' These words, taken from the *Shambhala Warrior Mind Training* verses, were in my mind at 3.30am in July 2015 as I and 12 others cut through Heathrow Airport's

perimeter fence and walked straight into the heart of the airport – onto the runway, where we built a fortress and locked ourselves to it to prevent planes from taking off, in protest against unnecessary airport expansion. The words circled in my mind as emergency vehicles surrounded us; I lay on the runway, in touch with the Earth, and gazed up at the open sky as the sun rose over London.

This was a peaceful, non-violent action in the face of the violence of climate change, which kills 300,000 people a year, predominantly women, the poor, and communities of colour in the Global South. They have been suffering various forms of violence for centuries; climate change is a continuation of this. We prevented 4500 tonnes of CO_2 being released from the atmosphere, equivalent to the annual output of 900 households, and changed the public discourse around airport expansion to include climate change.

The state responded by threatening us with yet more violence: prison. Thankfully, our sentences were suspended after much public outcry over such a harsh sentence. And thankfully, I have a spiritual practice to resource me through the challenges of confronting greed and narrow-mindedness in the fullness of its power.

Activism forms an important part of my spiritual practice, which I could broadly describe as a nature-based Western Shamanic Buddhism. At different times in my life, I've focused almost exclusively on activism and social change, or on spiritual practice. I had to immerse myself in both worlds, to explore their breadths and depths until I reached their limits. Finally, I came to see through my own experience that neither could exist without the other and I had to find a way to integrate the two. That journey is another story – here I will explore the interplay between social action and spiritual practice from a personal perspective, with a particular focus on what this means for the youth of today – and, therefore, the world of tomorrow.

"At different times in my life, I've focused almost exclusively on activism and social change, or on spiritual practice. I had to immerse myself in both worlds."

Buddhism and global issues

Social action is for me an expression of the five basic Buddhist ethical precepts I have committed to, presented here in both their positive and negative forms as practised in my tradition:

- Practising deeds of loving kindness, and abstaining from taking life

- Practising open-handed generosity, and abstaining from taking the not-given

- Practising stillness, simplicity and contentment, and abstaining from sexual misconduct

- Practising truthful communication, and abstaining from untruthful speech

- Practising mindfulness, and abstaining from intoxicants.

I firmly believe that structural violence is as important as individual/behavioural violence – it's just as real for those affected by it, and creates suffering on a vast scale – and it's just as important to challenge it. Structural violence refers to the systematic ways in which social structures harm or disadvantage individuals and certain groups, communities or classes of people. It's the suffering caused by policies, processes and social norms created by the structures of our society, including governments, organisations, institutions, the economy and financial system, and the wider socio-political system.

One of the most fundamental tenets of Buddhism is that of conditionality – all things arise in dependence upon conditions. Conditionality operates on multiple levels from the physical, inorganic and biological to the psychological and transcendental. But conditionality can also operate on a collective, social level. Buddhist traditions, with their emphasis on personal liberation and ethics on an interpersonal level, often overlook this.

It follow from conditionality that our actions (our *karma*) have consequences. This also operates on a collective level. *Karma vipaka* is the consequences of our actions. The fruits we reap as a result of our action. What is our collective *karma vipaka*? Climate change. Resource depletion. Extreme inequality. Economic collapse. Ecological collapse. We can change our collective *karma vipaka* by changing our collective *karma* and acting collectively.

Beneath the precept of not taking life is the principle of non-violence. I express this on an individual level by trying to avoid harmful behaviour, but also by being a pro-life force in the wider world, taking action collectively with others. For me, a deed of loving kindness is chaining myself to the gates of a fracking site so it can't pump toxic chemicals into the Earth; it's blockading a runway to prevent the release of thousands of tonnes of CO_2; its supergluing myself to the front door of a PR company highlighting its covering up of human rights abuses of dictatorial regimes.

The flipside of 'not taking life' is the cherishing of life, holding it sacred. It's a fierce solidarity with all of life and living beings, especially those without a voice – standing with them in their struggles, fighting with them for justice. Taking action when profit is being prioritised over life, an all too common occurrence in today's capitalist world. It's about honouring how deeply connected we are with everything and everyone else – because we are not separate, until we are all free, no one is free.

Kindness is a turning towards. Turning towards all beings, in their joy and flourishing and in their pain and suffering, not shying away from the pain and damage being inflicted upon the Earth and its inhabitants.

My life is an offering

I can practise generosity on this level too. The biggest gift I can give is myself, my life. Giving myself to the world, to liberation, to justice. The peace, liberation and development of ourselves is intimately bound up with that of our communities, society and the natural world. With this ideal as my bedrock, my life becomes an offering. The gifts I can give are my time, my energy and my love. And with ever-increasing levels of activist surveillance and repression, also my privacy, security, safety and comfort – even my liberty.

This world has not been given to us. We borrow it for a while before passing it on to future generations, who also borrow it. To be complicit in its destruction, to collude with the destructive system we find ourselves in, is a gross expression of taking the not-given.

For me, the principle of truthful communication extends beyond being honest in the conversations I have. It's about speaking truth to power. Power concedes nothing without a demand. It's about speaking up and calling out violence, oppression and injustice, not being willing to allow those things to happen without accountability from those inflicting it.

Truthful communication happens on the level of public discourse as well as interpersonally. We can change that discourse. In 2010 David Cameron infamously pledged 'No ifs, no buts, no third runway', referring to Heathrow amidst mass protest. He later reneged on that promise under corporate pressure, and commissioned an investigation into not *whether* to expand an airport but *which one*. The debate centred around Heathrow or Gatwick, with climate change conveniently ignored until our action highlighted the option of *neither*, because any new runway is incompatible with a safe climate.

Avoiding intoxication and practising mindfulness extends far beyond alcohol and drugs. We dull and intoxicate our minds with social media, TV, obsession over image and mindless consumption. The myths of capitalism can also intoxicate our individual and collective consciousness – that consumption makes us happy, poor people should just work harder, hard-working families are the only people who deserve a decent life, that migrants are the problem, that inequality is natural. To not be intoxicated by these myths is one thing. To avoid intoxication from the comfortable bubble that Buddhist practice can create is quite another!

The pitfalls of modern Buddhism

Western Buddhism is introspective and emphasises personal liberation. Without a conscious awareness and critical analysis of its socio-political context, it risks replicating the ego-image-obsessed hyper-individualism bred by consumer capitalism. As ancient wisdom merges with contemporary culture, a new expression of spiritual practice must emerge.

Mindfulness 'clear and radiant', as it is described in the precepts, is an awakened awareness. It is fully aware of the particular socio-political context we are practising in, of the violence and suffering around us – structural and otherwise – and turns towards it with love, compassion and fearlessness. To be fully aware and alive in our times is to understand the destructive power structures that condition us individually and collectively, to not be complicit in them, and to join the collective efforts to change them.

Progressive social movements shape society and the values it holds through collective transformation. Joining with such movements and engaging with the world and its suffering on a societal scale can help to mitigate the potential narcissistic tendencies of Western Buddhism and add a creative edge to practice, offering rich ground for spiritual growth and the propagation of spiritual values in society.

Spiritual paths often focus on individual change, which is a vital part of changing our world for the better. It's a great place to start, but a terrible place to stop. As Derrick Jensen wrote:

> Any revolution on the outside – any breaking down of current power structures – with no corresponding revolution in perceiving, being or thinking, will merely further destruction, genocide and ecocide. Any revolution on the inside – a revolution of the heart – which does not lead to a revolution on the outside – plays just as false.[1]

The pitfalls of social action

Equally, without reflection and self-awareness, social movements can replicate the very issues they are trying to change. Though well intentioned in its pursuit of a common good, replication of capitalist

---

1   *A Language Older Than Words*, Derrick Jensen (Chelsea Green Publishing, 2004), p.288.

productivism is all too easy to slip into when working on urgent issues. Groups falling into this culture can lack real community and support, leading to burnout, disillusionment and unhealthy cultures of overwork. In my experience, how valued and included people are can become bound up in how much they *do*, creating a tyranny of the energetic; we start to relate to each other not as human beings but as colleagues at best and disposable machines at worst. To avoid replicating unhelpful or oppressive tendencies, we must educate ourselves, acknowledge our privilege and use it wisely as allies, relinquish power to marginalised voices, ask what solidarity is actually needed and be willing to listen and let go of other agendas. All this requires work, time, deep emotional resilience and a lot of self-awareness.

Without the inner sustenance of a spiritual practice, the exhausting challenges of working for social change can become overwhelming. Limited resources; too few people taking on huge, complex issues; facing opponents with vast power and wealth; repression from the corporate, police and state powers. This can lead to corrosive cynicism, self-righteousness, conflict and burnout. Eventually, older, more experienced activists drop out, taking their experience and skill with them and leaving the younger remainers to continue. Perhaps this is one reason why it is often left to the youth to drive radical social change forwards, as well as their naturally keener sense of the future they will grow into.

The younger generation

This is particularly poignant today. We are the first generation to know enough about climate change to understand its devastating consequences, and the last with enough time to do anything about it. With impending ecological collapse also comes the threat of socio-economic collapse. Having to pay more for an education than ever, and with perhaps the most precarious chance of a secure job to pay it off, today's youth find themselves in a uniquely uncertain world.

We are acutely aware of this and are stepping up to the challenge in a multitude of innovative ways. Finding your place in a bewildering world of uncertainty is challenging enough even without having to respond to the cries of a world on fire. Spirituality of all faiths and none has much to offer this forsaken generation, and will play a vital role in recreating a sacred connection with the Earth, which will be crucial if we are to heal the broken relationship that has driven us to this point of crisis.

My own deeply spiritual connection with the Earth is a galvanising source of energy for action. Honouring the 'ecological self' allows me to see that I am not 'defending nature' but rather I am nature defending itself. Great power, energy and resilience can be drawn from connecting to the wider web of life. The more I deepen my sacred connection with the wider Earth community the more I find I am able to tap into a deep well of skill and resource that is beyond my own. In supporting young people to channel this sacred energy, spiritual communities can help to create a powerful force of life-affirming action; but they must first make the connections between their own traditions and the Earth from which they descend.

Spiritual communities also offer a radical, meaningful alternative to the often soulless, disconnected modern youth culture. Through my own experience of the young people's movement within Triratna, running events and retreats for under-35s, I have seen the appetite for depth and spiritual connection among young people – searching for meaning and community in a world that offers so little after many years of socio-economic policies that have eroded meaning and community spirit.

> "Great power, energy and resilience can be drawn from connecting to the wider web of life."

> "Spiritual communities can help to create a powerful force of life-affirming action; but they must first make the connections between their own traditions and the Earth from which they descend."

The violent riots of 2011 and the more recent outbreaks in 2015 and 2016 demonstrate the frustrations of a disenfranchised generation crying out for change through desperate, destructive rampage. Michael Meade wrote: 'If the fires that innately burn inside youths are not lovingly added to the hearth of community, they will burn down the structures of culture, just to feel the warmth.'[2]

Spiritual communities must create space for the young to come together and explore spirituality on their own terms, encourage and support them to create their own youth-led spaces. On so many occasions I've seen the transformative potential of such spaces and felt the benefits myself. It was only when I found peers to practise with that I was able to integrate my spiritual practice into my life.

To be relevant and meaningful to today's youth, any contemporary spirituality must listen and respond not only to the needs of young people but also to the needs of our times, as these will shape their lives and they will be responsible for transforming it.

The world is on fire like never before. Some of the destructive, violent structures of our society must inevitably burn if we are to survive. Building a life-affirming society from the ashes of the dying system will require great skill, creativity and courage. We need to create economic and social structures in our society and our communities that connect us and support us to evolve and mature spiritually. If the energy and vision of young people is not channelled, we risk the whole show being burnt just to feel the warmth.

So commit rebellious acts of kindness, speak with radical honesty, subvert the status quo with kindness and open your heart to the struggle, for the struggle is for life. A meaningful life, a life of integrity and connection, of cooperation rather than competition, of solidarity rather than selfishness, of generosity rather than greed. Let's stand together and pour love back into our communities, and join with others to dismantle the structures of oppression and reclaim our right to live as if the world mattered.

---

2   Quoted in *The Soul of Education: Helping Students Find Connection, Compassion, and Character at School*, Rachel Kessler (ASCD, 2000).

Chapter 11

LLEWELLYN VAUGHAN-LEE

SPIRITUAL PRINCIPLES IN ACTION

'What matters most is love.'

Llewellyn Vaughan-Lee PhD is a Sufi Sheikh in the Naqshbandiyya-Mujaddidiyya Sufi order. Born in London in 1953, he has followed the Naqshbandi Sufi path since he was 19. In 1991 he became the successor of Irina Tweedie, who brought this particular Indian branch of Sufism to the West. He then moved to Northern California and founded The Golden Sufi Center. Since 2000 his writing and teaching has focused on spiritual responsibility in our present time of transition. Vaughan-Lee is the author of many books, including: Spiritual Ecology: The Cry of the Earth; Darkening of the Light: Witnessing the End of an Era; For Love of the Real: A Story of Life's Mystical Secret; and Sufism: The Transformation of the Heart.

Llewellyn Vaughan-Lee writes:

The piece below was written in answer to a question from a 31-year-old person: 'What advice do you have for people my age in dealing with a world that tells us we are nothing but material mechanisms, and has almost no concept of the soul?'

I grew up in an England still dreary in the post-war years. It was a grey world aspiring to middle-class materialism – a TV, a washing machine, even a car! Then in the mid to late sixties, another color entered the spectrum of consciousness. The Beatles went to India to meditate with the Maharishi, and orange-robed Hare Krishna devotees could be seen dancing and chanting on Oxford Street in London. Spirituality in all of its flavors and colors began to arrive in the West.

This awakening spirituality was part of my adolescence. When I was 16 I began to practice Zen meditation, and experienced an inner dimension of emptiness completely different from the world of my schoolboy classrooms. When I was 18 I practiced hatha yoga (until I damaged my knee from sitting too long in the lotus position) and became macrobiotic, learning to bake my own unleavened bread. I studied sacred geometry and built geodesic domes. I attended one of the first Glastonbury Festivals, where the pyramid stage was supposed to transmit spiritual vibrations. Then, when I was 19, I met my spiritual teacher, a white-haired Russian lady who had just returned from India where she had been trained by a Sufi master. My heart became awakened to a love I never knew existed. Many friends at the time followed similar and different paths – exploring Buddhist meditation in the monasteries of South East Asia, reading Tibetan texts, chanting Hindu mantras, or whirling with Sufi dervishes. We felt that we were part of a spiritual movement that was going to change the world. Something was alive in a new way, a new spark of consciousness was present.

Looking back over almost half a century, I can see how the journey and story of my generation was to help bring these practices and teachings to the West, to help something come alive in our materialistic Western consciousness. Meditation groups formed, ashrams were built, and many of us practiced meditation, accessing different states of consciousness. We were both naïve and optimistic, expecting this infusion of spiritual consciousness to change the world. Sadly, or more realistically, while it changed *our* world, the world around us only became more enamored of materialism, technology, and the *toys of triviality*. And as the seventies moved into the eighties and then the nineties, many of the gurus became corrupted, mainly by sex or money, and many sincere seekers disillusioned. The innocence of those early years faded into the harsher light of daily life.

But something remained. There *was* a shift in consciousness – this new color in the spectrum remained – along with the different spiritual practices and texts that had come from the East. And those of us who remained true to our practices, who lived our meditation and spiritual values, held this shift in consciousness, integrated it into our daily life. We listened to our dreams and our heart, we were open to inner experiences beyond the physical. We lived the story of our soul.

Then, at the beginning of the twenty-first century, something within me shifted, and I was shown how spiritual values belong not just to the inner journey of the individual, but have a vital part to play in the outer world. Traditionally the seeker turns away from the outer towards the inner, seeking the truth that, for example, in Sufism can only be found within the heart. Through meditation and prayer, going deep within we find something beyond the illusions of the outer world – we dip into love's infinite ocean. We experience the reality of the Self and the oneness that belongs to all that exists – what the Sufis call 'unity of being', and for the Buddhist is experienced as Buddha nature with its awareness of the interdependence of existence ('dependent co-arising'). But I began to realize that this 'consciousness of oneness' was needed in our outer world, that our world was suffering from a misguided consciousness of separation, which is the consciousness of the rational self and ego: we are separate from the Earth and separate from each other.

This focus on awakening to oneness gradually evolved into my Spiritual Ecology work of recent years, giving a spiritual perspective to our present ecological crisis. When I began this work over a decade ago, 'oneness' was still a fringe 'spiritual' idea. Spirituality and ecology were rarely associated. Environmentalists thought spiritual practitioners were 'new age' and not activist enough, while apart from a few 'engaged Buddhists' and others, spiritual practices and teachings were focused on self-development and the individual inner journey. But I am very happy that in the last few years, oneness, interconnectivity, or what the Buddhist monk Thich Nhat Hanh calls 'interbeing', have become much more part of the mainstream, and central to understanding the ecological crisis – that we need to respond from an awareness of the Earth as a living organic whole.

As Pope Francis expressed so beautifully in his encyclical *On Care for our Common Home*, we need to listen to 'the cry of the earth and the cry of the poor'. We can no longer afford to live in a way of exploitation and division. We need to take full responsibility for our world and work together to return to a balanced and sustainable way of life for humanity and all of creation – to care for both the soil and the soul.

As I have mentioned, condensed into these paragraphs is almost half a century's journey of living, and also holding, a quality of consciousness radically different to that of the environment I was born into. In its broadest terms this consciousness is *the awareness of a spiritual reality whose values are very different to the ego-driven material focus of our present civilization.* Sadly the materialistic values of the fifties have now morphed into a global monster, exploiting and ravaging the Earth in a way that can only result in mutual self-destruction. And while there are those continuing this nightmare of 'business of usual' – the global corporations and politicians who pursue only economic growth or greed – there are others who have real 'care for our common home', who hear the cry of the Earth and the pressing need to live from a place of unity. Maybe we have already passed the 'tipping point' of unforeseen ecological consequences: temperatures rising, rivers and oceans polluted, and air made toxic. But as our world spins out of balance, spiritual awareness and its values have a vital role to play.

Yet I believe it is no longer enough just to hold this awareness – *we have to bring it into action.* The next chapter in this story of spirituality must be to bring these values, this quality of consciousness, into action to help a world that is becoming a soulless and environmental wasteland. I firmly believe that this is the calling for the next generation: for those who have the energy and passion to act from a place of service and love for the Earth. And especially important, from a place of unity.

This is the challenge facing those of the millennial generation who sense that life is something more than the accumulation of 'stuff', who have heard the cry of the Earth, which is also the cry of their own soul. How can we help the world in this time of transition? How can we participate creatively in our lives and communities? There is much work to be done, a work founded upon the principles of oneness and unity, a work that recognizes that all of life is sacred and whole. Life is calling to us and it desperately needs our attention; around us are what Thich Nhat Hanh calls 'bells of mindfulness', which we need to hear and then respond to – hear with our hearts and respond with our hands.

There are many ways to participate, to work towards ecological wholeness, from forming a community of urban gardeners, to developing new economic models based upon generosity and sharing rather than acquisition, such as 'pay it forward'. And I firmly believe that, while some global initiatives are vital, like reducing carbon emissions, most initiatives should be small groups of people coming together in different ways. Governments and politicians are too bound to the idea of continued 'economic growth' to commit to real change. Instead the world needs to be regenerated in an organic, cellular way, the way life recreates itself.

It is for each person to find the community and initiative that speaks most to their nature, their unique offering. And central to this work is that we are here to help each other and to help the Earth and all of its inhabitants – as in original instructions given to the First Peoples that we 'have to get along together'. I also believe that it is important for anyone committing to this work to develop their own spiritual practice – especially helpful is a meditation practice that is done every day. It can be a mindfulness meditation, watching the breath, the Christian practice of centering prayer, or a Sufi heart meditation. This practice can support and protect us, and inwardly guide us in our work.

And if I have learned anything from my own journey, I've learned what matters most is love. Love is the most powerful force in creation, and it is our love for the Earth that will heal what we have desecrated, that will guide us through this wasteland and help us to bring light back into our darkening world. As in the words of the poet Wendell Berry, 'The world...can be redeemed only by love.' Love links us all together in the most mysterious ways, and love can guide our hearts and hands. And the central note of love is oneness. Love speaks the language of oneness, of unity rather than separation.

We need a new story, one based upon the deep spiritual principles of oneness, care for the Earth and care for each other. This is a multigenerational work and it is for this younger generation to bring these principles into form, into action *now*. It will not be easy. The forces of greed and exploitation are more entrenched than we realize, the environmental collapse accelerating. But this is the challenge for those whose hearts are young and energized, who care for the planet and for the souls of future generations. This is the next chapter of the story of our time that is waiting to be lived.

PART 4

COMPLEX IDENTITIES

We are living in a globally connected age of complexity. That complexity and global influence is clearly reflected in our emerging identities.

In the West, the under-35s are the most ethnically diverse generation we have ever known. In the US, going on for half the younger population are now people of colour, and in the UK, mixed-race identities are the fastest-growing ethnic minority group.[1] Mixed-race peoples may well be the single largest ethnic minority group in the future. The growing popularity of DNA testing for ancestry demonstrates that, in reality, single ethnicity heritages are already an illusion.

In St Ethelburga's Sacred Activist programmes, when we gather a group of 20 young leaders, the identities in the room stretch across the globe. We meet many young people who have, for example, an Asian mother and European father, who were born in Hong Kong, grew up in Egypt and are studying in London. These patterns, coupled with the internet and communications technology, have produced a younger

---

1 'The Rise of Multiracial and Multiethnic Babies in the U.S.', 6 June 2017: www.pewresearch.org/fact-tank/2017/06/06/the-rise-of-multiracial-and-multiethnic-babies-in-the-u-s

generation who are *emphatically* global. Even if their DNA doesn't span the world, their social media friends and followers probably do.

In this collection, our contributors reflect a range of different routes into that global, interconnected identity. For Vero, Zoë, Kara and many others, their ecological activism has expanded their sense of self. Borders and nationalities make little sense if you live with the Earth in your heart in every moment. Bruna's work with displaced people connects her to the dramatic waves of human migration traversing continents, and brings her up against national identity as a limiting and sometimes inhuman barrier. Camille and Orion find it through understanding interlocking systems of oppression, and through dismantling binaries.

When you add into the mix the multiple religious influences that this global way of life inevitably brings, and the astonishing array of spiritualities accessible in any 21st-century city, it's clear we are witnessing a massive sea change.

As a member of Generation X, growing up as a religious seeker in London, by the time I was 25, the plethora of faiths around me already made it impossible to accept the truth claims of any one tradition. It just seemed glaringly illogical to believe in any one right way. Then the question naturally becomes, not which tradition is right, but which one suits me best?

Twenty years later the pick-and-mix approach is ubiquitous (though for some, balanced precariously with the tension of family expectations). Even those committed to a single tradition would these days think nothing of incorporating some yoga or practising mindfulness techniques originating in Buddhism. Being committed to a single tradition also no longer necessarily equates to being committed to a particular place of worship, congregation or guru. Many young people identify as, for example, Christian, Buddhist or Muslim, but remain unaffiliated to a specific community.

There is a freedom in this, and also many dangers. Dekila in Chapter 26 writes with passion about cultural appropriation and the dumbing down of spiritual practices taken out of context. Underlying those issues, a society that shops for spirituality is relating through a consumerist lens. The one thing that might keep the damage of rampant consumerism in check, or provide an alternative story, has itself become a commodity.

Perhaps young people have no choice but to shop for spirituality? As Bayo Akomolafe, the Nigerian ethnopsychologist, says:

> I know you don't mean to do many of these things: you do not mean to appropriate other cultural values, strip them of their embeddedness in context, package them into neat formulas or products and commercialize them. Or maybe you do, because you know no other way to approach the sacred.[2]

Seekers these days do not leave their home town to wander on time-honoured pilgrimage routes. We search on the internet and enter into the marketplace. But where is the line between seeking and shopping? And how do we prevent the capitalist forces that are shaping our experience and our behaviour from taking us even further down a perilous road to the gradual, imperceptible hollowing out of our deepest sources of meaning?

Clearly there is something wonderful about the rich mosaic of spiritual influences we come into relationship with at this time. In the early days at St Ethelburga's, those involved in interfaith dialogue were exhilarated by the way our exchanges opened minds and hearts to a whole world of ancient wisdom teachings. In the longer term, what will be the impact of that global mixing and unbundling on every level? Will neoliberal economics commodify and destroy the soul of religion? Without depth and commitment, will our inner lives become ever more distracted and shallow? Is it an impending train wreck – a slow wiping out of belief and spiritual practice? Or is it the dissolution that comes before a transformation – a caterpillar dissolving in the chrysalis before becoming a butterfly? Is it a tragic disintegration or does it herald the emergence of a new way of being with the Divine? What do you think?

---

2   Bayo Akomolafe, 'Dear White People', http://bayoakomolafe.net/project/dear-white-people

Chapter 12

ORION STEPHANIE JOHNSTONE

EXPLODING BINARIES

'Ferociously committed to our collective liberation.'

Orion Stephanie Johnstone is 35 years old and a queer, non-binary composer, theatre director, community organiser and sexuality educator who describes themself as 'ferociously committed to our collective liberation'. A graduate of Tisch School of the Arts in New York, Orion has held residencies at Pace, UArts and Montclair State Universities and they were Associate Music Director of the national tour of War Horse. Orion's current projects include being musical supervisor and contributing composer for a multi-generational choral concert event called 'Primer for a Failed Superpower', based on re-imagined protest songs from the past hundred years. They are co-director of Diana Oh's {My Lingerie Play} The Concert & Call to Arms!!!!!!!!!, a piece about dismantling rape culture, performed alongside creative direct action in the public square. Orion is a sex and relationships coach. They created a popular podcast, Sex for Smart People, dedicated to contextualising ideas about sex and dating within a larger social justice framework, and they are the Chief Director of Content and Community Architect for a new dating app for kinky people called KinkedIn.

An interdependent worldview is one in which nothing can be left out, nothing can be cast into the duality of 'this' or 'that', 'us' or 'them'. I wanted this book to include someone who identified as gender non-binary as it is an important part of that landscape of complexity. The number of people in the UK seeking treatment for gender identity issues has soared, and there are huge changes emerging in Generations Y and Z in how gender is perceived.

Orion's spirituality is based in a relationship with wholeness and a passionate exploration of inclusion. They are not only blazing a trail by living an expanded relationship with their own gender and sexuality, but also enthusiastically and joyfully seeking ways to support others. Sexuality is one area where many religious institutions are not keeping up with cultural norms and contributes to the mass exodus from institutions. Orion's story of rejecting the shame that religion instilled in them, and replacing it with a freedom of expression that is positively celebratory, is an exhilarating one.

Alongside exploding the binary of gender, Orion's commitment is to decolonisation, to anti-racism, to exposing the intersectionality of overlapping oppressions (also mentioned by Camille in Chapter 20 and Dekila in Chapter 26) – and to decolonisation of the body – the integration of spirit and matter, sacred and profane.

This shift in thinking from dualism to inter-relationality has, over the last two decades, percolated through many different disciplines. The millennial generation takes us a step beyond thinking, forging new ways to live it, to ground it in practical tools and embodied processes. Anti-racist work keeps us vigilant to the ways in which Western colonialist conditioning can warp that process. We need people like Orion, Camille, and those behind the Black Lives Matter movement, to notice when we create genuinely inclusive spaces or processes – and to pull us up when we only think we have.

Orion says: 'I look at anti-racism and decolonisation as spiritual practices.' Just as those who take their spiritual values and learn what it means to act them out in the world, those who are living their values in the world experience that as their spiritual path.

The work of building a world that is just, as well as sustainable, becomes religion, becomes 'spirit-centred justice'. Generation Y are teaching the world that faith that stays in the realm of the private and personal is over. The path is to take what one knows in one's heart to be right and true, refuse to be conditioned by those who have given in, boldly cut through resistance, both inner and outer, and live it. Every day. No matter what it costs.

Motifs in this chapter:

- Complex identities

- Natural leadership

- Protecting Earth

JH: Orion, let's talk about identity first. Tell me more about how you identify from the perspective of gender, sexuality, faith and culture.

Orion: First and foremost, I am someone who sits in the question: 'Who' and 'how' might we be together more bravely, in the light of our collective liberation? I am a white person who endeavours with every cell of my being to be anti-racist. I am queer, which is as much of a political identity as it is a sexual identity. Not 'gay as in happy' but 'queer as fuck you', as in: fuck your overlapping and intersecting systems of oppression. I'm trans and non-binary, and I love being playfully, robustly 'gender-full'. I do my best to operate from the place Kate Bornstein calls 'radical wonder and radical welcome'.

In terms of my roots, my father is a fundamentalist evangelical Christian pastor. I was an evangelical Christian until the age of 22 (I'm 35 now), and since then I've been finding my way home to the connection with spirit that feels really true to me.

My most core spiritual practice is curiosity. And humility. The humble admission that I don't know how things will turn out – that's where my hope is rooted.

JH: Tell me more about being gender-full or gender non-binary. Why is that important in our society at the moment?

Orion: I understand binary gender to be a colonialist concept, rooted in white supremacy and Christian supremacy. In many cultures around the world, gender has long been understood to be beyond male and female,[1] and non-binary gender shows up in other forms of nature too. Within many educated, privileged US communities there is a lot of discussion now about gender complexity, but it's important to name: this is not new. I was awake to myself, long before I had words for it. And I owe much to so many trans and gender non-conforming folk who paved the way by being open and visible about their full selves.

Using the pronouns 'they/them/theirs' feels deeply important to me. The 'she' pronoun had long felt like 'Oh, I could put on this dress but it clearly doesn't fit quite right, everyone can see it is awkward'. Whereas using they/them/theirs feels like putting on a piece of clothing that I feel deeply at home in. It is also a deeply political and spiritual way of living into 'queer' as a verb, because when folks know they can't assume my gender, then the ripple effect means folks will assume less about other folks' gender, which is one part of creating more safety and freedom for everyone, of all genders, and specifically for trans folks.

> "Using the pronouns 'they/them/theirs' feels deeply important to me."

---

[1] For example, the Māhū of Hawai'i acknowledge an intermediate state between man and woman, and the Dineh of the Southwestern US acknowledge four genders: feminine woman, masculine woman, feminine man, masculine man. The term 'third gender' has also been used to describe the hijras of India, Bangladesh and Pakistan who have gained legal identity. There are many other cultures in which the third gender is seen as a natural and legitimate intermediate being rather than as disordered or as a movement from one conventional sex to the other. In some Eastern cultures the intermediate gender/s are revered. The notion of reincarnation also allows for more fluid and mutable categorisation.

I think it's important to ask, what does the binary serve? What's the impact of transcending or dismantling it? What's it connected to? Much of the Western version of binary gender is really rooted in control over the feminine. Patriarchy is invested in keeping this rigid binary structure where men/male/masculine is given more power, and the other side of that duality is not honoured. Thus, we are all liberated when we can hold genders more fluidly. Whether or not we are all upholding each other in our gender complexity, that makes a very real difference to how open my heart is in any given context. But the experience of being unapologetically non-binary is often exhausting. I'm grateful to be rich in queer and trans community where I am fully seen. The rest of the world feels different and harder. But because of the privileges that I carry, it is statistically safer for me be out and open about who I am than for many folks who don't carry those privileges.

JH: I love that you use your privilege to blaze a trail for us all. That's really humbling. Tell me more about your journey into sexuality education...

Orion: I didn't set out to become a sexuality educator! As an evangelical Christian, I experienced different forms of spiritual violence that became deeply ingrained as shame. After my first sexual experiences I'd been expecting to feel awful and shameful but actually just felt deeply respected and celebrated and seen and honoured and beautiful. It was an epic journey from utter shame to utter celebration, and I was very open about sharing my experience. People started coming to me with questions and wanting sex advice. I was talking to about ten people per week, and it became clear that I was seen as a person it was safe to talk to about things that it doesn't often feel safe to talk about. I wanted to take that very seriously. So I began a deep study of sex, gender, relationships, communication and consent. Everything I have built as a sex educator started just as a resource for friends, and my coaching practice was formed so that I could have boundaries around the deep work with individuals.

JH: So where do spirituality and sexuality come together for you?
Orion: Spirituality to me has a lot to do with wholeness. And wholeness has a lot to do with decolonisation. I look at anti-racism and decolonisation as spiritual practices. White supremacy primarily hurts people of colour, but the violence that white supremacy does to white folks can boil down to a disconnect from body and Earth.

A lot of my spiritual practices are very simple. Am I listening with all of my senses? Am I listening with my full body? Do I know where the sun and moon are positioned in the sky right now? Am I conscious of myself not just in a man-made four-walled structure, but as an interdependent being on this whole vast planet in this whole vast universe?

My spiritual practice also has to do with looking at ancestry, including my Polish ancestry. In just about every lineage, there are Earth-based practices that were covered over by organised Christianity. So I'm learning more about that. Also, I'm fired up to learn more about my 'chosen ancestors', these warriors for queer and trans justice. I think of Marsha P. Johnson and Sylvia Rivera, and others who courageously paved the way. Engaging in the fight for collective liberation is deeply spiritual for me; I don't believe I can be in my own wholeness without doing so.

In my Christian upbringing there was this belief that you can either be a good person or a sexual person. It's been a long and painful, but ultimately gorgeous, journey to realise that who I am sexually is a core part of the good, whole person that I am. That did not come overnight, and my own journey was supported by the journey of so many others.

A part of that was learning about the practice of tantra. Tantra is an ancient practice that comes from cultures that are not my own. When I first began learning about tantra, I wasn't doing it from a conscious place but a more appropriative place. With that acknowledged, I am grateful for the enormous gifts from that practice – it was the first arena I saw where spirituality and sexuality can be one and the same – this deep listening to my body, which is deeply decolonising too, and

> "Full-on sacred *and* profane – those things are not the dichotomy the dominant culture would have us believe."

that pleasure is sacred! I don't mean just in the sense of, we're going really slow, have lit candles and are being really tender – but also any place that our erotic maps point us toward, with communication, from a place of wholeness. That was huge for me – how we can live into more permission to be our whole selves – full-on sacred *and* profane – those things are not the dichotomy the dominant culture would have us believe.

JH: So what is your real calling Orion? And what kind of world do you want to see?

Orion: Sometimes it feels painful to think about the world I would like to see, because the very real violence many people experience on a daily basis means it can be tempting to stay in the realm of harm reduction. Harm reduction is a way of being that I deeply respect – but I also believe that it is our duty to imagine and co-create a world that can hold all of us in a more just and liberated way, knowing that, as adrienne maree brown says, we can feel that world in our blood and our bones even if we can't fully comprehend it yet.

So through that lens of our mandate to imagine, I imagine a world where a culture of care is so strong that it's non-negotiable. I think of care as so deeply anti-capitalist. I think of moving at the speed of trust as a radical and revolutionary fighting back against all that is oppressive. I think of the abolition of prisons and of police systems. I think of radically re-imagining how we show care, and how we conceive of safety with each other, starting from a deep place of listening to the people around us, and widening who we mean when we say 'we'. I think of kinship networks that are far vaster and more nuanced than this model of privatise-your-compassion-in-nuclear-families that we have now. I imagine what it can be to operate from a place of abundance in terms of care, intimacy, safety and basic needs being met.

I can't envision a step-by-step path toward what I'm describing; however, I think my deepest calling, or what I'm here to do, is to embody those values with integrity and to boldly create containers for others to live into them as well, inasmuch as they want to. My deepest calling is to continually sit in this question of who and how might we be together more bravely, in light of our collective liberation. What that looks like for me these days is spirit-centred justice and justice-centred collaborative art-making. I find myself playing the same role in every space that I'm in, even though I move through radically different spaces – as sexuality educator, as political organiser, as theatre director and theatre maker. In every space, I'm doing my best to be facilitator and midwife of this more liberated world I know in my blood and bones is possible.

> "I'm doing my best to be facilitator and midwife of this more liberated world I know in my blood and bones is possible."

JH: What role do the arts play for you in bringing about that world?

Orion: I'm clear that art is not a luxury but is a basic cultural human right. The professional arts world today is deeply entangled in all of those systems of oppression, and especially capitalism, so it's challenging work in the arts and also to be in line with my spiritual and political integrity. I was working as a professional composer and theatre maker from about 2001 to 2011. In that ten-year period my work was deeply informed by my political values, but I wasn't really walking the talk. Just reading about collective liberation, human rights and queer rights – I didn't really feel empowered. When Occupy Wall Street happened, I dropped everything and was basically just there for eight months. I thought I would never make art in the same way again. I took a deep dive into studying how systems shift and widespread cultural healing happen, learning anti-oppression facilitation, and channelling my musical gifts into singing in the context of civil disobedience and direct action.

I learned a lot about organising in the truest sense – how we can listen for what's emerging and collectively channel the power that is here toward our liberation. Since the heyday of Occupy Wall Street, I've gotten asked to do some really powerful and gorgeous art-making precisely because I stepped away from art-making in order to focus on anti-oppression and pro-liberation more directly. Thus, I find myself having the opportunity to make a lot of art that is deeply in line with my values. I am really humbled by that.

JH: My last question is about ministry. Throughout our conversation I can see how everything you do could be seen as new forms of ministry, speaking to the urgent need to bring activism and social change together with spiritual values, and the need to offer that to others through sharing inspiration and through leadership. Can you say something about yourself as minister?

Orion: Yes. I am a community minister in every space I'm in, and empowering others to their own ministry, whatever that looks like for them. The world I'd like to see is centred in a culture of care, where everyone's power is celebrated, especially those who carry forms of power that are currently marginalised within the dominant structures. I'd love to see a world where everyone feels permission to be a 'lower case a' artist, and a 'lower case c' chaplain and a 'lower case m' minister.

Chapter 13

VERO LOPES DA SILVA AND ZOË VOKES

CITIZENS OF EARTH

'It's time to evolve our ideas of identity.'

Twenty-six-year-old Veronica Lopes da Silva is half-Portuguese and half-Ethiopian, and grew up between Pakistan, Sudan, Italy and Angola. Through years of being involved in campaigning on global and local economic, social, political and environmental issues, she has explored different ways of having an impact. She currently works for Global Generation, a youth charity based at the Skip Garden in London, engaging young people and the community on topics including sustainability, seasonality, biodiversity and cultural diversity. By creating opportunities for people to harvest, forage and cook together, Global Generation invites participants to explore their interconnectedness with each other and the living world.

Zoë Vokes is 26 years old and lives in Brighton. Though born in the UK, she shares with Veronica the experience of travelling widely throughout her childhood, and grew up in the Philippines, Nepal and Sri Lanka. Zoë has started a number of her own businesses and has been working as a freelance event and project manager on environmental events for the last two years. She has a passion to protect endangered species, particularly marine mammals, as well as safeguarding the lives of all animals around the world through awareness-raising, activism and public speaking. Zoë is dedicated to working for a future that sees the end of the anthropocentric worldview.

Vero and Zoë were participants on St Ethelburga's first spiritual ecology leadership programme. They both identify as spiritual but not religious, and both care passionately about protecting Earth. Vero is of mixed heritage and they share the experience of growing up in different continents and countries, exposed to many religious and cultural influences.

Both work in projects connected to environmental change or education, making their own contributions as leaders. However, my interest was less to do with their social contribution than how they have made sense of the many competing narratives around them. How have they forged their identities? How has their love and concern for Earth changed the way they understand themselves? How have their experiences impacted on their spirituality?

When living in intimate proximity with so many religious traditions and communities – some walking their talk and others not – discerning a path is a rich but complex journey. Vero says, 'There is much more space and openness for people to explore, to find their own tradition, their own practice, their own spirituality.' Our recurring theme shows up again – that of rejecting readymade answers in favour of active inquiry and following one's own instinctual wisdom.

Their identities are naturally global. Zoë says she 'tries to live with the confusion and beauty of not belonging anywhere, but also belonging everywhere', and Vero once longed for 'a connection to a particular land' but now cultivates a cosmocentric perspective. For both, their relationship with Earth has become a guiding light reflecting their sense of what is sacred, shaping their values and governing how they live. Through that lens, everything is included. There is no space for spiritual life and ordinary life. It is all one.

I wanted to interview them together to draw out a conversation about the gifts and the constraints of that experience.

Motifs in this chapter:

- Complex identities

- Protecting Earth

JH: You both have very interesting multicultural heritages and have grown up in a variety of different countries. I'd love to know what that experience was like for you and how it impacted on your identity.

Zoë: The whole experience was a really rich one for me, but it was also challenging. It definitely made me a stronger person as well as exposing me to many different cultures, and it had a huge impact on my identity – or rather my lack of identity. I don't feel British, but I'm not from anywhere else in the world. It's something I've really struggled with for many, many years of my life. Now I see myself as a citizen of the world, not as a citizen of any particular nation state. In fact, I feel like countries as boundaries are slightly pointless. At the end of the day we are all human and we're all living on this beautiful planet that is in a lot of distress. That is what we need to be focusing on. Borders don't really make sense and are going to make less and less sense as the world becomes ever more obviously interconnected. I'm proud to be a citizen of the Earth, not a citizen of the UK or the Philippines or Nepal or wherever. I am someone who tries

> "I am someone who tries to live with the confusion and beauty of not belonging anywhere, but also belonging everywhere."

to live with the confusion and beauty of not belonging anywhere, but also belonging everywhere.

Vero: I definitely resonate with the idea of belonging nowhere and everywhere at the same time. My mother left Ethiopia for the first time with my dad and moved to Islamabad where I was born. Thirty years later, there is a distance between her and her 'home'. My father's identity is also complex. On paper he is Portuguese, but my grandmother was Cape Verdean and my grandfather was Portuguese and together they lived in Mozambique, where my father was born. From the US, to Austria, Germany, Canada and Angola, my family has spread in search of better education and opportunities.

Growing up, I always wanted to *belong* somewhere. Over time, I've noticed a shift though. In our work at the Skip Garden we explore the universe story and the cosmocentric perspective as a way to also encourage young people to reflect on their identity on multiple levels. That has actually helped me find my own place in something much more significant than in arbitrary and strategic borders drawn up by others. The 'third culture kid' and 'international' identity has always felt vacuous to me. What I really longed for was that feeling of having a connection to a particular land. Through the cosmocentric perspective, I rooted myself in the awareness of belonging to something far greater – the Universe.

Zoë: For me, reconnecting with the Earth as a whole also brought me comfort. I recognised that was somewhere I belonged and it made me feel like I could connect honestly with any piece of land on the Earth.

Vero: My longing to belong and my struggle to find an appropriate 'category' made me realise that we have constructed identities that fit uncomfortably with my worldview. I think it's time we evolve our ideas of identity.

JH: It seems to me there is real power in those narratives.

Zoë: And yet society still dictates that this isn't acceptable. You have to belong somewhere. Like, what can I call you? Where are you from? Well, that's a difficult question for me to answer because I don't fit into your specifically defined categories. I think for many people it brings up the fear of the unknown.

Vero: I began to challenge the idea of national identities when I saw how it can be used, by people in positions of power, as an obstacle to genuine solidarity and to obstruct us from seeing common ground between all. The world would look drastically different if we based our relationships on the understanding and truth that one's fate is tied to that of others – and that we cannot stand to the side while another suffers. I would like to see a world where our interconnectedness is not only recognised and respected but also celebrated.

JH: So how did these experiences impact on the development of your spirituality?

Vero: I didn't grow up in a religious household, and, though my mother is Ethiopian Orthodox Christian, her relationship to what she refers to as God is also a very personal one. That was an important example to have growing up. I still felt societal pressure to conform to traditional ideas of religious identity though. When I lived in Italy, Sudan and Sri Lanka, I sometimes almost envied those who felt deeply rooted in their religion. But I also saw how mainstream religions can and have interacted with big power and politics. I understood the danger posed by such a powerful tool in the wrong hands. This made me more fearful and resistant to religious institutions as opposed to personal relationships with God or with the Earth or with spirituality. That left me wanting to be open and explore what it all means to *me*, and not follow a predetermined path. So now, it feels like an active inquiry – there is no end in sight.

JH: So you saw the dark side of religion, or the misuse of religion, but still allowed all those different influences to lead you into a really active, sincere inquiry. That sounds very real. Zoë, how is it for you?

Zoë: Huge similarities but some differences as well. I was exposed to so many different religious traditions growing up. Catholicism in the Philippines, then Buddhism and Hinduism in Nepal, as well as

Christianity more widely, Islam and Judaism – not just as a result of being in a particular country but also because of our international friends. So I had a really varied experience and feel very blessed to have been exposed to all these traditions.

Nepal has a very special place in my heart. I think I may have lived there in a past life. It's funny that I can talk of past lives as well. I'm sure a lot of people wouldn't really be on board with that! I wouldn't call myself a Buddhist, but the experiences I had of Hinduism and Buddhism in Nepal were very beautiful. One of my favourite places in the world is Boudhanath, a Buddhist stupa in Kathmandu. On the night of Buddha Jayanti, the Buddha's birthday, the whole mandalic structure is lit up with oil lamps – it's absolutely stunning.

I think that the experience of growing up with lots of different traditions allowed me to explore different practices and beliefs and then take on what resonated with me and leave what didn't. I searched for a long time for something I felt really fitted me. For now, I've concluded nature is my church and the Earth is the equivalent of God to me. I devote my work and practices to this beautiful planet, and my ministry is about being a vehicle for Her protection.

Vero: That's interesting. My experiences were a bit different. Learning about people's relationships with Catholicism in Rome, with Islam in Sudan, where Sharia law is enforced, and the role played by Buddhist monks in Sri Lankan politics – I was faced with examples of what can happen to even the most inspiring and beautiful principles and teachings when they are not truly embodied, and how dangerous this can be in a political sphere. That exposure has personally closed me off to a certain type of relationship with religion.

I now hope to have an active relationship with ideas, people and the world around me which allows me to approach new ideas with curiosity and openness.

Zoë: Oh no, I definitely had that experience too, particularly with Buddhism in Sri Lanka. I put Buddhism on a huge pedestal and thought it was untouchable. But when I got there... I met with monks and talked to them and was deeply, deeply disturbed by their responses. That's partly what made me feel okay about finding my own way. I felt comfortable acknowledging that I don't necessarily agree with any one religion, nor do I feel an affinity with any particular one, because for me, no single one is perfect, and I definitely have a difficult relationship with institutionalised religion.

JH: Do you think there is a possibility that you might stumble across a religion or a community that you might commit to? Or are you committed already to the path you have chosen outside of any particular tradition?

Zoë: That's a really interesting question! I'm inclined to say no, that I won't ever pick a specific tradition. I see the value in elements of so many different traditions. I studied religion at university to try and grapple with all of this. What I would love more than anything is to find a community of like-minded people who are deeply spiritual, have deep connections to the Earth, who are understanding of many religious traditions and can incorporate some of the practices into their lives without necessarily having to become part of an institutionalised religion. That would be a community I would feel very at home in.

Vero: In the past I wondered if I was missing *something*, but now I don't feel the need to commit. That doesn't mean I reject the idea of seeking altogether. There is something really beautiful about seeking. By this I mean seeking not because you're missing something, but because you never know what you might discover. There is something about exploring multiple stories because they can reveal different aspects of reality or of yourself, tell a different piece of the story, or even just make you think of something in a new way.

JH: Can you say something about your practices? How do you practise your spirituality?

Zoë: It's hard to know what is defined as a practice and what is just a part of who you are. I try to meditate regularly. I try to be grateful – I keep a gratitude journal. I've started to give thanks before every meal. There are practices that are a bit more hidden and not so obvious – like trying to come from a space of love when I speak to people, trying to be understanding of people's differences or difficulties. And then there are things I do – I burn incense and sage and I have Nordic runes, which never cease to be a guidance and remind me of the interconnectedness of everything. And I like to do a ritual for big decisions or events. When our family dog died a few years ago, we had a puja and that was an important part of the grieving process for my whole family.

Vero: Oh, that's such a hard question! [lots of laughter] In a way my 'practice' is my life. It's in how I approach life and its obstacles. It's how I introduce ritual into my life. Since being fortunate enough to be working in a community garden, it's the act of harvesting vegetables and coming back to the kitchen and cooking with love for those I love, and then returning the peels back to the composter or the worms, and going to check on the chickens. It's a lived practice – that's what I strive for. Maybe that's because I don't want to replicate what I've come across in the past – those who practise by going through the motions. They could describe their religious practices clearly, but I wasn't always convinced they actively incorporated their principles into their everyday personal, social and political lives. I don't want compartmentalised elements of my life – I want to strive to embody my beliefs in everything I do.

> "I don't want compartmentalised elements of my life – I want to strive to embody my beliefs in everything I do."

JH: There's something very beautiful about seeing your practice and your life as one. I like that a lot. On a different theme, how has it been for you growing up at a point in human history when there are so many global crises? How has that impacted on your spirituality?

Vero: I believe there's a need to find common ground, and rise up to the challenges of our time – and the stories we tell are very important. Unfortunately, a lot of the stories we tell divide us or define us. Our religious and national identities can also be used to divide us. I believe part of the solution involves standing with openness and a willingness to practise revolutionary deep listening – accepting we are far more complex, so much more than just one story. I want to continue to explore what it means to be *human* and recognise my responsibilities to my community, other living beings, as well as our home. I don't necessarily even have to describe it as 'spiritual' – it's really about striving to become a whole, complete, conscious, engaged human.

Zoë: I really relate to that. I've felt a lot of pain and grief for the state of the world – socially, environmentally, politically – on almost every level there is pain. This was a recurring theme for me growing up. I really felt the pain of the world. If people or the Earth were suffering – I felt that pain.

> "I've felt a lot of pain and grief for the state of the world – socially, environmentally, politically – on almost every level there is pain."

I'm getting better at acknowledging the grief and turning it into action. Deciding actually that's something I feel strongly about, so what can I do about it, how can I help, what can I change? The fact that the world is messed up can be a positive trigger – it can give you that drive and ambition to help, the clarity around what you want to do or who you want to be. This pain softens you, and in many ways I see this 'softening' as connected to 'spirituality', and ultimately a big part of becoming more *human*.

Vero: There are days when it all feels like too much – the violence, injustice, inequality and exploitation of humans, our home, and the other species we share this home with... But I have to remind myself that we're on a journey and it's not just downhill. We need to be telling ourselves the stories of success too – positive examples of how we *can* work together and bridge those boundaries and face our future together. Nothing positive can really come out of a space of fear. We need to be acting from a place of love. And we need to acknowledge that a lot of amazing things *are* happening. And when you are involved – whether you're at an eco project, working in a refugee camp or organising within your own communities to tackle issues such as racism and sexism – it can feel like you're in a little bubble and removed from the reality out there. But there are many others, all combining together to form a powerful network tackling the issues of our times – rooted in communities, but feeding into something much greater.

JH: It would be great to hear you both talk more about your relationship with the Earth, what the Earth is for you.
Zoë: This is an easy one for me! I feel a deep love and connection to Earth. Earth, capital E and without 'the'... I often feel putting the article 'the' in front creates distance and doesn't reflect the closeness of the relationship we all have with our planet, and everything on it for that matter. For me, Earth is our mother, our life giver, our sustainer, our common home. A living being that we, as humans, are intimately and inexplicably connected to. I see all of Earth – plants, animals, rocks, rivers – as inherently of value, worthy of our admiration, respect and protection. This is the only home we have, and it desperately needs our attention, love and protection. Earth is simply part of my extended family, and I try to live my life in a way that reflects that every day.
Vero: I started campaigning on environmental issues during my time in university in Scotland, but I don't feel I was fully conscious of the possibility of developing a more intimate and conscious relationship with the Earth. My relationship with this home is now evolving, and it's one I'm excited and very privileged to be nurturing. Like other relationships, it's one that requires time, care, love and respect.

JH: And how do you see the spirituality of the future?
Zoë: I see the spirituality of the future as one that is much more fluid than how we understand it now. I think it's going to be more about spirituality and not necessarily strict religious institutions. I'm excited for the spiritual future, I feel it has so much energy behind it, so much potential for positive transformation.

Vero: I have also noticed pockets of openness in my experiences, and I hope that this is an opportunity to move past the age of religion as a tool for domination, oppression, violence or separation...and move into a space of greater respect, understanding, deep listening and mutual learning in the future.

Chapter 14

ABBAS ZAHEDI

REINVENTING CULTURAL IDENTITY

'We all need some sense of Utopia to invest in.'

Abbas Zahedi is a multi-disciplinary artist based in London. His practice ranges across sound, moving image, installation, performance and participatory events. Abbas's current practice is influenced by the predicament of being a second-generation migrant, in a hyper-connected world. Abbas has exhibited his work at shows and festivals in London, Oxford, Cambridge and Venice. He was an artist with the Urban Dialogues programme of exhibitions and academic salons (2012–2016), in association with Sotheby's, White Cube and King's College London. In 2015 he performed poetry from his work at the Bradford Literature Festival and was a featured performer at the Hammer and Tongue finals in Camden. Abbas has used his practice to develop a number of grassroots initiatives and was awarded a fellowship from the School for Social Entrepreneurs in recognition of his innovative approach to working with migrant communities in the UK. Abbas is married with a young son.

I first met Abbas through a BARBEDOUN event (see below), and liked the way he used his overflowing imagination and constant live stream of new ideas to host gathering spaces that felt very fresh and animated. For me, Abbas, as a second-generation migrant, represents an experience of both connection and disconnection. Despite the complexity of living Islam within a non-Muslim collective, Abbas survives a city that makes him feel he doesn't belong and withstands the call to radicalisation at university. He knows the experience of marginalisation, but emerges looking at the world through a lens of multiple stories and identities living side by side in a fertile soup.

There must be many people who share these experiences. What I appreciate with Abbas is his resourcefulness. He responds to everything through the dazzling kaleidoscope of his creativity – processing his experiences, reflecting them back to others, making art installations, designing new spaces and gathering people. Like Nick George in Chapter 17 and Sukina Douglas in Chapter 18, Abbas plays the roles of 'Gatherer' and 'Maker', offering spiritual nourishment for a complex and multicultural world.

Looking through his eyes, I experience a vision of both the challenges and the immense creativity of cultural diversity that I struggle to express. I hope something of it comes across in this passage.

Motifs in this chapter:

- Complex identities

- New spaces

- Natural leadership

Social entrepreneur, cultural alchemist, performance poet and culinary innovator – Abbas is an artist who pursues his art, as a way of 'overcoming binaries forged against the chaos of losing culture and familial familiarity'.

Abbas's projects include BARBEDOUN, a pop-up bar that hosts imaginative supper clubs, events and artistic installations. Drinks are all alcohol-free, creating an inclusive alternative setting for young Muslims and others who don't drink. He is a curator of open-mic nights where spoken word, music and prayer are woven together to create spaces rich in texture, community and spiritual energy. His audiences are a young crowd who resist simple definitions – urban 'cultural nomads' with multiple identities and roots all over the world. Abbas is also a new father to a beautiful baby boy called Yasin, undergoing the initiation of parenthood, and beginning to see his own leadership and social contribution through the lens of making a better future for his son to grow up in.

Starting a conversation with Abbas is like stepping into a swirling space, alive with ideas and possibilities, questions that taste like a medley of ingredients, poetic rhythms and deep philosophical inquiries. The future is here somewhere. I can taste it and sense it, like a song that you hear for the first time and, with a rush of excitement, know is going to be a hit.

Abbas was born in Camden – his parents came over from Iran and settled in the UK following a series of medical complications. Whilst growing up he attended Holland Park School, one of the most diverse secondary schools in the country.

His experience, like many others, has been of treading a path between different heritages, seeking for a sense of identity and belonging in a landscape where a million competing narratives exist side-by-side in the rich but potentially bewildering soup of cultures that is 21st-century Britain. 'We don't grow up solidly in one culture. We had a domestic culture at home, and all these cultures outside which were externalised. We are often forced to navigate this all on our own. The domestic culture is prominent in childhood, then with adolescence; what happens outside starts to impact how you see yourself and how you socialise.'

The values and mores of those two realities rarely fit together seamlessly, leaving many with a sense of cultural schizophrenia (also referred to by Sukina Douglas in Chapter 18). Simplifying identity and 'othering' all those who are different is a dangerous response that underlies many societal ills. 'People want to reduce their own identity to one thing. Anything that's not that becomes the opposite. Then you have this binary. It's very tempting to do this because it offers security and taps into a basic human instinct for finding a tribe. You're safe here because you're in a pack.'

Talking with Abbas is like sensing into two distinct parallel universes. One where a new relationship with identity, complexity and social-mixing lead us to a deeper sharing and valuing of culture, a multi-dimensional connectedness and a fresh respect for individual uniqueness. Alongside it another reality where, driven by fear, identities contract and harden and where everyone not like us is the enemy. 'You can create separate communities online where you find people like you and it reinforces very limited, reductive ideas of yourself. These insular communities present a sort of freedom yet they have very little connection to lived reality.'

Our conversation makes me aware of my privilege – the privilege of unquestioned belonging. I begin to see the magnitude of the challenge for those who are not so lucky – and to see the range of responses – the adaptive and the destructive, the resourced and unresourced. 'Often the offspring of migrants are in very precarious situations, very vulnerable, and that affects how they see themselves and how they move within society.'

Abbas's own story is not short on tragedy. His father died when he was very young, and he lost his mother to a heart condition during his teenage years. When Abbas was at university studying medicine, his younger brother developed the same condition and also passed away. 'I was dealing with so much turmoil inside of me. Without my parents, I lost contact with the culture I was raised in. My primary mode of trying to acculturate myself became a religious one. This was how our identities were being framed at the time by the media and local communities.'

> "I was dealing with so much turmoil inside of me. Without my parents, I lost contact with the culture I was raised in."

In the post 9/11 era, groups like Muslim Brotherhood and Hizb-ut-Tahrir were very active on university campuses, and although he never joined any of these groups, his experience of being surrounded by their discourse was not unusual. 'When you have a group of people who don't have a strong sense of who they are, growing up in a context of cultural confusion, many people took religion on as a full identity. The way it manifested was through becoming very conscious of the rules and regulations of Islamic practice. How to behave and how to conduct ourselves socially, what's correct to consume and what not to consume – looking back, it feels so strange now.'

Abbas describes how this obsession with rules began to feel like a kind of 'religious anorexia', similar to some of the young people he met in his medical training who meticulously controlled food intake as a way of compensating for other aspects of life that felt beyond control. 'It was as if our experience of the external structure of society was breaking down and couldn't be relied upon for support. So you take on control within yourself and start to impose limits on your behaviour to provide structure. If you sense the society is not open to you and you can't really plug yourself in and connect to things, you feel marginalised and it's not an experience you can control. I don't want to make this comparison in a disrespectful way, but this anorexia, this obsession with controlling the minutiae, was one kind of response. When I look back on it now it really makes me sad, because we were at university – a time of our lives when we should have been flourishing and exploring, but we spent so much time regulating ourselves and being policed by our peers.'

In my imagination, I see the thousands of young people from every country in the world who Abbas has met or rubbed shoulders with in his lifetime weaving their way through an intensely multicultural landscape, fighting their own battles, experimenting with their own solutions, dealing with unique but similar challenges of belonging and identity, and seeking a way to be, a place to call home. 'You try to create your own Utopia or imagined homeland – through community, through a constructed identity. Because I lost my family, I lost that domestic cultural connection, so my experience of being uprooted is heightened. But in other ways it actually opens me up to try and establish new things. You could say in the spaces

I create I've tried to build a new kind of family that's not based on ethnic, linguistic or spiritual ties *per se*. It's just whoever is around at the time and feels like they don't have a space, and I'm just like, "Let's create one!"'

One of the many things that really touches me in this conversation is when Abbas talks about the loss of the symbolic, and how the Islam he encountered at university contradicted or invalidated the religious heritage of his parents' homeland. 'Islam has been part of Iranian culture for hundreds of years, it's infused and had time to develop a certain cultural coherence. So, the rituals of Ancient Iran and Islamic Iran are somewhat joined together now for most people. Take our spring festival, Nowruz, for example – it's a tradition from the Zoroastrian era, but Iranian Muslims just put a Qur'an on the table and that makes it okay. So, they deal with it in a very pragmatic way. But the modern approach to religion is more fixed and rationally centred. It focuses on acts rather than the spiritual or symbolic dimensions. There's more logos than mythos. When you lose yourself culturally, you also lose your symbolic framework, you lose your metaphysical symbols, you lose the mythos. My mother was very much into poetry, and in Iran I was always presented with incredible architecture, food, culture and music – it was so rich. I assumed that this stuff was religious, but in the religion they were telling us about in the UK music was *haram*,[1] drawing figures was *haram*, so many things became *haram*. Yet I'm seeing miniature paintings of the prophet's night journey in Iran, and thinking, how can that be *haram*? It didn't compute. So I started to become more curious about the cultural dimension.'

Like many second-generation immigrants who choose professions based on a need for stability, Abbas started studying medicine, but after his brother died in 2009, he found himself prioritising his artistic practice as a means of healing. A few years earlier he had attended a talk at his university where he and his friends were encouraged to understand the challenges they faced as

---

1   Forbidden.

part of a 'crisis of modernity'. Inspired by this, Abbas became interested in classical art forms and went to study with traditional artists, calligraphers and stonemasons, which became a new source of inner nourishment. 'That was a critical influence – coming to see that we've lost our symbolic language, that this is behind some of our cultural difficulties, and prevents us from trusting ourselves. My aim was not to go back into a traditional mode of being but rather to develop a tactile sense for it and have a foundation from which to move forward and do something contemporary.'

If you ever have the pleasure of attending an event Abbas has curated, you will find yourself in an atmosphere of the experimental, of openness, connection and conviviality, surrounded by cultural creatives and inspiring, independent-minded people. You won't want to go home – these are people you will want to talk to through the night until sunrise. In a world where the forces of consumerism and religious extremism compete to erode our sense of meaning, cultural and spiritual malnourishment are fast becoming endemic. Abbas offers something as intangible as a fragrance – much-needed spaces where there is the taste of something real.

But this phenomenon of cultural malnourishment, this need for belonging, is not just the prerogative of the neo-diaspora nomads. In the new post-truth political landscape, it's apparent that it goes much deeper than that. White British people also feel marginalised. Identity issues are ubiquitous and no one is immune. Stephen Jenkinson, founder of the Orphan Wisdom School, says: 'What we suffer from most is culture failure, amnesia of ancestry and deep family story, phantom or sham rites of passage, no instruction on how to live with each other or with the world around us or with our dead or with our history.'[2] The millennial generation are the authors of slogans like 'find your tribe and love them hard'. You see the adaptive, resourced response to identity challenge in social entrepreneurship, in digital creatives, in the hipster movement, in arts and music, and the non-resourced response in those vulnerable

2   https://orphanwisdom.com/teachings/making-wisdom/

to binary points of view that lead to joining ISIS or the English Defence League.

'Hipsters,' says Abbas, 'are a white middle-class response to multiculturalism, a seeking of identity, for people who feel they lack that. When you go to Hackney, you see English people taking elements of culture from other groups, dressing differently, eating particular foods, setting up businesses. These guys were telling me how interesting Iranian food is and how they would like to learn to cook it as a means of enriching their own experience. I realised they are also searching for something culturally relatable amidst this mix

"Much of what we refer to as culture is kind of just the mechanics of an industry looking for something new."

we grew up in. Their childhood may have consisted of eating turkey drumsticks and now they want rosewater and saffron, or Szechuan pepper in a Korean burrito. But even then, so much of what we refer to as culture is kind of just the mechanics of an industry looking for something new, but that's a whole other story.'

According to Abbas, many in his generation are seeking Utopia. 'Society has lost something with its increase in consumerism, materialistic marketing and brand awareness. People are trying to create their own. People creating these small Utopias, small communities, cottage industries and businesses. I guess we all need some sense of Utopia to invest in. Even ISIS, as perverse as it is, is about going abroad and fighting for this great utopian ideal that you can't locate anywhere else. The result is the destruction of so much heritage and tradition. Yet even the disposable nature of popular culture creates this endless churn that leaves us without a sense of foundation. When it comes to food, concepts such as eating local, organic and sustainable are becoming more mainstream – how do we apply those principles towards our broader culture? These were the kinds of questions I was asking. Then I discovered I had drinks-makers in my own family heritage, and that became the basis for BARBEDOUN. Learning about the history of my own neo-diasporic situation, I wondered, why do I have to know who Justin Bieber is? I'd rather just listen to a friend who plays guitar and sings a song for me. I'd rather listen to people in my local area whilst sharing a drink or a meal together. With BARBEDOUN I could create a space to do that.'

"Why do I have to know who Justin Bieber is? I'd rather just listen to a friend who plays guitar and sings a song for me."

I ask Abbas what he wants to be remembered for. And what he wants for his son. 'In simple terms, I want to try make his experience more cohesive than my own – to give him the tools to relate to others in a more complex way from the outset, and to resist simple binaries of identity. That's where a lot of darkness comes from. If you just see everything as part of this one shared reality, you will learn to appreciate a much more sophisticated way of dealing with other people and realise how much we have in common. When someone is giving themselves a particular identity, at the expense of everything else that they have in their heritage, within themselves, within their own capacities, within their own interests – it's just so limiting. Yes, security can come from that, but that security is rooted in fear – creating security for yourself over the other. So yes, for my son, anything that helps us to move away from a fear-based approach and to appreciate one another in more nuanced ways. When he is growing up I can teach him about his heritage, I can teach him about the other cultures that are here in society and in the world as a whole, and give him enough of this cultural nourishment so that he won't have to deal with the kinds of issues we had to.'

I'm always deeply moved by the stories of people who turn adversity into a source of social good. The unimaginable pain of multiple bereavements when still so young could have generated such a different story, but instead has fuelled a deep questioning, a pushing of boundaries, an unrelenting experiment in going beyond dualistic thinking into a culturally interdependent landscape. I respect that. It's visionaries and creatives like Abbas who open the door for us to taste that new way of being – exploding the limitations and definitions that keep us apart from each other, and simultaneously reaching for that lost mythos, re-creating it, redefining culture, home, place, connection, faith and nourishment.

My hope is that Abbas and others like him can hold true to that vision, screen out the noise and junk and keep attuning to the rhythm and rhyme of a future where multiple narratives serve only to highlight our uniqueness and our inter-relatedness with each other. While elsewhere around us in the post-truth era, those same narratives, divorced from mythos and meaning, distorted by the consumerist weapons of mass distraction, risk devolving into what Macbeth described as 'a tale told by an idiot, full of sound and fury, signifying nothing'.[3]

Abbas is right. We don't need Justin Bieber. We need the kinds of spaces he creates. We need a neighbour with a guitar, singing songs from the heart about the beauty and intricacy of the challenges we face. And maybe we also need rosewater and saffron with a twist of mint from his bar.

3　*Macbeth* 5.5.17–28

Chapter 15

KINGSLEY L. DENNIS

THE PHOENIX GENERATION

'The younger generation are accessing their instinctive intelligence rather than reading from the tired old script of conditioned information.'

Kingsley L. Dennis PhD is an author, researcher and sociologist. He is the author of many books, both fiction and non-fiction, including The Phoenix Generation and The Sacred Revival: Magic, Mind and Meaning in a Technological Age. He is also the co-editor with Ervin Lazlo of The New Science and Spirituality Reader and co-authored with John Urry After the Car. Kingsley worked in the Sociology Department at Lancaster University and is now a visiting fellow at the Centre for Mobilities Research. He has authored numerous articles on social futures; technology and new media communications; global affairs; and conscious evolution. Kingsley currently lives in Andalusia, Spain where he continues to research, write, travel and live a sustainable lifestyle.

Kingsley L. Dennis writes:

The world is re-arranging in order to come together in countless new ways – with innovative changes in how we collaborate through people-centred action. Rather than seeing this as a revolution in social terms only, I consider this profound shift as a revolution in the human being – or rather, as a revolution in human *becoming*.

We are shifting from one set of C-values, Competition – Conflict – Control – Censorship, to a new set, Connection – Communication – Consciousness – Compassion.

Importantly, change on this planet will come through us, the people; and the attitudes, awareness, compassion and sincerity that we embody and manifest. Already there are countless examples of how this wave of change is occurring across the planet. Such examples include how young people are interacting with new technologies, developing constructive social networks, and communicating and collaborating across diverse cultures. The power of connected individuals is fuelling the 'We' feeling and bringing young hearts and minds together from across the globe. Such changes are showing that a different *type* of consciousness is arising, which marks the younger generations. The young people of the world today, and all those generations that will come after, are born *as change* rather than being born *into change* – this is a significant difference.

This transition is more radical than the shift from agrarian to urban life during the first Industrial Revolution. This is a revolutionary transition from national-cultural consciousness to planetary awareness and consciousness. What this entails is not only a structural shift but also a qualitative one; that is, a shift in our values, psychology and consciousness. What I am seeing is a younger generation that are accessing more their instinctive intelligence rather than reading from the tired old script of conditioned information. This instinctive intelligence is beyond dogma, boundaries and stereotypes. The younger generation are giving expression to an internal faith, and respecting that faith can manifest in various cultural forms that, whilst seemingly different, are in fact in connection with the same unified source. This inherent understanding is crucial as we, as a species, seek to move beyond our old conditioned tribal beliefs.

As the younger generation grows up and integrates into and participates in their respective societies, there will naturally be changes in many diverse areas of social life; such as healthcare, politics, media, technology use, innovation and spiritual practice.

It is my sense that a new awareness of spirituality is already emerging where old institutional dogmas are being replaced by increasing individual gnosis. We are moving toward the empowerment of the individual – of each human being – alongside a greater sense of connectedness to the whole. This will usher in great change across the planet – not overnight, but with time.

PART 5

NEW SPACES

Young people are gathering in new ways. They are creating vibrant, non-hierarchical, networked spaces, bursting with a sense of community and life force. They are coming together in an explosion of different micro-communities, dreaming into being 'the more beautiful world our hearts know is possible'.[1]

Through the work of St Ethelburga's, I've been touched many times by the atmosphere and aliveness of the spaces that young people create. Rumi's Cave, Wake Up London, our own spiritual ecology gatherings – when young people come together in service to something greater than themselves, dynamic, nourishing spaces result. While my own generation beat a hard-won path towards a new style of relating and co-creating, Generation Y do it seamlessly. When personal agendas are put aside, energy flows through an organic web of connections – unconstricted by hierarchy – and magic happens.

A particular flavour of inner nourishment becomes available in those places. If you're reading this, I'm sure you've experienced it. It's present in the relationships, in shared stories, aspirations and solidarity. There is a joy in it, and a purpose.

---

1   *The More Beautiful World Our Hearts Know Is Possible*, Charles Eisenstein (North Atlantic Books, 2013).

This spiritual nourishment shows up in communities drawn together through spirituality, but isn't limited by that label. These spaces blur the line between spiritual and not. Harvard Divinity School's pioneering report *How We Gather* analysed many youth-led spaces – some religious or spiritual, many not so – looking at the patterns they reveal.[2] Instead of asking the question churches ask – How can we attract young people into our communities? – they asked: Where are young people already gathering and what characteristics do those places have? How are those spaces fulfilling some of the same functions as faith communities do?

They found the themes of community, personal transformation, social transformation, purpose finding, creativity, accountability and 'something more' (their terminology for the spiritual) showing up in many different combinations, making visible the DNA of a much bigger movement that is emerging. Looking at the leadership of these spaces begs the question, what does ministry in the 21st century look like? How are new kinds of ministers trained, supported and kept accountable in their roles?

Along with many more of our contributors, the young people in this section could all be seen as ministers born from a new mould. Ruth creates community and meaning without religion. Nick brings together healing, activism and art. Sukina shares her Islam in a diverse, urban milieu, meeting young people on their own terms. They are all architects of new spaces, planting the seeds of a new era.

---

2   *How We Gather*, Casper ter Kuile and Angie Thurston (Harvard Divinity School, 2015).

Chapter 16

RUTH MOIR

REINVENTING MINISTRY

'In the UK, for the first time, there are more non-religious people than religious people. So where are the chapels and who are the chaplains for this time?'

Ruth Moir is 33 years old and was born in Aberdeen, Scotland, into a non-religious family of farmers. In her early twenties, Ruth wrote a business plan with a friend for developing an unused church space in Edinburgh into a community arts hub. The plan succeeded and they ran the space together for several years. More recently, Ruth became Community Creator for Sunday Assembly. Sunday Assembly looks a lot like church but is completely secular and inclusive. Started in 2013, Sunday Assembly now has over 70 meetings around the world in eight different countries, where power anthems replace hymns and inspiring lectures replace sermons. Their three key values are: Live better, Help often, and Wonder more. Ruth is also one of the founder members of Alt*Div, a community of self-directed learners who are part of the Open Masters programme. Alt*Div aims to offer an alternative to Divinity School for those who are not identified with specific religious traditions, and to re-imagine spiritual formation for a changing world.

Ruth and I met over a breakfast of porridge and blueberries in a tiny artisan coffee shop near Kings Cross. Our conversation, punctuated by the loud hiss and gurgle of espresso machines, was a memorable one. Ruth was wearing enormous gold earrings, which, like their owner, were delightfully sparkly in the mid-morning sunshine. Ruth is great fun to talk to and exudes tremendous warmth. The role of building new communities of meaning, so essential to the expression of our evolving spiritualities, is imprinted within her, a fundamental part of her *raison d'être*.

In her childhood, church didn't deliver an experience of God – only one of community. So as a young adult, Ruth begun instinctively separating out the elements of religion – ritual, inner work, ethics, accountability, connection to the Divine, and supportive community – and innovating her own creative solutions. She sits in the 'spiritual but not religious' camp, and is diving into the question of what ministry means for that fast-growing segment of society.

Alt*Div is one response to that question. It also embodies a significant new millennial-led way of 'doing' education. Global communities of peers form around a shared interest, build their own curricula, define their own goals and use community to journey together and stay accountable. One of the first things Ruth learns is that, like an anthropologist immersed in a community, this style of education can be fully integrated into life and work – not a separate process happening on the outside.

Ruth also beautifully articulates the dissolution of a fundamental binary in our religious thinking – that of sacred and profane. Rather than de-sacralising the world, this is a re-sacralisation of the wonder and beauty of everyday life. Drinking tea with a friend in need becomes 'a moment of giving, of humanity and love'. Like many in this book, present in her lifestyle and the way she lives her faith is the feeling of a deeper integration of these two opposites, the reconciliation of which could be so fundamental to our future.

Motifs in this chapter:

- New spaces

- Complex identities

- Natural leadership

JH: Ruth, it's such a pleasure to meet you and to hang out together in this lovely coffee shop and chat with you. I'd love to hear a little of your story.

Ruth: Well... I originally grew up in the North of Scotland on a sheep farm. I didn't need the word community as it was just there. Unfortunately we had to leave the farm, and my father got a job in England, which meant we had to leave the farm and the rest of the family, who are all Scottish, so suddenly we were without community.

Our family weren't religious, then when I was 11 or 12, I had a sleep-over with my friend and went to her Methodist Church with her the following day. I walked in and there was cake, there was tea, there was singing, people supporting each other, people being in community. I was in awe!

JH: I can really understand that. If you've lost community and then suddenly here is this space where people come together in a supportive atmosphere...

Ruth: Exactly. At the time, God was quite an alien thing for me because I hadn't grown up with it. So for me it was purely about people getting together. I went home quite enthusiastic and said to my mum, 'It's great! We should go!' She replied, 'But I don't believe in God...', and I said, 'I'm sure they won't mind!'

JH: That's so funny!

Ruth: I think this is where some translation needs to happen as we become a less and less religious society. What methods are there for bringing people together in caring, loving, sustainable communities?

I started going to this church's youth group and learnt about Christianity. I never found a god through it, but I did find a total respect for the church and the amount of space they gave me to question and express doubt. When I stopped going to the youth group, my friend's parents became meditation teachers and I learnt to meditate through them, which is still a central part of my life and my main spiritual practice alongside writing.

I then studied anthropology and focused on communities. My first research project was on Quaker communities, looking at the sacred and the social. My second research project was on 12-step programme communities for people with eating disorders, about the concepts of wellbeing, language and healing within these spaces. Then I went to New York, and when I came back I was trying to work out what to do with this anthropology degree... Then we found a deconsecrated church owned by a charity that was looking for someone to do something with it.

JH: Gosh, what a great opportunity – seems like it had your name all over it.

Ruth: Yes! My friend Jane and I put together a business plan, and got the space. We renovated it using our overdrafts, and friends donated paint and sound-proofing and scaffolding towers, and we made it into an alternative community arts space in the old town of Edinburgh. We'd both lived in New York and wanted to bring that energy to Edinburgh, so we called it The Bowery. We made a place where artists and musicians could collaborate and create new projects. We had ukulele nights, writers groups, life drawing classes, art exhibitions, craft fairs, live music and free popcorn. One artist made a 'disco toilet' where the cubicle had a mirrored disco ball, lights and music that started when you opened the door, we had life drawing classes with full set designs, we had vegetarian taxidermy...

JH: Vegetarian taxidermy?

Ruth: With oranges. [laughter] We had a real narrative of fun.

JH: I can see that's important for you!

Ruth: So that was The Bowery. Eventually the landlords took it back, which was really sad. And that created a real crisis moment for me and pushed me to think about what I really wanted to do.

At the time, I was involved with Creative Mornings – free breakfast talks where someone in the creative industries gives a talk and you can meet other folk – they happen all over the world. Sanderson

Jones [co-founder of Sunday Assembly] came and spoke. The first thing he asked was, 'How many people have thought of starting up a church without religion?' I sat there thinking, 'I thought that was *my* idea!' So when he spoke about Sunday Assembly, I was intrigued. I went along the following week and there were 450 people singing power ballads, wanting to create community for folk with or without faith, sharing a space, thinking about life, tapping into their values and going into the world thinking about how to live out those values.

When Sunday Assembly announced they were looking for a Community Creator, my friend Neil elbowed me in the ribs and said, 'They're talking about you!' I applied, and now I'm a secular minister or 'Community Creator'. It has pulled together many of my interests: in community building and creating spaces for secular spiritual practices, helping people look at their inner lives, and creating spaces to tackle social isolation and create positive social change in the city.

It's not just the Sunday meeting, we also have peer support groups where people come together to work on something they want to change in their life. We have community action days where we partner with charities in London – recently we were lending muscle power to a community garden project. We have retreat weekends. Some people just love coming on Sunday, that's all they do. But others are in the band, the choir, some people run a climbing group, or the 'Wonder Club'. There's a lot going on.

JH: So this is a secular community and I'm wondering about how spirituality fits for you. What does that word mean to you?

Ruth: For me it's the parts of life that fit in between disciplines. Spirituality's not psychology, it's not anthropology, it's not religion. It's the bit that sits in between, the threads that run through and pass around them. And

> "Spirituality's not psychology, it's not anthropology, it's not religion. It's the bit that sits in between, the threads that run through and pass around them."

it's the inner work. I'd say it's how you're living your life in relation to your values. In other words, the processes involved in how you live a life of integrity.

In terms of spiritual practice, I meditate and I journal every day, I write 'morning pages'.[1] They are my two main practices. But I think this is where some translation needs to happen as we become a less and less religious society. Perhaps it's using the language of inner work practices or integrity practices. I still don't have a translation for that, but this is the work I'm most interested in.

I think one of the reasons that faith-based communities have given people solace is because they are a place to really sit with yourself and have those mirrors and reflections back on you and your way of being in the world – so you can learn and grow.

JH: Interesting! So you take the spirituality away and break down the different elements within a faith tradition that nourish people – obviously community is one of them, and a framework of values. Practices – like prayer or silence or inner work – and then the business of living those values in the world of action – how you give, how you contribute to society, how you put those values into practice.

Ruth: Yes, and I think no matter what inner work you're doing it can get lost in translation without accountability. That is why community is so important to me. It's my community that holds me accountable for my work – how I'm

"It's my community that holds me accountable."

moving through the world, whether I'm doing that with integrity and care.

---

1   A creative practice involving free writing first thing in the morning, taken from the popular book *The Artist's Way* by Julia Cameron.

JH: So, alongside Sunday Assembly, you're also involved in Alt*Div, which sounds like a really fascinating initiative. Tell me more about that.

> "The idea is to create an alternative divinity school; looking at how we can support each other's learning and become the soulful community builders that I believe are so needed in the world."

Ruth: Yes, I've been a founding participant of Alt*Div. The idea is to create an alternative divinity school; looking at how we can support each other's learning and become the soulful community builders that I believe are so needed in the world.

JH: So Alt*Div is a response to the need for new kinds of ministry?

Ruth: It's an alternative to traditional theological education. It's different because it's formed at a grassroots level. It's not tied to any institution. We are a group of artists, activists and community organisers. It includes people from a variety of spiritual, faith or no faith backgrounds. We create our own curricula, we plan the learning and we hold ourselves accountable to working on it, to harvesting the lessons learned and celebrating the milestones.

JH: What are the origins of Alt*Div?

Ruth: It was started by Alan Webb and Sarah Bradley, who run the Open Masters community. They wanted to explore new ways of doing ministry 'where the ancient meets the emergent'. It's about soulful community building and also about the links between social justice and soulful community. It's for people who feel they are doing the work of ministry without calling themselves ministers.

So in the summer of 2016 our first Alt*Div cohort came together in New Mexico. Eighteen of us from lots of different countries and different backgrounds. We spent a week thinking about our learning plans, the questions we wanted to dig deeply into, and how we were going to be together as a community.

JH: What's your learning been so far?

Ruth: Well, it's been really interesting. One of the things I've learned has been about the need for braver spaces. As a community, naturally, we had to learn how to work with differences and conflict. I had to examine my own relationship with conflict. And I saw the importance of creating spaces for braver kinds of conversation. That was pivotal for me as a community builder. Now in a way I feel excited by conflict because it gives us an opportunity to have difficult conversations in a bigger setting and learn from them.

Also, about three or four months in, I had a bit of a wobble. I felt overwhelmed with the difficulty of creating change and I experienced burnout for the first time. I wasn't sure I could do this MA on top of my job. I was putting pressure on myself from an academic point of view and not achieving what I'd wanted. I realised I was thinking of an Open Masters as a personal project rather than seeing my everyday life and my work as part of my learning process. One of the challenges I've had is to recognise that I've been used to an education system where we think learning has to come from outside. My peers had already figured that one out! They reminded me that my job is my Alt*Div. For me it's similar to anthropological research, which I think requires you to put yourself in the frame in order to reflect on what your observations and responses look like.

JH: So the learning is fully integrated into your life?
Ruth: It is!

JH: So can you say a little about what ministry is for you?
Ruth: Do you know the story of the origin of the word 'chaplain'? It comes from the Latin word for cloak and the word grew out of the story of St Martin, a Roman soldier, meeting a man begging in the rain and cold. He tore his own cloak in two and shared it, half for the beggar and half for himself. To be a chaplain is to give comfort and shelter. I think modern-day ministry and community building are about creating those braver spaces for people to come together and have the conversations that are so important to life, that allow

people to be the best person that they can be at that moment. In the UK, for the first time, there are more non-religious people than religious people. So the question for me now is, where are the chapels and who are the chaplains for this time? And how can we best create and co-create the spaces needed for people to be in supportive communities?

JH: Earlier on you spoke about seeing nature as a reminder that the Earth is sacred. What does the word sacred mean to you?
Ruth: That's such a great question! For me it has something to do with recognising the beauty in everything. When I studied anthropology, we talked about the sacred and the profane. There was this binary distinction, which doesn't feel right at all; the profane can feel incredibly sacred. Your friend making a cup of tea for you when you need support is not profane – I consider that to be an incredible, touching moment of giving, of humanity and love. So what is it to hold those moments as sacred? Maybe these moments that we use the word 'sacred' for remind us to wonder. The words 'wonder' and 'sacred' go together for me, again this is a challenge of interpretation.

JH: Yes, and many would say that binary distinction is the root of our environmental crisis – separating Heaven and Earth, rendering Earth as profane...
Ruth: And the social justice crisis – when you look at political divides in the world and where humanity is divided into sacred and profane, look at white supremacists for example. Dividing the world up into binaries affects how people see other human beings and the universe. So what is it to challenge ourselves and our ideas of binaries?

JH: That brings me to another question. Reflecting on my visit to Sunday Assembly, I was struck by the invitation to celebrate life, which comes across so strongly, and wondered where that sits with the fact that we are in a devastating global crisis? I know you engage with environmental issues, with social justice, with

racism, in your volunteering activities, and the value you have of 'help often' also comes in here. But I was aware in the Sunday meeting the whole emphasis is on celebrating life. I was aware that held a danger of creating the feeling that the difficult things are being denied. How do we celebrate life within the context of crisis? For me somehow not naming the crisis left this question.
Ruth: That's a really interesting point. We had a time when the UK was going through crisis after crisis – the Manchester bomb, the Grenfell Tower disaster, the Westminster attack, the Borough Market attack – and I noticed when something big happens in our communities, our attendance goes up. I think it's because people need to re-engage with the world as somewhere there can be positivity.

When there is a tragedy we start with silence, with a moment to reflect and then with a reflective song. So we are saying, this is real, this is hard, and life still keeps going. From an organisational point of view, the reason Sanderson [one of the two co-founders of Sunday Assembly] is so engaged with celebrating life is that he lost his mum when he was a child. Death taught him that we have this life and don't know how long or short it will be – so how are we going to use it? We are in a global crisis and we are still living, and we still have the ability to make positive social change.

JH: If you were hosting it there would be vegetarian taxidermy...
Ruth: Ha, ha, yeah...and disco toilets! But I do think Sunday Assembly often gives people that boost to get through the week that is really needed in these times.

JH: How do you see the future of ministry? And your own ministry in the future? You are growing up into that crisis, with a particular inquiry and a particular gift that you are bringing. How do you see yourself navigating that potentially very difficult future?
Ruth: How can you predict the unknown? All I know is I'm taking my own journey more seriously as I grow in the role. I'm realising how easy it is, with any kind of ministry, to put others first rather

than yourself. It's the old analogy of putting the oxygen mask on yourself first before the child. So navigating the future will definitely include that. As Audre Lorde says, 'Caring for myself is not self-indulgence, it is self-preservation, and that is an act of political warfare.'[2]

I do think that community building is going to become more and more important. So there is something about tooling myself up for what is needed and the new communities that emerge out of what's happening in the world.

In terms of navigating that, I think we all need to continue to learn together. I don't think I would be doing the job I'm doing today if I was without the support of my Alt*Div community. In the UK there is no Divinity School where you can go to become a non-religious minister. I do wonder what it will take for Europe to take this kind of ministry seriously and how I can support that happening.

---

2   *A Burst of Light: And Other Essays*, Audre Lorde (Ixea Press, 2017).

Chapter 17

NICK GEORGE

IF I WAS SUCCESSFUL...

Credit: Susan McLaren

'Find your tribe, work with your tribe and lean on them.'

Nicholas, a Christian, lives in Lynchburg, Virginia with his wife and their two young children. A qualified counsellor, he founded The Listening in response to something he noticed in his work with young people: a powerful need to be heard, within a community setting. The Listening connects the worlds of youth mentoring, civic engagement and the performing arts, including spoken word, poetry, dance, theatre and musicianship. The goal is to identify young people who are experiencing a turbulent adolescence as well as those with an interest in creativity, and offer them a positive support system. The Listening also offers safe space for the wider community to have brave conversations and explore diverse perspectives.

Unlike Sunday Assembly, The Listening is not attempting to substitute for a place of worship, but is nevertheless a space where spiritual nourishment and human connection are offered freely. Nick's project is another great example of how the millennial generation is recreating meaningful community outside organised institutions. His vision is to create safe spaces to explore difference and diversity, by bringing together art, healing, activism, community and faith. He performs the roles of 'Gatherer', 'Healer' and 'Maker'.

Safe spaces, brave spaces and freer spaces are much needed if we are to open things up and enable the shifts in perspective that enable change. Nick points toward the needs of those growing up in a church, but encountering a plethora of other spiritual influences, or exploring forms of sexuality their religion doesn't endorse. 'Where do you go to grapple with that?' The use of personal story here comes as no surprise. Story is such a powerful tool for generating empathy and honouring our uniqueness whilst also making visible our common humanity.

I particularly wanted to include Nick because his experience of bullying and attempted suicide as a teenager is sadly an increasingly common one. Suicide in the younger generation is rising steadily. Religious belief systems often include strict injunctions against suicide, but as young people disaffiliate, those injunctions will be of less and less use. The need for those in caring professions, ministers of all traditions and types, old and new, and young people themselves, to understand and respond will grow.

As a friend once said to me with eloquent simplicity, 'There are many challenges. Many people are suffering. In the end, our only joy and sense of belonging will be through awakening to this work.'

For me, Nick is a wonderful example of someone who has survived a painful journey and stepped forward into his own unique form of leadership, acting with a big heart and great creativity to support others and to meet some of the needs of our times. I hope he can serve as an inspiration to others – and particularly to those who find themselves in dark places.

Motifs in this chapter:

- New spaces

- Natural leadership

JH: What was faith and spirituality for you when you were growing up?
Nick: My family comes from the West Indies, from Trinidad and Tobago. Growing up we went to a church in New Jersey. It was a very dynamic atmosphere, focused on young people and creativity, engaging local youth in recognising the Divine in our creativity. We sang in choirs, wrote and acted in plays. That kind of thing. That's the environment much of my current beliefs were founded on.

JH: So what is faith for you now?
Nick: I think faith is always there, whatever it is you believe in – whether you believe in God, many gods, She as God, your inner spirit as god-like, or science or music. Whatever it is, it's what we connect to that allows us to keep going – whether the path is smooth or rocky. Faith is the reason to keep going.

JH: So, tell me about The Listening.
Nick: My experiences growing up definitely impacted my journey. Dealing with bullying in school, I found that, second to my faith, creativity and art was what helped me get through. Whether it was listening to Michael Jackson or Linkin Park or Ron Kenoly on my way to school, or scribbling in my notepad. Were it not for my guidance counsellor in middle school who suggested Maya Angelou to me, I wouldn't have thought of using writing that way. Those were the tools that God gave me to allow me to cope.

Fast-forward a bit to undergrad, coming to school in Central Virginia. It was during the 2008 elections, and my school, Stateside Liberty University, brands itself as the 'most exciting Christian university in the world'. It is very much regarded as the safe haven for students of conservative thought and the moral majority. As a believer, I thought that would be the best place for me too.

But it was during the election season of 2008 on the eve of this country's first non-white president that I began to see both my faith and my social convictions clash in

> "I began to see both my faith and my social convictions clash in ways I hadn't expected."

ways I hadn't expected. I saw believers acting very unsavoury, and combating with each other around the election campaign.

I've never been one to discourage passion. But we needed a way to engage with our passions, with the things that we care the most about, in a safe environment. Not for the purpose of changing anyone's thought or converting anyone's beliefs but just understanding and listening to each other. Therein lies potential for change. Not in what we believe but in how we regard each other.

One of the things I find people tend to be passionate about – regardless of what they believe in or what they look like – is what they listen to and how they create. If you find yourself in a karaoke bar and they play 'Carry On My Wayward Son', anybody will at least be able to get along with that, with the melody, with the tune. Beauty transcends those barriers, dance transcends those barriers.

So The Listening was spawned from that conflict. Our main question throughout these years has been: If you had a room full of people willing to listen to you, what would you say? Now that's a very fun question to ask, but, reflecting on my own history, not a lot of young people have that question asked of them. With this project I wanted to merge two very strong interests of mine – community engagement – including mental health – and youth mentoring, with all of that being carried on a platform of performing arts.

JH: So what kinds of things do you do?
Nick: Our main format for community engagement has been open mic. The theme for our first open mic for this year is going to be 'Miseducation' – challenging the ideas of what we thought we knew, inspired by the book written by Carter G. Woodson, *The Miseducation*

of the Negro, and Lauryn Hill's album, *The Miseducation of Lauryn Hill*. Both of those productions look at what the Negro's experience in America was, or what love was, and both dismantle that and reflect on their own experience, realising that there had been such major miseducation going on. Love is not what you're taught it was, being black in America is not what you're taught it was.

For some people, growing up Christian and deciding that you identify more as a non-conforming, non-religious practising individual, if that's your truth, you went through a major miseducation process having grown up. Or if you're shown life is about loving one way and then you recognise that now you are bi-curious, homosexual, whatever. Or the 15-year-old who's just learning about mysticism and agnosticism or Wicca or what have you, who's just learning about these things and questioning. Where else can they grapple with that? The Listening is safe space to wrestle with those ideas creatively and compassionately.

Young people have smartphones so they can find any answer they want, but learning happens in a safe community, in a brave community that is able to meet those challenges, and not even necessarily to find answers but to pursue the questions together.

> "The Listening is safe space to wrestle with those ideas creatively and compassionately."

> "Young people have smartphones so they can find any answer they want, but learning happens in a safe community, in a brave community."

JH: I want to ask you about role models and mentorship. It seems to me you were really lucky in terms of your role models when you were growing up, and you had great mentoring at times when you really needed it. I'm just wondering where that fits with your vision?

Nick: Yes, I've been very lucky, very blessed. This year, I lost three very important women in my life who served at our church back in New Jersey (Elnora Haynes, Irma Peoples and Michelle Lewis). These women were just a few of the passionate individuals who were a part of our family at the Newark Gospel Tabernacle. They believed in the voice of the young people, in the power of the young people, and they didn't give up on any of us when we were starting to go crazy, even before puberty, just dealing with inner-city life stuff. They loved on us, hard. And they had no salary, no recognition, no outer reward.

Our youth leaders and youth pastors were incredible people. I played keyboard for maybe half of my life. In high school I was in a Shakespeare group, in a performance group. Our teachers gave their time so generously outside of teaching hours to make those things happen for us. So I've been incredibly blessed. With The Listening I wanted to do what my guidance counsellor did for me: open the door to see how these arts can be used to heal.

JH: And that forms a part of what you want to offer in The Listening, mentoring for young people?
Nick: Yes. Each person is matched with an adult, college-educated and upward, who has knowledge or experience working with young people, but has also had a direct relationship to how art has been a part of their own growth. I wouldn't like for any young person to be matched with someone who didn't have both some sort of mental health counselling or psychology experience, understanding more of the finer details of people, but they are primarily people who have been directly impacted by the arts.

For decades, for centuries, people have been using the arts to cope. So why not make it happen officially? There's arts therapy, there's music therapy, but before we get to the clinical level let's just be people. If we can work at this level, where we're just people and we're just talking, I genuinely believe (and there's evidence to support it) that mentoring relationships do help in more ways than one:

from academic to social, cognitive, cultural, and more. So that's separate from what we do to engage the community. Community engagement invites everyone; the youth mentoring specifically wants to work with young people.

JH: You've mentioned the mental health needs of some of the young people you support, and I know your own background was originally in psychology. You've also talked about suicide attempts when you were younger. I know suicide is on the rise among the younger generation. Is there anything you'd like to say about that experience?

Nick: One of the main lies about suicide or depression is the idea that you're by yourself. And when I was going through my experience, you couldn't tell me different. I knew for a fact that nobody could understand, that nobody else was going through it, that I was by myself and what's the point? Like I might as well go. Not die, because you don't necessarily use that language, just not be here.

It's my hope to show young people that you are less alone than you think. That darkness, it's yours because it knows you, but there are so many different tools in people. I think that's maybe key to why I want The Listening to be regarded less as an organisation and more as a community, because the people that have been part of The Listening bring their own stories, bring their own challenges, and I think it's together that we're able to defeat some of these feelings.

JH: One final question. What would be your message to the young people reading this book, who want to make a difference with their life?

Nick: Find your tribe. A lot of us lose a lot of time, waste a lot of resources believing this false narrative of the self-made man. There may be a lucky few, but generally it can't be done alone, and it won't be half as fun without your community, your village – not behind you but *with* you. That can be a family of fellow believers, or practitioners, or your blood family, or a group of people who have the same shared experience and passion – whatever it is, find your tribe, work with your tribe and lean on them.

If I was successful...

If I was successful, I would have never been able to travel to Trinidad and Tobago, Nicaragua, or Costa Rica.

If I was successful, I wouldn't have been able to see TobyMac, The Roots, Janelle Monae, Snarky Puppy, Johnnyswim, Kirk Franklin, Thousand Foot Krutch, Family Force 5, Lecrae, Andy Mineo, Tedashii, Trip Lee, Sho Baraka, Miles Hodges, Alysia Hodges, Joshua Bennett, Young the Giant, or Stevie Wonder perform live.

If I was successful, my parents would not have seen me graduate college.

If I was successful, I would never have written and published my first collection of poetry.

If I was successful, I would never have had my heart be broken, learn to glue the pieces back together, and venture into the world of love again.

If I was successful, I wouldn't have seen the man my brother has become. I wouldn't get to walk with my sisters through this life.

If I was successful, I couldn't get to see my cousins get married.

If I was successful, I wouldn't be able to create the perfect waffle-eggs-and-sausage bowl.

If I was successful, I wouldn't have been able to watch The Wire.

If I was successful, I would never have heard 'The College Dropout' or 'Good Kid, Maad City'.

If I was successful, I would have missed thousands of starry nights, waterfalls, cloudy horizons, rainbows, sunrises and sunsets.

I would've missed fresh snow, summer rain, snow days, holidays...

If I was successful, I wouldn't get to see what I look like with dreads, or with actual facial hair.

If I was successful, I would've missed the return of French Toast Crunch.

I would've missed the iPhone.

I would never have come up with the inspiration for The Listening.

If I was successful, I would have never met my wife, never had our first kiss, our first night together.

I would have never met our children, Naomi Alese and Noah Michael, never looked into their eyes, never heard their first cry.

If I was successful in my suicide attempts, I would have missed so much.

Chapter 18

SUKINA DOUGLAS

THE NEED FOR NEW KINDS OF LEADERSHIP

'Credibility comes from authenticity, from being in your truth.'

Sukina Douglas is 36 years old and a hip-hop poet, spoken-word artist, creative writing teacher, activist and a community leader. She was born in Bristol to Afro-Caribbean parents and converted to Islam when she was a student. Together with Muneera Rashida, she formed the innovative hip-hop duo Poetic Pilgrimage, which used the art of rhyme to deliver a message of peace, unity, interfaith relations and freedom. Sukina edited a Muslim hip-hop magazine and presented a lifestyle show on Islam Channel. She later became the manager of a progressive youth-led Muslim community centre called Rumi's Cave in North London, which blends spirituality, art and social action. Sukina leads poetry workshops and teaches creative writing, using spoken and written word to explore the different perspectives and experiences of young people growing up in diverse urban cultures.

I first met Sukina several years ago at an open-mic night at Rumi's Cave. I happened to be passing this tiny, tea-shop-sized gathering space that had recently materialised in Kilburn, my home neighbourhood in North London. My attention was caught by what sounded like a hip-hop-style poetry slam with a strange hint of religious devotion emerging from the darkened space. After peering in through the windows intrigued, someone eventually took pity on me and squeezed me into the back row. The miniature space was packed with a young, mostly Muslim crowd, and there was Sukina at the front, pouring forth a passionate stream of ancient-urban spiritual self-expression. I stayed for the rest of the night of course, and was welcomed into a community bursting with poetry, music, prayer, friendship and delicious food in a very novel combination.

At the time, Rumi's Cave was one of the first really innovative youth-led spaces I'd encountered. Through an eclectic mix of artistic, thought-provoking and caring programmes it was clearly meeting some of the spiritual needs of this multicultural crowd in a very different way to a mosque. Their work includes Rumi's Kitchen, which offers free food and friendship to homeless or disadvantaged people and various routes into activism. I love the combination of spirituality, creativity, giving and a fluid, non-judgemental community. Finding Rumi's Cave played a part in the exploration that led to setting up the St Ethelburga's Sacred Activists programme and eventually to this book.

What stands out for me in this interview is that, despite being a convert, Sukina's visibility as a performer means she is often approached by younger people for advice about Islam. Echoed by Emmanuel in Chapter 6, young people seek out those they can relate to, often needing what their peers can offer above that of their elders. Sukina has heard that call and stepped into her own journey of leadership. My experience of her is of someone living a continued exploration in how to bring her faith and creativity together in service to God and others.

Motifs in this chapter:

- New spaces
- Sacred activism
- Complex identities
- Natural leadership

JH: What do you want to tell me about young people and faith?

Sukina: I think we are in a really important place in our experience as human beings. It's an important time. You have to find your place in it all. We don't all have to be mobilised in exactly the same way, but we all have a part to play in the next stage of our human existence. I don't think anyone has the privilege of sitting on the fence. If we are here, and if our souls have manifested in this time, it's because we're supposed to be part of this change.

> "I think we are in a really important place in our experience as human beings. It's an important time. You have to find your place in it all."

JH: How have the many challenges and crises we see around us in the wider world impacted on your faith journey?

Sukina: In the Qur'an it talks a lot about how a believer should never despair. I think it's really important that we don't allow ourselves to get into despair, because ultimately every soul is here to have an experience. I think it's about always having that dual perspective. We need to act. If we see something that's wrong, we need to be striving for justice, but also remembering God is in control. My perspective isn't the totality of the bigger picture. That's what my faith has given me.

JH: What's the relationship between your faith and your music and poetry?

Sukina: Hip-hop and the kind of art I'm engaged in is very much about the narrative of your life. That's the reason it became so popular, it represented voices that are never heard on mainstream platforms. The voice of the underdog, the voice of the voiceless. Credibility comes from authenticity, from being in your truth. People regarded Poetic Pilgrimage as making Islamic rap, but we never really saw ourselves in that category. Obviously faith comes into it, but our Muslimness can't really be divorced from who we are. Spoken word and poetry, the way I write it, is outpourings from the heart. My heart feels full sometimes and I have to release it. My faith and my relationship with God, the way I live my life and my activism, are all part of the narrative of my life. My faith informs my heart, which in turn informs my music.

JH: Tell me about your conversion to Islam...
Sukina: Being from an Afro-Caribbean background, I felt there was a massive gap in our understanding of our history. I was in a way trying to restore myself and my identity. I hated feeling that I had no traditions or customs. We were told, 'Your ancestors were slaves, you ended up in the Caribbean, your grandparents came to England, here you are.' I didn't feel rich in my identity and my culture, so I think for my early years, it was about that.

In the last month of my degree, I had to do an essay about Malcolm X. When I read about his pilgrimage, I had such a strong feeling. I almost felt like there was something wrong with me! I didn't know why I was feeling that way. I mean, Islam was not on my bucket list of things to do – it was a complete diversion. I wasn't in a traumatic place in my life. I was getting ready to live it, you know. I was about to hand in my dissertation, and my plan had been to spend the whole week in bed drinking champagne! But by the time I went to hand in my final assignment, I was wearing hijab and ready to say my *shahada*.[1] With Islam came this more outward gaze. I was ready to be aware, to look at the world on a wider scale.

---

1   Declaration of faith, repeated when someone converts to Islam.

JH: What do you think is different for your generation?

Sukina: Well, one of the things is social media. It's a blessing and a curse for my generation. For example, Syria. We're receiving tweets from Syria, videos, images, and all of them are live. The urgency of that kind of live experience has a big impact. It comes with a burden though. You've seen it – you know it and you can't hide from it. It also comes with the opportunity to act immediately. If I see people are fundraising, I see these are the organisations to donate to, maybe someone else posted about

> "Social media is a blessing and a curse for my generation."

sending some containers of donations which just arrived there – it's that kind of pace. We can act – which is good – but sometimes the speed and pace can create a particular kind of hype. Then it dies down, because now we're focused on another disaster somewhere else. Social media is a good thing, but it's also a trial for my generation.

This rise in my generation of depression and anxiety, mental health issues, and suicide – I think it's because we are really overwhelmed. We are overwhelmed, and we don't know how to respond.

JH: How would you describe the relationship between faith and action? How do those things come together in you?

Sukina: There is a *hadith*, a tradition of the Prophet Muhammad, that says, if you see an injustice try and change it with your hand. If you can't change it with your hand, change it with your tongue. If you can't change with your tongue, change it with your heart. But the most praiseworthy is the first. So basically if you see injustice, and can change it with your hand, then make that change.

JH: Has your relationship with activism changed as you've gone deeper into your faith?

Sukina: Yes it has. Once, when I was in retreat, just engaging in *dhikr* and reading the Qur'an, dissolved in God, I got very sensitive and couldn't really deal with the problems of the world. Now I'm back in

London, back to earth, so to speak, I'm still trying to navigate that space between 'I can't cope, my heart's not ready' and 'You're here and you're present and you've got a role to play'. There is work that needs to be done.

There are times when you feel there is a lot of darkness, a lot of instability, with what we are going through right now collectively. We shouldn't just come together based on what is dark, but also based on light as well.

JH: Tell me about Rumi's Cave. It seems to be quite an unusual space. It's not a mosque, so in some way it's outside of the normal religious structures, but it's a magnet for many young Muslims and has a real sense of community about it. What does it mean to you and what do you think the potential is for spaces like that?
Sukina: I think the reason why Rumi's Cave really worked was because we had three key elements. One was faith and spirituality, which was what Sheikh Babakir brought. One was art and creativity, which is what I offered. Then we also had the charity and community aspect. I think those three things made it really successful. And it was led by us, by young people. I was 30 years old when I started there. Sheikh Babakir wanted me to be the manager, to be the face of Rumi's Cave, not him or another elder. He said, 'This is your project, you run it the way you want.' That was really intimidating at first. But he gave me the space and he trusted me, and that was the biggest thing. He was really clear: 'This is your generation, you know your people better than I do, you know what you need.'

JH: Do the people that attend, do they go to mosques as well? Or is Rumi's Cave an alternative to the mosque?
Sukina: No, not everyone goes to mosques. When we started to do Friday prayers at Rumi's, I was much more comfortable there. I just felt intimidated whenever I went to a mosque. I felt very judged. In my mind I was always preparing some kind of argument for someone. Particularly around the time that I was more visible on Muslim television, when I used to present a show. Rumi's Cave was

a better option for me, and I know that it was for so many other people as well. I used to see girls outside the Cave put their hijab on outside and then come in. I used to say to them, 'Don't do that, just come as you are, otherwise there is no point.' They talk a lot about the cultural schizophrenia that a lot of Muslim youth experience.

JH: Cultural schizophrenia?
Sukina: Being two completely different people, you know – at home you are Muslim boy, speak Bengali or Urdu or Somali with your mother and everyone thinks you are this good boy. Outside you are in a gang or sell coke or you have a girlfriend, or multiple girlfriends or go clubbing. But it doesn't serve anybody if you're not able to be real. If you are able to be real, then at least we can have a conversation about it.

JH: So is the mosque working for the younger generation?
Sukina: I don't think so. The way Muslims engage with mosques in a city like London is like, 'Okay, it's one o'clock, I need to pray, I'm in Walthamstow, google where is the nearest mosque in Walthamstow and go and pray.' Or, 'Oh, it's seven o'clock, I need to pray Maghrib, I'll pray in central London.' There is no sense of community. It's a really bad metaphor, but sometimes I think people treat mosques like a public toilet. You go in, you do what you need to do, then you go out. There is no camaraderie. It is not enriching. It is really unhealthy to have a mosque where I can't see the face of the imam. If I have a problem, I am not even going to know who to talk to. All these kinds of structures come from back home, but don't work here. The imams often don't know how to deal with women. They don't know how to deal with the youth.

JH: What do young Muslims need to face the immense challenges of the times?
Sukina: I think a lot of things are needed. First, we really are in need of leadership. We are in an impoverished place when it comes to faith-based leadership native to the UK. The reason I say that is,

when you go across the UK and attend Friday prayers, oftentimes the sheikhs or imams are not really addressing what's happening in society or connecting the faith to what's happening in our lives. They're not giving us advice about how to engage with this world that we're in. The sermons just focus on a particular story from the Prophet Muhammad's life (peace be upon him). It's not that these things aren't important, but the role of these stories, these metaphors and parables, is to give us the strength and guidance to know that what we're going through is not different to what people have been through in the past. But if we're not taught to see them as tools for us to manoeuvre in this life, they just become dead stories that don't mean much. Or you develop a community of people that are nostalgic and half dwelling in an imagined Arabia where everything was perfect. That's problematic.

We need our British scholars, whatever their background, to strive to be relevant, to be aware of current affairs, what's happening in the world. And what's happening in the youth. What do they want? What are they listening to? What are their trials? Often the Friday prayers aren't even in English. They are in Bengali or Arabic or Urdu, and often kids from that background don't really understand their language enough to make sense of it. So everyone is missing out.

I think what religious leadership means or meant in a village in Pakistan is completely different to what leadership means in London today. What is required is completely different. Some old uncles from the village in Pakistan – they don't understand me, a 21st-century Jamaican Muslim hip-hopper, they have no idea what I am going through! We don't just need someone to come and do prayers for a newborn child or for the dearly departed. We need leaders to give us the tools and guidance to live in this world. That is what we're lacking. That's to do with religious leadership, but we also need other kinds of leadership, from community centres, people engaged in education, legal affairs.

Not all young people will feel comfortable going to an imam. We need people who are confident enough to be present in our communities and offer support where necessary. I'm not saying there aren't these things, but I can count on the fingers of one hand the scholars and sheikhs who are relevant, that I can go to and listen and feel transformed when I leave their spaces. When it comes to community leadership that's a new thing. Many of our

"Some old uncles from the village in Pakistan – they don't understand me, a 21st-century Jamaican Muslim hip-hopper, they have no idea what I am going through!"

community are not used to having leadership outside the traditional religious realm, so having someone who is a leader but from an arts background or activist background, these things are quite new – but very important!

Young people need somewhere to go where they can come as they are, where there will be adequate support, and also compassion, so when they are ready to make a journey deeper into faith, they have a community that can back them.

When I first became a Muslim, I was contacted by a lot of Muslim youth, even people whose fathers are religious scholars, asking me questions about Islam that I'm not really qualified to speak on, though I do my best. They saw us (Poetic Pilgrimage) in some position of leadership because we're on stage and we've got a platform. They thought we were people they could look up to and ask for advice. But we never set out to be role models. What it shows is that Muslims are looking for members of the community who aren't necessarily in high religious positions in the community. They need people they can relate to.

Chapter 19

PARKER J. PALMER

HOW THE GENERATIONS
CAN DANCE TOGETHER

Credit: Sharon L. Palmer

'Until the young and old are connected like the poles of a battery, there's no power.'

Parker J. Palmer founded the Center for Courage and Renewal. He is a world-renowned writer, speaker and activist who focuses on education, community, leadership, spirituality and social change. He has reached millions worldwide through his books and more recently his podcasts on the popular platform curated by Krista Tippett, On Being. One of his more popular podcasts is the lively intergenerational conversation between himself and Courtney Martin, who is seen by many as one of the key voices of her generation. Parker was also mentioned as a source of intergenerational inspiration by several of the young leaders included in this book.

Parker holds a PhD in sociology from the University of California at Berkeley, as well as many awards and honorary doctorates. His books include Healing the Heart of Democracy and Let Your Life Speak. The Leadership Project, a US-based national survey of educators, named Dr Palmer one of the 30 most influential senior leaders in higher education and one of the ten key 'agenda-setters' of the past decade. Parker is a member of the Religious Society of Friends (the Quakers). He is in his late seventies and lives in Madison, Wisconsin.

JH: **Thank you so much for taking the time to speak with me Parker. It's such a delight to meet you – if only on Skype! There's a great deal in your work that's very relevant to the themes of this book – about how we discern a vocation, about the relationship between inner life and outer activism. Also your vision for holistic education, and as you so beautifully describe it, 'how the generations can dance together'. Where shall we start?**

Parker: Well, let's talk about the role of the inner life in social change. If you look at the great movements that have transformed the face of the world – the women's movement internationally, movements for liberation in Eastern Europe, South America or Latin America, the Black Liberation movement here in the US, or the movements for LGBTQ rights – what you find is that these movements are started by people who have had every form of external power stripped from them. They have no status in the eyes of the law or larger society, no credibility. They have no access to traditional forms of power, no political leverage and no money. This is where we normally locate power, somewhere in the external world. Where do these people get power? The answer is, the only place where no one can take it away from you. That's the human heart. The human spirit. The inner life.

What animates these movements is the inner life, the decision to live 'divided no more' – the moment of recognition where people say, I am no longer going to speak or act externally in a way that violates the deep truth I know inwardly. To contravene it is to live a divided life – to act one way on the outside whilst knowing something else on the inside. To bring those two together is to be divided no more. We come to that place only by taking an inner journey.

> "Increasingly young people are rejecting indoctrination."

I worry about young people who are given hardly any help in understanding what an inner journey is or how to take an inner journey. We give young people very little help in understanding that linkage between the inner and the outer. They get no help in their education – because education is externally oriented. We certainly don't give them help in our religious institutions, which are more interested in somebody standing up front and telling them what the 'objective truth' of their tradition is. 'Here's what you need to believe, now go believe it.' That's not inner growth, that's indoctrination. Increasingly young people are rejecting indoctrination.

Unless we understand our own inner landscape, our action is likely to do more harm than good, no matter what our intentions. You don't have to go all religious on people to deliver this message. Socrates said that the unexamined life is not worth living. Well I'm old enough now to amend Socrates.

JH: [Laughs] The advantages of age!
Parker: I say, if you chose to live an unexamined life, then please do not do anything that involves other people! You'll do damage if you do. So if you take any of the people we associate with the great social movements – Nelson Mandela in South Africa, Roşa Parks in the US civil rights movement or Dorothy Day in the Catholic Worker movement – these are people who made a decision to live 'divided no more' and acted on it.

But we have to frame this message in ways that build bridges with a rising generation of people for whom the old language of religious tradition doesn't work any more.

JH: That's so beautifully expressed, Parker. The decision to live divided no more. That this is the power behind movements for justice. And it's also very relevant for young adults who have less conventional power in life and grow up potentially colluding with a system created before they were born, that no longer works for them. It's clear that young people are facing a future that is very broken and quite dark. Can you say something about how those principles might be important at this moment in time?
Parker: Bill Moyers[1] once famously said, 'The only answer to the power of organised money – the big driver behind everything from

---

[1]   The American journalist and political commentator.

climate change to Trump – is the power of organised people.' I deeply believe that. So part of our inner-life work, having made this initial decision to live divided no more, is to live in a way that gathers others around us, people who join what I call 'communities of congruence', where we can support each other in what turns out to be the very risky decision to express one's identity and integrity in the world.

Now if you're a straight, white, middle-class, well-educated and older male like me, there aren't a lot of dangers out there. But if you are a person of colour, or gay, bisexual or transgender, for example, it's very dangerous to come out with your own truth. So there's courage involved in raising your flag and saying: 'Here I am, this is what I care about, and I invite other people to rally around this flag and join with me in a community that can help sustain this difficult and dangerous decision.' But that is exactly how every social movement has advanced. And there's a lot of inner work that goes into the formation of community. I have to control my ego, I have to fight jealousy – who's getting too much attention or too many of the rewards – I have to negotiate things with other people who, for some strange reason(!), don't always see things my way, even though we care about the same things.

One of the things inner work does is to reinforce the conviction that *no punishment anyone can ever lay on me could possibly be worse than the punishment I lay on myself by conspiring in my own diminishment.* To me, that's very important. I'm astonished at the number of times we make deals in life that are, in fact, ways of conspiring with our own diminishment. We say, 'In order to get or keep this job, I will tuck away that part of me that finds this work morally offensive.' Or, 'I'll tuck away that part of me that finds the corruption within this company morally offensive.' Or the part of me that finds the way women, or people of colour, are treated in this workplace offensive. Those are self-diminishing decisions. Make enough of them in the course of a life and you get smaller and smaller and paler and thinner – until you're merely a wisp of your real self.

So the next step in the development of a social movement is doing the inner work necessary to come together in community. The power of organised people. This is the only way we can deal with these huge issues facing the rising generation of young folks. It's only the power of organised people that can change anything.

That's a critical part of spiritual formation in the younger generation.

JH: Agreed! How we build community is such an important theme. And many millennials do this very organically, coming together in new ways. So what qualities do you see young adults bringing to the table at this point in history? What do you see emerging from the millennial generation that inspires you?

Parker: Remarkable things. Things that really give me hope. I've been privileged in the last decade to be deeply involved in young activist and leadership retreats. So I've gotten to meet a lot of young people, under the age of 40. I'm 79, so that's really young as far as I'm concerned! Young activists have a very different motivation behind their activism than the one we had in Berkeley in the 1960s. In the 60s, we had a sense that if we worked hard enough, by the end of the decade we could pretty much solve racism and the whole nine yards. It didn't happen. The utopian illusion fell apart, and when it did, a lot of people just threw up their hands and went to work on Wall Street. They said, 'Okay, idealism doesn't work, so I'll turn to pragmatic realism and get the biggest slice of the pie that I can.' So some of the folks from Berkeley in the 1960s ended up 40 years later helping to create the great crash of 2008 via corruption.

In the 60s we got hung up on quick outcomes. But many in the younger generations know they can't solve the problem overnight. But they 'Do It Anyway' – which happens to be the title of a wonderful book by my friend and colleague Courtney Martin, about her generation of activists. They do it for the reward that follows on intrinsic motivation, into which is woven their integrity and their identity. So that's one incredibly valuable thing some millennials are bringing to the table. They have a lot more wisdom in that way of approaching social problems than there was in my generation.

JH: In my tradition we have a saying, the Prophet Muhammad (peace be upon him) said, 'Even if the world is going to end tomorrow, still plant a tree.' It took me a few years to understand the wisdom behind that. That it's not about outcomes, but about living with integrity.

Parker: It absolutely is, yes. And the most important seed that any one of us has to plant is the seed of our own integrity.

JH: So what advice would you give to the younger generation about faith, and about discerning how to make an authentic contribution? How can that path of integrity, integration, authenticity be found at a time when there are so many challenges?

Parker: I'll borrow an idea from Gandhi here, who called his autobiography *My Experiments with Truth*. The only way I know to keep discovering, rediscovering and expanding your discovery of vocation is by experimentation, or so it has been for me. As any scientist will tell you, a lot of experiments fail. In science that's not regarded as a terrible thing. You *learn* through failure if the experiment is carefully crafted. Sometimes you learn more than you do from a successful experiment.

JH: Good point!

Parker: So one of the things we need to do for young people is validate failure – carefully crafted, carefully held failure. This ought to be going on in higher education, but instead we *punish* failure. We make people feel ashamed of it. I'm convinced that's one of the reasons we're so stuck. People are afraid to fail – yet it's only through conducting experiments, many of which *will* fail, that we're going to get anywhere.

JH: We're in the biggest potential failure humanity has ever known in a lot of respects. Young people are witnessing and contemplating failure all around them. Systemic collapse, due to how we have chosen to live.

Parker: Yes, that's right. But things might change if we learn to name and claim our failures before they overcome us – that's why the validation of failure seems so important to me. Here's a quick story. I once had lunch with seven male faculty members. Someone got to talking about a course he had failed in college, the failure of which led him closer to the vocation that he now loved. His parents wanted him to be a doctor but he took organic chemistry and failed it – which freed him to pursue his love of 18th-century French literature, the subject he now taught. Everyone at the table, it turned out, had a story of failing at something when they were young which had brought them closer to their true vocation.

So I asked, 'How many of you have told your story of failure to your students?' Not one hand went up. So I said, 'You have students in your classes who are failing, and they feel ashamed, they feel lost. Would you please tell them *your* story of failure redeemed? It would be enormously encouraging for them.' As I tell my students, my vocation didn't really come together, consciously and coherently, until I was in my early fifties...

JH: That's very encouraging!

Parker: ...so I really get annoyed when adults take an 18-year-old and ask, 'What's your life plan?' I want to shake them and ask, 'What was *your* life plan at age 18? Did you even have one? And if you did, how close is it to what you're doing today? I bet it's on the other side of the moon!'

JH: Yes, there is something very important about validating mistakes. And also in older generations acknowledging the places where collectively we have failed. Failure can weigh people down. My sense is, the way to let go of that is by making the learning fully

conscious, integrating it so it can be shared. Then it becomes a resource that others can draw on.

Parker: Exactly. That's also the point when it comes to the dance between the generations. That's one of the reasons intergenerational work is so important. Older folk have a lot to share with the young, and we have a lot to learn from the young. I like to say that until the young and old are connected, like the poles of a battery, no power gets generated. The young sink into their tribal enclaves, the old sink into their tribal enclaves, and everything goes dead. Stasis. When the poles of the battery get connected, there's electricity. One kind of electricity happens, as you just suggested, when the elders can talk to the youngers about what didn't work for them. There are clues in that for the young but there's also redemption for the elders. How do you redeem a bad life experience? You find some way to serve others with it. In my own life I've had three deep dives into clinical depression, with suicidal imagining. That's one of the most horrifying and seemingly most unredeemable experiences a person can have – it's some of the worst darkness a person can know. How do you redeem *that*? You redeem it by telling your story, so that people who are currently suffering, or live with those who are suffering, can see there's life on the other side.

> "The young sink into their tribal enclaves, the old sink into their tribal enclaves, and everything goes dead. Stasis. When the poles of the battery get connected, there's electricity."

In Western cultures, maybe in all cultures, we have this conspiracy of silence around the hard things of life. We have to bust that open. I think that's a part of what young people are doing.

JH: What other ways do you see that elders can support young people as they face this very challenging future?

Parker: Many people in my generation bemoan the collapse of our traditional institutions. You know the kind of thing I mean: 'Oh, I remember a day when everyone went to church and kids were all raised with Christian values, and the pastor was one of the most important people in town. Now all of that is going to hell in a handbasket.' Right? But the younger generation isn't spending any time at all mourning the collapse of traditional institutions. Some of them may be applauding that collapse! More importantly, a number of them are inventing new institutions – new forms of church, for example.

So I say to the younger generation, 'Good on you for attempting this experiment!' It interests me. I find it hopeful. I want to encourage these emerging new creations – different ways to do church, different ways to do politics. This generation is social media savvy and very effective. Take the Occupy Movement in the US. Many people say it came and went, so it was a failure. But I say, no, Occupy introduced a meme or a trope into our culture that liberal economists had been trying to introduce for decades and failed. They put the language of the 1 per cent on our lips.[2] More people began to see how wrong it was and started to wake up.

> "I say to the younger generation, 'Good on you for attempting this experiment!'"

We need much more osmosis between the generations. We live in age-segregated societies, in silos. We physically separate the elderly in housing and care facilities. There are a million young people out there who are yearning for someone in the older generation to simply pay attention to them. When I was young, that kind of elder-attention and mentoring was much more available.

JH: What's the most important thing you have learnt from the millennial generation?
Parker: I learnt just how much fun they are! I find them energising and encouraging. That's important because a lot of older people are

---

2   'We are the 99 percent' was an Occupy slogan in 2011. The *1 per cent* refers to the top 1 per cent wealthiest people in society that have a disproportionate share of capital, political influence and the means of production.

afraid of young people. They're afraid that young people don't like them, or that they won't have anything to talk about. Or they find the dress styles or hair colours of younger folks to be a little scary! But the real fear of older people is that young people see us as over the hill – while on the other side of the fence, many young people are afraid their elders are not interested in them.

When I taught college, I sent my students out to seek conversations with people in the fields that they were interested in. If you're interested in becoming a banker, go to the local bank and ask for half an hour with the bank president – not to ask for a job, but just to know their story, to learn from them. The students would say, 'Nobody is going to give me any time for that!' And I'd tell them, I wager that half of you will not only get that 30-minute convo, but that it extends into an hour, or they invite you to lunch. Because who doesn't love talking about their own story?

I love to be with young people. It saves me from stagnation. It saves me from recycling my ideas with a lot of old white men who are cynical or in despair. The antidote to this fear that keeps us apart begins with walking into our fears and simply getting together. We fear that reaching across the great divide of age won't work. Believe me, it will – I know because I've seen it happen time and time again, when someone has the courage to take that first step!

PART 6

CHALLENGING ORTHODOXY

To say the younger generations have been badly short-changed is an understatement. It's not just that millennials have worse economic prospects than their parents, start life burdened with student debts, can't afford to buy their own homes, and are paying the price for baby boomer pensions. Those are side issues. The reality is that they are inheriting a world that is increasingly bleak, unjust and dystopian. Water and food security are precarious. The oceans are full of plastic. Bee and insect populations are plummeting. Extremism is gaining traction. Societies are disintegrating. We are facing real survival issues. And the elders, those in positions of influence, allowed this to happen. They dig their heads in the sand while the world burns.

Activist parents who sold out, religious values that don't translate into action, faith leaders who are hypocritical, ego-driven gurus getting rich on fake wisdom, institutions that are stuck in the past, churches that care more about falling congregation numbers than about the real issues, MPs with no ethics, politicians who fail to follow through on promises, hierarchies that block any kind of change, corporates that exploit mercilessly, power that is relentlessly abused. As Adam Bucko (whom we met in Chapter 5) says, 'There is much to be angry about in today's world, whether you are young or old, but certainly if you are young. Adultism reigns.'[1]

But the younger generation *are* rising. The Arab Spring. The Standing Rock water protesters. The March for Our Lives protest against US gun laws – this was the largest-ever protest in US history. Who organised it? Teenagers. There are many examples of youth-led revolts sweeping away old assumptions, freeing up our minds, making space for the new. The younger generation have always been the harbingers of change. It's just that now we need them more than ever before. Beneath the surface there is also something quite different happening from what occurred in youth movements of the past. Gen X-ers fought to stop what they saw as wrong or to gain the power to do what mattered to them. Gen Y are in a different business. The gradual shift in worldview we are experiencing globally, across many disciplines, is taking us from hierarchical to networked ways of working, from dualistic frames to systems-thinking, from binaries to interconnected wholes. We see this in our sciences, in ecology, business, community building, and more.

This is not just a one-fight-at-a-time battle for justice. It is a broader attempt at a more fundamental redistribution of power, away from corporates, politicians, religious leaders and those at the top of the hierarchies, towards the people, towards participatory decision-making, towards co-creation, towards diversity engaging our collective intelligence. The challenge to authority is not insubordination. It is evolution.

Gen X rebelled against their parents for as long as it took to get what they wanted (or until they grew up). Gen Y are more likely to be friends with their Gen X parents, sharing power, relating to them openly, both sides redefining where authority lies in the parent/offspring partnerships of the 21st century.

Millennials are the uprisers, but also the reinventors, the pioneers, the prototypers. There is much as yet unformed, still to be

---

[1]   *Occupy Spirituality: A Radical Vision for a New Generation*, Adam Bucko and Matthew Fox (North Atlantic Books, 2013), p.4.

revealed. Perhaps it's Gen Y's job primarily to rip up the plans and make space for asking deeper questions. Maybe we'll need Gen Z a little further down the line, to ground the most efficacious of these new forms, to rebuild structures in more life-giving patterns? Right now, it's just one big experiment!

Chapter 20

CAMILLE BARTON

OUR COLLECTIVE LIBERATION

'I'm hopeful – but it's going to be messy!'

Camille Barton is a 26-year-old movement artist, diversity consultant, producer and founder of the Collective Liberation Project, who is passionate about how the fusion of art and politics can lead to social change. Improvisation, prefigurative politics and Afrofuturism are at the core of her art. While living in the San Francisco Bay Area she worked as a youth worker and dancer and also trained in restorative justice, non-violent communication and peer counselling.

In 2016, back in the UK, Camille began leading workshops on White Allyship and set up the Collective Liberation Project (CLP). CLP designs experiential workshops based on a compassionate activism approach, educating about oppression and equipping people with the tools to transform the behaviours that perpetuate racism and sexism in themselves and in their communities. Camille also manages projects for festivals such as Burning Man, Nowhere, Boomtown Fair and Symbiosis. She co-produced The Sisterhood, Glastonbury festival's first women-only venue, incorporating a strong focus on intersectionality and providing a platform for women of colour.

Like others in this book, Camille is a creative and passionate advocate for 'liberation from our collective oppression'. Her art and anti-racist work are innovative and alive. In this conversation however, my hope was to highlight her experience of the older generation, as that is an important part of the picture.

Camille voices her frustration with the disconnect between believing and doing that she sees in Generation X – the hypocrisy of those espousing values that are not fully lived. She grew up in North London with her mother, who was of Nigerian and Guyanese descent, and her father, who was white British. Her parents were meditators, influenced by the influx of spiritual traditions from the East, and raised their family with an openness to all faiths. But for Camille their spirituality is very individually focused, and reflects the way Western materialism has subtly corrupted the Eastern teachings that arrived in the 1960s and 70s: 'the social action part has been removed'. She articulates how 'a strange conservatism became part of [her parents'] lives' as their youthful energy for change somehow morphed into a sense of helplessness. In other words, they sold out.

Camille's journey through rejecting her parents' tradition, adopting her own meditation practice, exploring Yoruba spirituality alongside many other influences, and pursuing her bold movement art, has been fuelled by a need to live her values in a world that demands to be engaged with. 'My spirituality is about how I live every day. It's not just confined to my meditation cushion. It's something I'm trying to bring into the world.'

Throughout her narrative is another recurring theme – the impossibility of working daily for social change when the odds seem entirely against it. The need is to keep doing the right thing. Be fearless but realistic. Acknowledge, but not stare too hard into the face of a future that looks potentially very dark. Camille names with great honesty what must surely be a collective feeling: 'It's really, really scary.' Yet she bounces back with hope and optimism in the next sentence. This is the place many young people occupy daily. Like Courtney Martin, whose book about the new generation of activists[1] tells us to 'just do it anyway', Camille knows that to think too much about the end results is a recipe for a nervous breakdown.

---

1   *Do It Anyway: The New Generation of Activists*, Courtney Martin (Beacon Press, 2010).

Despite that, there is a determination to live her values and celebrate living them, with spirit and integrity, because that's what is needed but also because it brings a sense of wholeness and fulfilment that could not be attained via more selfish pursuits.

I've been grateful for the honesty of young adults like Camille and hope I can continue to learn from them.

Motifs in this chapter:

- Challenging orthodoxy

- Complex identities

JH: What was your experience of spirituality when you were growing up?
Camille: Well, there was always an open space for exploring spirituality, as both my parents are 'Premies'.[2] My dad ran away from an evangelical Christian family and found himself in an ashram at 17. He's very anti-religion and believes that connecting with the divine truth within is the only thing. My mum believes it's all about connecting to the Source, and there are many ways up the mountain. They're both 'avatar neutral', they believe that Krishna, Muhammad, Jesus, Buddha were all living masters teaching universal truths, and that religions and dogma were created afterwards. I grew up being very interested in different belief systems, seeing the universal elements within them, but also being quite critical of the ways that power has been codified around belief.

JH: How would you describe your spirituality now?
Camille: It's an ongoing journey. I've had a meditation practice for about ten years, but not from Prem Rawat's teachings. I've been quite resistant to it for a long time as I wanted to define *my* thing – maybe that was my own kind of rebellion! Now I'm also trying to connect to Orisha-worship and my indigenous Yoruba spirituality.

---

2   Followers of the Indian spiritual teacher Prem Rawat.

My spirituality is about how I live every day. It's not just confined to my meditation cushion. It's something I'm trying to bring into the world. Eastern traditions are being watered down and commodified to fit a Western capitalistic framework. The social action part has been removed. Now it's all about finding inner peace and accepting that life is suffering – then you don't have to worry about how you're making money or the impact you have on other people, because it's all about you and your individual salvation. I think that's a load of crap!

> "Eastern traditions are being watered down and commodified to fit a Western capitalistic framework. The social action part has been removed."

I've gone against my parents' generation where spirituality is seen as a private thing they do on their own and has no connection to the real world. For me, it's super-important that spirituality and action aren't separated. My spiritual practice allows me to do the social justice work I do. It gives me more fuel, strength and compassion to make change.

JH: How did that understanding come to you? Are there any particular moments you can describe, of realising the way your parents' generation was practising spirituality didn't really make sense to you?

Camille: I always felt like an activist, even before I knew what the word meant. Apparently I was talking about gay rights when I was six. I felt deeply upset about the state of the world as a child. And I didn't like my dad's job in the oil industry. I noticed a lot of Premies were deeply spiritual people but had jobs that were destructive. When I talked to my dad about it, he would say, 'Well, if I'm not doing it, someone else will.' For me that just wasn't good enough. His sense of apathy is partly because he believes that this material realm is an illusion and the only thing that's real is the inner world. I just don't think that's true. This plays into capitalist individualism and allows a lot of people with privilege to say it's not real anyway and we can't make the change, it's always going to be like this.

Considering both my parents were quite radical in their youth, it felt like this strange conservatism became part of their lives. They didn't feel they had the power to create change in the world and were quite happy continuing to just go inside and observe themselves rather than actively engaging.

There's also the other extreme where activists feel they have to change everything and can't rest or have any kind of joy or connection until this is all fixed. I don't believe that either. I'm trying to find the middle ground.

JH: Tell me about the work you're involved in now.
Camille: I've been developing an organisation called the Collective Liberation Project. We lead somatic and experiential anti-racism trainings. It's about understanding white supremacy and actively starting to dismantle it in our communities. It's about providing education and space for people to bring their feelings into it. I've noticed in a lot of activist spaces there's not really any room for feelings. It can be quite militaristic – this is our agenda, this is our mission, feelings don't matter.

Oppression is deeply emotional. It's not enough just to have facts and figures, and to believe 'I'm not racist or sexist'. It has to be unlearnt and processed through the body as well. The organisation is an experiment in using an activist lens but bringing a somatic and emotional component in so people can stop talking hypothetically about things that are happening in the world and start applying it to themselves and ask, 'How am I reproducing this? Where do I see this in my family and my workplace?' Allowing people to see that a lot of work can be done if they tune in to how these things relate to themselves rather than seeing them as issues that exist out there. It's about engaging with it on a micro and macro level.

JH: So how did that work come about?

Camille: In California I saw a lot of West Coast energy that was based around saying yes to things and creating new things, rather than just saying no. I'd seen a lot of just saying no in England, which was so boring!

I lived in a cooperative called Raven House with ex-students from Berkeley who were involved in activist work, and I was doing some organising with the Black Lives Matter movement. I was really inspired by that. This is the current civil rights movement. It was incredible to be part of it.

I worked as a youth worker in a continuation school that was using restorative justice. Most of the students had been in the juvenile detention system at some point, either incarcerated or in foster care. For me, being a middle-class, mixed-heritage person who grew up in Muswell Hill, it was a clash of worlds. It was beautiful, really humbling and I had to learn a lot.

Then, back in the UK, Brexit happened and this whole right-wing wave emerged. There are definite differences but, institutionally, the same stuff is happening in the UK. It's just less talked about, less understood and people don't have strategies to address it.

JH: How does your work come together with your spirituality? You expressed so beautifully earlier that you don't see spirituality as separate from the world, so how do they come together for you?

Camille: For me, it feels powerful to live my values. Spiritually, it affirms my belief that things are changing and can change. When people come to a workshop and something shifts in them, that feels really powerful, to see that these things aren't entrenched for ever.

I suppose the reason why I'm a good facilitator is because I basically meditate my way through facilitation. When things come up, I observe them. There are big reactions that come from people – it's heavy stuff – but because of my meditation practice, I'm able to observe and decide how I'm going to respond. I don't have to react, because

"It feels powerful to live my values."

my meditation practice gives me space to notice and understand that this is coming from a person suffering, and enough compassion to hold the various needs in the room.

Sometimes if I'm in a down place, I can get into a headspace of thinking everything is so dire, is it ever going to change? But then if I'm in a good place, I can feel, regardless of what the end goal is, the journey of living in line with what I believe is what it's really about. If I stay present with that, there's more power and longevity than by weighing the scales – that's a mental health hazard waiting to happen. I'm content with that for now, and I'll take tomorrow as it comes.

JH: Talking about tomorrow, how do you feel about the future?
Camille: I've noticed that sometimes I'm choosing to skirt around the amount of fear and anger that I have about the state of the world. I just keep trudging on. But I do need to give more space for grieving, for fear and uncertainty. It's just all such a big question mark right now. I've studied international relations, I have a pretty good grasp on power relations and the flow of history, and I know that in times of austerity and recession, fascism rises. I know that it's linked to the economy, I know there've been other moments in history that are comparable even though I haven't lived through them. But at the same time – it's really, *really* scary. I oscillate between wanting to throw myself into the beautiful struggle of trying to create change and other moments where I want to run away and dance for six weeks in Brazil. I need to do both. That's a coping mechanism for continuing to inject my life full of joy, beauty and inspiration.

I am hopeful though. I believe in being hopeful, and I am hopeful, even though it might not be rational. It feels like an exciting time to be alive. It's now or never.

I find myself thinking I should become a CIC, get loads of funding, train more people. That could be good – but that's a certain kind of success model rooted in a very Western way of doing things. It's not necessarily what my heart wants. I want to learn from communities who are using different models, learn to live in a way that's not just for the individuals in your family but the wider community, the land that you live on, the food that you eat, the celebrations that you have, the honouring of ancestors – how this can all tie in to a web that sustains us or sustains the planet. Here, we have such an atomised, individualistic society, most people don't even have close relationships with their families, let alone with others. Intimacy and connection is a precious and limited thing. I feel I've got a lot to learn about how to build connections, how to not have disposable relationships, really give reciprocity and be sustainable. What I've been taught to do by this culture is to think, 'I'm an individual, I'm living my life and I'm having a great time.'

JH: What's your relationship with African spirituality? You mentioned the Yoruba tradition earlier – how has that been in your life and how has that fed into what you do?
Camille: I haven't had much connection to it until recently as I wasn't proud of my African heritage because of internalised racism. Growing up in a very white area of London, it wasn't something I felt I could celebrate. Happily, that's changed now, and I'm in the early stages of learning about the Orishas and trying to understand what Yoruba people were doing before colonisation – our practices and rituals. I'm going to Brazil soon, to Bahia, where that legacy is most thriving.

When Western people go to the continent, Africans sometimes ask, 'What religion are you?' Many of my friends would say, 'I don't practise a religion.' And they'd say, 'But what do you believe?', and they get confused: 'I don't believe in anything.' To many Africans, that doesn't really make sense because there's an understanding that you are giving power to whatever your beliefs are. In the West, we believe that we're not believing anything, but actually what we're giving power to is science, Western rationalism, capitalism and individualism. That's what we're praying to, we just don't see it because it's so normalised.

JH: That's so well articulated. Do you ever feel the need to have a single tradition, or are you at home with that diversity of influences?

Camille: I do feel a pull to honour my indigenous heritage, because part of the pain of colonialism is feeling that's been stolen from me. The beauty of chaos magic is that we may not have all the texts and the rituals word for word, but we can take the core and re-create it into something that is applicable now. That's what is relevant for me. Even if I was to learn from Yoruba elders in Nigeria or from a Babalawo in Bahia, I know that my context as a British-raised person means some contextualising and re-creation is necessary for me to make sense of it and responsibly interact with it. I'm a fan of reclaiming and respectfully revisioning for the times.

JH: Power is a theme that's weaving through a lot of what you do, and the millennial generation are really engaging with the need to share power, rejecting hierarchical power structures in favour of something more fluid and organic. I'm wondering how you relate to power and what you feel needs to change in relation to power?

Camille: Big question! We need truth and reconciliation processes for all the different abuses that have been happening. The first step is for people to understand how people come to oppress each other so easily. The first oppression everyone faces in a Western context is ageism. That's normalised in school systems. No one wants to be at the bottom of the ladder. We get resentful because it doesn't feel good to be oppressed, so we oppress someone else.

JH: As a young adult, do you feel empowered or discriminated against?

Camille: I think the intersection of being black, queer and female-assigned, having piercings, tattoos and being quite young-looking – people are surprised when I come into a room and they realise I'm leading the training. It can be quite confronting, especially for older white men. I definitely get pushback. Is it the age thing, is it the race thing, is it the woman thing? Maybe it's all of it. I don't know.

Unless I really trust someone, I don't like being in a hierarchical structure. But running my own organisation means I have autonomy, and that's important to me, especially in such a precarious economy. If I was in a different generation and could get a nice job in the third sector, buy a house, buy into capitalism – maybe I would have done that, but I can't. I don't want a zero-hour contract. I don't want to scramble to get one of these jobs that seem like a golden ticket but really are underpaid and you're doing two other people's jobs and then you have to deal with subtle racism, even in sectors that are meant to be progressive. Right now, I just don't want any of it. I'd rather have a modest income, work for myself, have a bit more autonomy and then choose who I want to collaborate with.

JH: I know in communities that are trying to operate on interconnectedness, it isn't always deep enough. Sometimes there can be a false interconnectedness that's created, where privilege isn't really noticed. Where white Western people or older generations believe the environment we create is inclusive when actually it's not. What's been your experience of that?
Camille: That's a really big thing that has been a consistent part of my life. In my parents' Premie community, I noticed an unwillingness to acknowledge racism and the different lived experiences that people of the global majority have in the UK. It became apparent to me that many spiritually conscious people haven't dealt with their inherent racism or sexism. I've had bad experiences going to meditation classes and hearing white Western Buddhist teachers say, 'Suffering is inevitable, you can't worry about the troubles of the world. It's not to do with you, it's always going to exist.' Once, I put my hand up and said, 'Er, sorry, I think that's a bit messed up that you can say in this privileged group of people we don't have power to create change! There are lots of things we can do to create change. This pacifying, individualistic approach is a departure from the core message of Tibetan Buddhism and does a disservice to the amount of privilege we have to change things.' In the break of the class I was cornered by an older man who said in a passive-aggressive, whispery tone, 'I bet

you think you're really big and clever, don't you, making everyone feel bad and uncomfortable like that.' He really went off on me and I ended up having a cry and not coming back.

There've been lots of times like that. We want to be close and there are many ways in which we are similar. We are all human beings and spiritual beings. And yet there are lots of differences in the material realm. We should celebrate those differences. I think often we pretend these things don't exist because it's easier for the dominant group to get what they want rather than having to be uncomfortable and hold the space for the complexity and messiness of all our different needs. It means our conversations are going to be longer and maybe we're going to need more emotional support, but the closeness we create will be more real. But yes, it is hard and I struggle with it. It's experimental because we don't have a road-map. I'm hopeful – but it's going to be messy!

"It is hard and I struggle with it. It's experimental because we don't have a road-map."

Chapter 21

MATT YOUDE

YOUTH MAINSTREAMING

'When they call you forward to lead and take responsibility –
answer the call.'

*Matthew Youde is a 29-year-old Catholic, born in Caerphilly in Wales. He has
been involved in youth work for many years, in both interfaith and single-faith
Catholic environments. In 2008 he joined the United Religions Initiative (URI) as
a volunteer supporting the Global Young Leaders Program, helping to organise the
first international gathering of URI youth in Mayapur, India. Since then he has been
a Trustee on URI's Global Council and a trainer at Young Leaders Program events,
and now serves as Associate Director of Global Programs for Youth Leadership
Development.*

Matt is an ardent advocate for youth mainstreaming – for integrating youth perspectives into policy making, governance and programme planning across all sectors and spheres, to ensure those who have a greater investment in the future are represented in all forms of decision-making. The purpose of youth mainstreaming is to overcome the marginalisation of young people in society (alongside the marginalisation of women, people of colour and LGBTQ people). Its purpose is also to enable decision-makers to benefit from the different perspectives young people bring. This approach seeks to increase our collective intelligence by increasing diversity, and also aids the intergenerational transfer of knowledge and skills.

Matt's perspective, which I'm sure many millennials share, is a response to watching the leaders of previous generations sleepwalking into the multiple global environmental and economic disasters we now face. Within the millennial generation there are many with a real appetite for radical change. It is important that those people gain access to leadership roles where they have the means actually to implement that change. If their elders are not responding fast enough, then the least they can do is make way for those who will.

Matt's narrative reflects the frustration that those in positions of influence are largely reluctant to sacrifice their own attachments and self-interest in order to tackle our most pressing issues. We are lucky to have young people willing to speak out and to continue working within a system that has failed them, rather than strike out on their own as many do. Although I'm sure many readers will agree with him, Matt's narrative also raises questions about how the generations can best work together – how to draw on the strengths of the younger without alienating the older.

Motifs in this chapter:

- Challenging orthodoxy

- Complex identities

- Protecting Earth

JH: Matt, I'd love you to share a little about this idea of youth mainstreaming, which I know you're passionate about. And about the relationship between Catholic social teaching and supporting young people.

Matt: It comes from a wider church tradition of focusing on communities that don't typically get served. Those who can slip through the cracks. So historically there have been chaplains for refugees, minorities, young people, women, etc.

JH: So there is a recognition that young people are marginalised within society and marginalised within the Christian tradition as well?

Matt: Yes, both. There is one core teaching, or charism, called the lay apostolate, which is about the role of people who are not priests and lay religious being active in the Church. That kind of lay leadership was seen as something young people could take up and embrace. And the other charism was indirectly part of Catholic social teaching called the preferential option for the poor, which is essentially affirmative action to tackle discrimination. You make a greater effort for those groups you identify as marginalised and needing more help. So, the work for young people came from identifying them as a group that needed some preferential attention.

JH: Can you say more about what youth leadership is for you?

Matt: The Western corporate understanding of leadership is the default, and means positional leadership – board members, chair people, directors, and so on. Youth leadership usually means the foot soldiers essentially. It's what I call social leadership – cleaning rivers, doing voluntary work. Now that's not a bad thing to be doing, but that seems to be the ceiling of leadership for youth. When I started working in interfaith, around the time of the Copenhagen climate talks, youth leadership programmes had a lot of intersection with the environmental movement. That's how many young adults got involved in interfaith. But what that did was relegate youth leadership to campaigning and advocacy.

JH: Making a contribution but not necessarily having the power to change much?
Matt. Yes, exactly.

JH: And what would you like to see?
Matt: Two things. More younger people in positional leadership roles – boards, CEOs, etc. I'm not talking about youth creating their own spaces to do that together, although that's been a wonderful flowering of creativity, prototyping some potentially new way of doing things in society. But ultimately these separate places that millennials have created are not the answer. Your multinationals are still doing what multinationals do. They're not changing fast and we're at a critical moment, especially for the environment. So there comes a point where it's no longer an incremental change from the inside but a more dramatic shift in thinking that's needed. Some of these places that have real power, that's where young people need to be in decision-making roles in order for us, quite frankly, to save the world.

> "Multinationals are still doing what multinationals do. They're not changing fast and we're at a critical moment, especially for the environment."

> "Some of these places that have real power, that's where young people need to be in decision-making roles in order for us, quite frankly, to save the world."

We need to be in governmental leadership, we need to be in business leadership. Not just on the fringes experimenting with new ways of doing. We need to do that too – and God knows there are enough of us – we're the largest generation to have ever existed! But our thinking, our different approaches, need to be in those places of power. Then secondly, there is the campaigning version of young leadership, which is an umbrella for all the efforts to try and get us there. So for me, youth leadership is both a goal and describes a set of programmes and special initiatives, every effort that's made to shake things up and get youth into those places.

JH: So young people need to be in positions where they can influence, in places of mainstream power, in order to save the world?

Matt: Yeah, and it's a very broad statement to make. I'm not going to paint an entire generation of young adults as one mind or one voice, but there are some trends in values and in what's important to my generation. If you combined those social attitudes with power, a lot of things would look very different. Everything from civil rights and equalities to environmental standards, business ethics, and so on.

JH: Talk a bit more about those values...

Matt: Okay, so most polls show that young people are generally more relaxed about everything from interracial marriage to LGBTQ issues, experience more urgency around environmental standards and decarbonisation, and are far more active on anti-colonial and neo-colonial policies.

I do think the business community is way out ahead of the charity sector in adapting to millennials. They are flattening their organisational structures in response to millennials' needs. They realised millennials care less about financial security than we do about purpose (although I take that with a little pinch of salt – I think there is over-sampling of a certain class of young people).

Essentially we need a shifting of money and power from where it is currently to where it needs to be. For example, [in one family foundation I was connected with], the family built its money from oil essentially – whale oil and then ground oil – and have a foundation that gives away $200 million dollars derived from interests in investments. When younger family members gained more leadership within that foundation they completely decarbonised the investments and now it derives its entire endowment from low- or zero-carbon investments. That's real power, that's what young people can do.

People of all generations can do this of course, but statistically we're more likely to.

> "The business community is way out ahead of the charity sector in adapting to millennials. They are flattening their organisational structures in response to millennials' needs."

JH: What's it been like for you as a young person growing up seeing the increasing crisis that has been unfolding and watching elder leaders struggle to create change?

Matt: Incredibly frustrating.

JH: So what would your message be to senior leaders?

Matt: We're not that scary. Share power with us. Don't be an obstacle to social change.

JH: One last question. What would be your message to young adults who are reading this?

Matt: Your voice and your leadership are needed. They are urgently needed, otherwise this world isn't going to survive. You do have to step up. You're going to meet some resistance but you have to push through that. There are people out there who are allies. Seek them out, find them, work with them and, very much more importantly, when they call you forward to lead and take responsibility – answer the call.

Chapter 22

AMRITA BHOHI

THE MARRIAGE OF INNER AND OUTER

'There's a freedom because we know something is over. We can redefine everything.'

Amrita Bhohi is passionate about working with the energy, creativity and vision of younger generations and coming together in service to a different future. After completing an MA in Ecological Economics at Schumacher College, Amrita worked on the global Eradicating Ecocide campaign and at the policy think tank, the Royal Institute of International Affairs (Chatham House). In 2013 she organised TEDx Whitechapel, which was named as one of the most popular and radical TEDx events in London. Now, she leads the Spiritual Ecology Programme at St Ethelburga's Centre for Reconciliation and Peace, which explores how practical environmental and social action can be rooted in a recognition of the interconnected and sacred nature of life. Her work focuses on facilitating training workshops and supporting practical project development, mainly working with emerging leaders in the next generation.

Amrita has been instrumental in helping shape the strategy at St Ethelburga's towards young leadership. Her spirituality is rooted in service. Identifying with a particular tradition or community seems secondary to her commitment to act in service to the whole. Amrita has a visionary quality about her. She tracks the escalating crises around us with a questioning mind, fully awake to the limitations of mainstream thinking, and with the clarity of one who is not caught in the prevailing paradigm but holds her awareness unwaveringly on the underlying transition and evolutionary opportunity.

She also has the ability to gather and inspire her peers, articulating a call to action that really speaks to the heart. She is passionate about the potential of Generation Y, the possibilities for reinventing everything and laying the foundations of a culture based on a different set of values. She also witnesses the many obstacles and blocks her peers face – both spiritually and in their careers and social contributions – and increasingly acts as a guide and mentor to those around her.

In the few years that I've known her, she has rooted herself with increasing depth in what will clearly be a lifelong mission to work with her generation (and those that follow), inspiring them to put spiritual values into action through building leadership capacity and through the work of spiritual ecology.

Motifs in this chapter:

- Challenging orthodoxy

- Complex identities

- Protecting Earth

- Natural leadership

JH: So tell me a little about your relationship with your spirituality.
Amrita: I was born into the Sikh tradition, but as a second-generation Indian. Like many of my age, I didn't understand much of the language or customs and so didn't make a personal connection to it beyond the social norms of going to the temple on Sundays with my family. There were efforts to engage young people, through Sunday School for example, but it still felt something difficult to

relate to in my life growing up in England, where the cultural values and context were so different to India.

However, something that I took for granted and became aware of later was that it grounded me in a certain worldview. The spiritual dimension was something that I never questioned; unlike many of my peers at school, growing up within an Eastern tradition I always knew and understood that there was a reality beyond the material. This was something I appreciated more and more as I got older. At university, for example, there was a sense of being 'lost' and 'searching' that I experienced in my peers. But I always felt guided and rooted in the values and wisdom I inherited and didn't feel I had to search for anything, it was always there.

In my late teens I had started exploring spirituality mainly through reading books, and as a result of a traumatic family crisis that made me begin to ask deeper questions about life. But after graduating from university, I really began the journey of experiencing it for myself. I'd always been interested in meditation, so I tried out a ten-day silent Vipassana meditation retreat. Which just felt so right. Looking back, I think it really unlocked something for me. I made a connection with my heart and soul that was really beautiful. It felt like a new beginning. I experienced the world differently and felt so much more alive, more in touch with my life force, more in touch with the Earth. It just felt so natural meditating.

JH: Do you identify as a Sikh?
Amrita: Yes and no. My spiritual journey and development over the past ten years has been influenced by two other paths as well as Sikhism: Buddhism and Sufism. And the paths and teachings all somehow feel as one within me. Interestingly, it has been the direct, personal inner spiritual experience that has brought me back to Sikhism over the past few years. I've fallen in love with Sikhism, the philosophy and the practice, and feel more and more identified with it as a significant part of my heritage and who I am. I think I'm more of a Sikh than I'd realised, even though I am not really rooted within a Sikh community, which is interesting.

JH: What is it in the Sikh tradition that most resonates?

Amrita: The warrior tradition and the fundamental teaching of oneness, those two things are the heart of Sikhism for me. Humanity is one. We're all one family and we're all interconnected. In my earlier life I related more to the peaceful, non-violent tradition of the early gurus, but as I've got older I'm now really intrigued and inspired by the tenth Guru. He changed the whole face of Sikhism and turned it into quite a military tradition where warriorship, fighting and killing were at the heart of what it meant to be Sikh. I always used to find that a bit hard to relate to. But now I see it as fighting for justice, giving your life for truth for justice in the world. Being willing to do that with a certain amount of ferocity and the power of the sword. Sikhs are supposed to be saints and soldiers. Do their meditation and prayers, and equally do their service in the world. That is such a symbol of how I see my spirituality and actually how I see the spirituality of other young people as well. A kind of marriage of inner and outer – the warriorship and the oneness.

JH: I can really see the saint and warrior in you! And also see just how much it's needed in the world.

Amrita: I couldn't be a part of any spiritual path that didn't also speak about the need to bring the light of spirituality into the world and to address the issues of the time. I can't really relate to keeping spirituality private, especially in a world today where we are collectively facing such grave issues – it doesn't make sense to me. I think I always felt a sense of responsibility and privilege growing up in the West. Maybe it was an awareness of the relative poverty of my ancestors in India. From a young age I felt very aware of the wealth and opportunities available to me, and I felt a real sense of responsibility to give back. How can you be aware of the imbalance in the world and not feel that we need to do something? There is so much that needs to be done. The inner oneness is also out there in the world. Living it means seeing the person in the slum as us.

JH: So how has it been growing up in a world with that kind of inequality present? With those grave problems? Facing that future?

Amrita: It is so intense. It's so in your face. For me it's been a process of progressively realising how deep and systemic the problems are. When I travelled to India, to Africa – seeing there is real poverty in the world and yet we have so much wealth. How do we allow this to happen? Then realising the magnitude of the environmental crisis, the economic crisis, and wanting to look more deeply into the roots of these social and environmental issues. Learning about the economic system and how this drives so much of the destruction and suffering. The more you learn, the more you see how bad the situation really is and how interconnected it is. It's in every single aspect of life. It's all-inclusive, completely systemic. Things are really broken.

JH: Was there any particular moment that stood out for you in coming to understand that brokenness?

Amrita: There were many! A really pivotal experience for me was that I had an opportunity to intern at Chatham House, which is a high-profile think tank. I went to roundtables, events and conferences with people from government, business and corporations – all very establishment, very conservative. It was fascinating and deeply shocking realising how out of their depth all of these people were. They just don't know. These problems are so severe and they are grasping for solutions, totally out of their depth.

Secondly, they are dealing with it all at such a symptomatic level. All they are able to do is respond to the crisis in the immediate sense, like a nuclear disaster happened so we need to just fix that up quickly. No one is asking whether nuclear energy is viable, or what are the wider consequences of this, or should we have nuclear energy in the first place. I've been at conferences about the financial crisis with the CEOs of big banks essentially talking about how they can continue doing what they're doing with new regulation basically. I was deeply shocked. I just sat there and said okay, obviously we're not going to find any solutions here. This is not where I want to work.

No one is asking the right questions. So, yeah, that was a really critical experience for me, realising how inadequate and impotent mainstream thinking is and how systemic the problems are. I wanted to be asking philosophical questions or ethical questions. I felt really unsatisfied about the depth of inquiry, no one challenging the norms. So much of this has just become normal, this is the way the world is. We can't even begin to think differently. So I felt like a real outsider there and realised that maybe I was on the more radical edge of the spectrum! But then luckily I found the New Economics Foundation and Schumacher College. I found I fitted in much better there!

JH: So I can see why you would bring the warrior side of the Sikh tradition and the warrior side of your own nature to bear on all of that.

Amrita: Yes, definitely, I feel it is so needed! I find myself often challenging and fighting the dominant narrative and system, speaking and standing up for the deep injustices being subjected to people and especially to the Earth today. And standing for a world that honours the sacredness of all life. Along with many others who are doing the same.

JH: So what do you see as the response of your generation, growing up with that?

Amrita: Well, firstly I know there is an enormous energy for change. That young people have the energy and the desire and the passion to make these changes. The challenge is how can we use that energy, how can we channel it, ground it. How can we make it go somewhere and make it build something? And not have it ebb away because there are no opportunities to use this energy, and you end up getting another ordinary job to pay the bills, because often young people are in such debt. There are so many constraints to living this practically. I'm one of maybe 100,000 people who is lucky enough to have a paid job in this area, doing what I love and believe in. I think many young people coming out of university are just searching and lost, you know. But the energy is there.

When we did our TEDx conference, when we first came on the stage, I walked on and there were all these young people, and this energy smacked me in the face. It was so overwhelming! I really wasn't expecting it. It was like, wow!, something could actually happen if we really used that, you know? So that's what I feel – an energy to make change, to take action.

But it's not a simple journey to go on. I've noticed with peers and friends there's a lot of stop-start doing this, working a bit in the system, working a bit out of the system – not really having one special path. I noticed that pattern a lot with my peers. Again it kinda breaks my heart, this lack of channelling your energy to one thing, that you can dedicate yourself to in the long run, really build something with. Likewise with the spiritual dimension, often there is a big searching going on. Which is natural. But a lack of opportunity to say this is what I want and I am just gonna go for it in the long run. You know, a bit of psychedelics, a bit of spiritual practice, a bit of shamanic stuff, a bit of whatever.

But when we apply ourselves to these issues and just do it with all our heart, and all our energy and all our commitment... When I'm working with my peers on that level, everything just comes. It's like magic. All that talent, incredible talent, vision, creativity – mind-blowing. That's when all the spiritual searching or instability becomes irrelevant, because we all know this is what we're here to do.

> "When I'm working with my peers on that level, everything just comes. It's like magic. All that talent, incredible talent, vision, creativity – mind-blowing."

JH: How would you describe that thing you're here to do?

Amrita: To be in service to building a new reality, a new society based on the values of oneness. With care for people and the planet at the heart of it. Included in that journey are all of the challenges of working with the system, going into the corridors of power. When I'm working together with others in that way, I feel such a sense of adventure, of what might be possible. But more recently, my expectation about what is possible has definitely changed, become less.

JH: What changed?

Amrita: The landscape in the world, the lack of political direction and action on these issues. It's definitely getting worse and you can't ignore that. I've been interested in these things since I was 20 – for almost ten years – and you wonder when the system is going to start imploding. When is this norm going to start breaking down? This normal thing that we do, that destroys the planet. Everything revolves around this question about how long that is going to last.

JH: That is the question everyone's asking! How long is it all going to last? Let's go back to spirituality again. Can you say more about how you bring your spirituality to bear on this work?

Amrita: I would say at the deepest level I've come to see that it is simply my spiritual practice to be of service to the world. Yes, I have this deep soul longing to help, to make a difference. But even if the outer world situation were great, it would still be my practice. And that's quite liberating. It means the outer circumstances are in some way irrelevant. I don't have to be so concerned about results. As long as I'm coming from the right place and I'm doing it with the right intention, the rest is God's will. I don't have any control over whether things are going to change or not. And as things get worse and my actions seem to have less and less impact in the greater scheme of things, I just keep on doing it because it's my practice.

On another level, I think the extent to which you can make real change in the outer sense is very dependent on your inner state. Your ability to integrate your own shadow, and ability to differentiate when you're coming from ego and when it's a genuine desire to help. Working with other people more, I've come to really notice that – when ego-dynamics get involved. It's fundamental. I think all of our futures are dependent on our ability to get over ourselves and work together. It's as simple as that. As long as we're stuck in our own individual ideas of how it should be, we're never going to move forward. We need to get over ourselves.

> "I think all of our futures are dependent on our ability to get over ourselves and work together. It's as simple as that."

When we disconnect from that part of us that knows we're here for the sake of others, we lose something. When I'm with peers and we're all connected to that place, it's extremely powerful. Something comes through. But the minute other stuff comes in, like insecurities, power dynamics, it's a mess!

JH: So true! For me, the real heart of what you've been talking about is your experience of the power within your own generation. That hunger for change, that willingness to act. And the more embodied awareness of the interconnected nature of reality, whether that worldview comes from spirituality or simply through growing up with globally connected social media, etc. Can you say a bit more about your experience of that?

Amrita: The people who I admire the most excel within the system but are there to change it. It's action balanced with heart, with vision and with spirituality, and that is such a powerful force. The ability to speak to the old on its terms, as well as coming from this whole different space. I think that's needed.

But also an enormous amount of creativity, wild creativity, in all sorts of forms. The blending of all sorts of things. Nothing is excluded. We can run a conference on a particular theme but also have poetry and myth and art – it's a kind of holism which is so rich. A more interdisciplinary edge, we are interested in bringing things together and not seeing things as separate. I love that. It's so exciting and really of the future. And joy and fun as well. We are on an adventure. We are all attempting this huge thing. There is so much unknown. And it brings out something special in everyone.

JH: That fascinates me – that joy. There is a particular quality I notice in your generation, something so palpable and distinctive. I've come to think of that as life re-creating itself. Pure life force.

Amrita: For me it's been about realising anything is possible. Many of us have gone through this process of seeing through the illusion. It's all just conditioning. You realise, 'I don't have to fit into that world!' So it's like, wow!, we can just like make it up, create it however we want. Like, what is the definition of work today? We can just make that up. Make it work for you.

There's a freedom. Because we know something is over. It's not going to look like that now. I feel quite free in a sense of not needing to fit into that. My life isn't going to have a preordained trajectory. We can redefine everything. Because clearly nothing's working. So let's just remake it all!

JH: That's so inspiring! Why do something simply because it's been done that way before? Look where doing things that way got us!

Amrita: Exactly. At one point I really rejected the old, discovering how bad things were, I felt I didn't want anything to do with that. Some of my ideals were maybe slightly inauthentic because they came out of rejection, out of a wound.

JH: What was the wound?

Amrita: Just seeing the pain, the pain of what this system has caused. How destructive it is. Not wanting to be a part of that. But the deconditioning is so necessary and so important, for all of us. That's what enables me to go to an event and stand up and say what's not being said. Because I've gone through that process in myself. Deconstructing the narrative it's all based on, that nobody questions. It's about being skilled in how we choose to challenge it, I suppose.

JH: So what would be your message to other young adults in connection with spirituality and action?

Amrita: Don't stop believing it is possible. That vision you have in your heart of a different world, don't stop believing in it. We can create that. I truly believe even if it's just a group of us, even if it's just glimpsing in a small way that it's possible. Keep believing in it.

And if you don't already have a spiritual practice – get one. And commit to it. That is such a fundamental part of all of this work. If we're not coming from the right place then even our positive actions are a kind of illusion, and any change will only be superficial. If we're not going to recreate the patterns of the past and truly allow something new to come through, allow that vision to come through, it's all about the place we come from inwardly.

> "That vision you have in your heart of a different world, don't stop believing in it. We can create that."

Spiritual practice is also a real protection against the chaos of the times. Unless you have a way of making sense of it all, you'll go crazy.

JH: And, lastly, what would be your message to the older generation?

Amrita: Don't be scared. Don't be scared of the challenge, don't be scared of the energy, the creativity. There is something completely new coming though, and there's this huge unknown zone, which can be really scary. But just be open to it. Ultimately that's how the transition is going to happen, isn't it? We can both meet in that unknown space. Maybe that's where the power is.

Chapter 23

BHAI SAHIB MOHINDER SINGH

SHARED SOCIAL RESPONSIBILITY

'It is the youngest members of a family that serve to challenge orthodoxy.'

Bhai Sahib Dr Mohinder Singh Ahluwalia OBE, KSG is the third in line of Sikh religious leaders of Guru Nanak Nishkam Sewak Jatha, and is Chairman of the Nishkam Group of Charitable Organisations. Bhai Sahib (which means 'Elder Brother') is active in interfaith dialogue, social regeneration, heritage conservation and education. He is Patron of the ground-breaking Sikh ethos multi-faith Nishkam School, Chair and Trustee of the Museum of World's Religions UK and Co-Convenor of the International Charter for Forgiveness and Reconciliation. He is passionate about empowering individuals and organisations with common religious values to selfless service. Internationally, Bhai Sahib is a recognised 'Interfaith Visionary', holding the Juliet Hollister Award from the Temple of Understanding whose past awardees have included His Holiness the Dalai Lama and Nelson Mandela.

Bhai Sahib Mohinder Singh writes:

The younger generation are a beacon for the future. Not only can they envision a better world; they have the power to change the world. Sometimes, it is the youngest members of a family that serve to challenge orthodoxy and suggest new approaches to tackle what seem to be intractable problems. They have energy and passion and unimaginable potential to do good. Equally, they have the potential to become nihilistic and apathetic, depending on the contexts and conditions they find themselves in.

As economic, environmental and social problems become intertwined on an unprecedented scale, millennials demonstrate enormous drive and commitment to fight for causes that they are passionate about. Globally, from events in Egypt to mass migration across the Mediterranean, they have utilised social media to put the spotlight on issues that mainstream media may not have had access to or have not deemed newsworthy. And so, young people have become an alternative and powerful voice. With this power, however, comes the responsibility to ensure that social change is pursued, not for self-aggrandisement, nor to perpetuate the vicious circle of violent extremism and retaliatory action, but for the common good and to build sustainable peace.

Young adulthood brings with it many compelling impulses and convictions. Often, these are joined by the inclination to seek instant gratification or results. Senior leaders can offer insights honed from decades of lived experience, for which there is no substitute. They have the potential to provide a steadying hand and stable backbone. Such intergenerational engagement is vital for us to co-create the kind of robust and resilient architecture that is needed to foster a better world for us all.

If peace is the goal, senior leaders must be genuine and not hypocritical in working towards it. There is no room for lip service. Importantly, they must be there to create opportunities for dialogue and action. They must provide support with love and respect and guide young people to think with both the heart and the head. I would also add that the two-way dialogue can become a richer and deeper three-way one, by connecting with the Spirit, with God, with the spiritual reserve blessed to each human, irrespective of age. This can transform the tone and direction that any collaboration takes.

All of us have a shared, social responsibility to lovingly raise and engage with young people, who will be new parents and grandparents of tomorrow. Today, they are fully armed with technology, the might of connectivity and recognition of the brutalities of our world. Yet, indulgence in technology at the expense of real human contact also leaves a huge vacuum. We risk rearing a generation less accustomed to contact with real (rather than virtual) communities, for such contact crucially shapes and sustains us as whole people. Family breakdown has further eroded the social fabric, as well as the tender fabric of a child's personal world, the consequences of which are difficult to measure.

With so many complex problems and uncertainties confronting us, from the microcosmic to macrocosmic scales of our lives, we must indeed inspire, motivate and empower young people to be true agents of social change. Like a mirror, they present all humans with a reflection of our potential to live with values, virtues and integrity of character. To walk the talk, however, we must be genuine about what we think, do and act, as we support them to become society's beacons and future hope.

PART 7

PROTECTING EARTH

The Bedouin Tent at St Ethelburga's, designed to host difficult conversations, has been privy to many dialogues between divided groups, on themes such as Israel–Palestine, Brexit and migration. Surprisingly, one of the most polarised conversations I ever witnessed in that space was focused on faith and the environment. It was a year before the climate change summit in Copenhagen in 2009. In our small dialogue circle there were environmental activists, awake to the immense urgency of the situation, anxiously trying to impress on everyone that time was running out, and that immediate action was required. There were also those who believed that acting from a mindset of separation would merely replicate the same problems and solve nothing. These people were adamant that a shift towards a consciousness of interdependence was needed first. That was their priority. When those two positions became apparent, a gulf opened up between them. The deadlock and hostility in the room were palpable. There seemed no way forward.

Generation Y is resolving that split. Their action is beginning more and more to emerge naturally from a sense of an interconnected whole. Xiuhtezcatl (Chapter 24) knows Earth as a living, spiritual being. Zoë (Chapter 13) relates to Earth as her Divine Mother. Kara (Chapter 10) draws her sense of spiritual potency from her connectedness with the wider web of life. Dekila's (Chapter 26) heart is firmly bonded with the Earth's habitats, wildlife and processes. As we touched on in Part 4, 'Complex Identities', a whole generation of people are emerging who are not just connected up globally via technology, travel or ancestry, but have integrated into themselves a new, stable, vastly expanded sense of self – one that is much beyond the individual, intimately entwined with our planetary home. This is a profoundly important and much-needed shift.

The wisdom teachings at the heart of all our religions offer a worldview that is similar. Contemporary engaged Buddhists, for example, have been widely influential, inspiring many activists (Buddhist and otherwise) and helping evolve a shared language for our interbeing with each other and with Earth. In St Ethelburga's community of spiritual ecologists, it's rare to find someone who hasn't been influenced by Thich Nhat Hanh's invitation to fall in love with Earth, or Joanna Macy's concept of the 'ecological self'.

Many of the young people I interviewed are also very drawn to indigenous wisdom. There is a hunger to learn from the old ways, from those who have not lost their connection with Earth or strayed from the lived experience of interdependence. When Native American elders like Pat McCabe and Tiokasin Ghosthorse teach younger audiences at St Ethelburga's, a magic happens. Ancient teachings are met with respect and welcomed by hearts attuned to the future, hearts that recognise the value of what is offered. In these moments, something beyond the individual is nourished and comes alive. This is Earth calling to Herself.

Young people are also taking seriously their own relationship with place, recognising the importance of heritage, story and belonging, or deeply relating to a particular land. This often goes hand in hand with a growing awareness of the damage of cultural appropriation – the need to honour where traditions and practices originate, and to locate ourselves in what is indigenous for us, rather than borrowing indiscriminately from others.

Within religious institutions, whilst many are doing good work, one can't help feeling there remains untapped potential for faith leaders to galvanise, to help transform the mindset that has commodified the physical world and precipitated the devastation of our ecosystems. Young people, both affiliated and otherwise, drawing on the hard work of many older environmentalists, are rapidly changing the way they see themselves and breaking down the age-old dualism between Heaven and Earth, reclaiming creation as sacred. They are standing up, speaking out, and often leading the way. For a growing portion of the unaffiliated young people we meet through St Ethelburga's, nature is becoming their holy book. They are replacing priests with permaculture, church with the local Sunday morning farmers' market, prayer with interspecies communication, and worship with 'forest bathing'. While institutions lose their appeal, the beauty of the natural world remains a reliable doorway for many into a relationship with the Divine or with something beyond ourselves.

So where will this take us? Is spiritual ecology becoming a new tradition in itself? Are millennials laying the foundations for a new Earth-based religion? And/or does the environmental crisis have the power to unite the religions of the world (and the generations) towards one common goal of protecting the beauty of creation, while we still can? At what point – if ever – will the crisis be seen severe enough to shock our institutions into change? Can they abandon the competition to convert the unchurched and reinvent themselves as hives of spirit-centred activity, reaching out beyond the labels of this identity or that, affiliated or not, to simply serve the God of their understanding by picking up the mantle of stewardship? Can they link the wisdom of their own teachings to the needs of the wider world, and share it freely – because it is needed – and not in exchange for people signing up to any kind of membership? What would it take to rewild all the land the world over, that belongs to places of worship, so the more-than-human world could find desperately needed pockets of sanctuary?[1] Going further, what would it mean

---

1   This is the aim of the Alliance of Religions and Conservation's project, Living Churchyards.

to rewild our religions, to reconnect them inwardly and outwardly to Earth as a living, animate, spiritual being? What would that mean for religion? What would that mean for Earth?

This is a defining moment in the history of humanity. Whichever way you look at it, if we are to transform this global catastrophe, a radically different relationship with the created world must surely become a central note in the lived faiths and spiritualities of the future. But maybe that transformation works both ways and our faiths can be reborn, reshaped, reinvigorated for a new era? Perhaps this is the call, the hidden opportunity in the heart of the darkness?

Working with the young spiritual ecologists in St Ethelburga's programme, I sense a new form of spiritual leadership emerging. Some of our programme alumni in coming years will undoubtedly become the founders of new eco-retreat centres or land-based new monastic communities in the future. Despite being committed to their own faith practices and traditions, they are unlikely to set up communities that link to religious institutions directly, but rather to build inclusive spaces, informed by their own spirituality, but open to all. Their purpose will be to work with the Earth, but I see them drawing deeply from their own faith, and learning openly and respectfully from the spiritualities of others.

This doesn't have to mean a watering down of tradition, but rather a remodelling of what religious community is, so the global need comes first, fully integrated with the private, inner journey of souls. Faith teachings and practices (supported by new modes of powerful mentorship, outside of hierarchical structures) are then lived as deep and formidable resources in an *applied* setting, bringing joy, meaning, wisdom, discipline and transformative power into our global change-making. Faiths no longer compete with each other, but share their unique contribution as one part of a harmonious whole, speaking and acting together for the ways of love. At this late stage in the day, we may not be able to circumvent some of the damage our way of life has already created, but as the Prophet Muhammad said,

'Even if the world is going to end, if one of you has a sapling in his hand, let him plant it.'[2]

It has brought me great hope and great happiness to work alongside some of the young pioneers involved in this work. I sense a very particular quality of regenerative energy that bubbles up within these remarkable souls – a spark in their hearts that holds an imprint of the future – a future that feels like a song, like a beautiful lost memory, coming alive again in a new way. That future is already with us, being implemented in many small ways, around the edges of the dominant paradigm.

Listening to the young voices in this section, Arundhati Roy's famous words are revived within me: 'Another world is not only possible, she is on her way. On a quiet day, I can hear her breathing.'[3]

---

2   Prophetic Hadith, Musnad Aḥmad, 12491.

3   *An Ordinary Person's Guide to Empire*, Arundhati Roy (HarperCollins, 2004), p.86.

Chapter 24

XIUHTEZCATL MARTINEZ

YOUTH VOICES ARE POWERFUL

'It's important to start now.'

Xiuhtezcatl (pronounced shoe-tez-caht) Martinez is an 18-year-old indigenous climate activist and hip-hop artist. At the early age of six, Xiuhtezcatl began speaking around the world, from the Rio+20 United Nations Summit in Rio de Janeiro, to addressing the General Assembly at the United Nations in New York City. At the age of seven, he began songwriting and performing. He has worked on grassroots projects to get pesticides out of parks, coal ash contained, and moratoriums on fracking in his state. In 2017 he was part of initiating a youth-led lawsuit against the US federal government for their failure to protect the atmosphere for future generations.

He has won numerous awards, including the 2013 United States Community Service Award from President Obama, and was the youngest of 24 national change-makers chosen to serve on the President's youth council. He is the youth director of Earth Guardians, a network of young people in 30 different countries, working to address climate change. Xiuhtezcatl also recently published a book, We Rise: The Earth Guardians Guide to Building a Movement That Restores the Planet, and a new solo album, Break Free, addressing racial injustice, climate change, police brutality and indigenous rights. Alongside this, he is still finishing his studies at high school in his home town of Boulder, Colorado.

There are 21 plaintiffs involved in the unprecedented lawsuit against the Obama administration for the inadequacy of its response to climate change, *Juliana* v. *United States*. Most are teenagers, but some were as young as nine years old when the case was first initiated. We know the world has gone terribly wrong when we see children leading radical action against world leaders who have failed them.

But we also see the power of a generation rising up.

Xiuhtezcatl is a part of that uprising. He seems unstoppable. Bill McKibben of 350.org calls him 'an impressive spokesman for a viewpoint the world needs to hear'. Whatever hopes or personal ambitions teenagers have had in the past, Xiuhtezcatl shows us that none of them make sense any more. All routes to a purely personal pursuit of happiness have been rendered absurd. The only possible response to coming of age in the 21st century is action – action that honours the interwoven nature and holiness of creation.

Growing up immersed in the indigenous Aztec rituals of his father, and advocating for social and environmental justice with his mother, Xiuhtezcatl had a deep grounding in sacred activism. Naturally, he felt called to be part of the Standing Rock fight against the Dakota Access Pipeline. Standing Rock began as a youth-led movement, its unparalleled global response due to the energy of its youth overriding the pessimism of their elders. It was also a place where bridges between movements were built, and bridges between spiritualities. It demonstrated an inclusiveness that can be a hallmark of youth-led action, and also reflects the importance of indigenous voices in revitalising our understanding of interconnectedness.

These days Xiuhtezcatl's diary is rammed, and it's hard to get an interview with him as he travels constantly, speaking and mobilising his generation. Despite his punishing schedule and the overwhelming odds, Xiuhtezcatl says, 'There's never been as much hope as there is today.' That hope – and the potent willingness to act – are the gifts of Generation Y and Z activists, making them a force for change to be reckoned with.

This interview is a slightly shortened version of one that originally appeared in the *Earth Island Journal* Spring 2017 issue conducted by Managing Editor Zoe Loftus-Farren.

Motifs in this chapter:

- Protecting Earth

- Sacred activism

- Natural leadership

You're only 16, and you've already been an activist for a decade. How did it all start? How did you develop this unique awareness of climate change, let alone this intense commitment to address it?
My mama had been involved in activism – she started an Earth Guardian school in 1992 in Maui, Hawai'i – and all of my siblings were involved in speaking and activism, performing and making music about it. My father had been an ambassador for Mexico, talking about culture, environment, and spirituality. So there was just a great amount of awareness in the way that we lived our lives as a family, in trying to use as few resources as we could, and [we were] just very aware and conscious.

[There was] also my connection to my roots, my ancestry, the indigenous part of me that felt a sense of responsibility as a person to protect and connect and be a part of something. And I guess growing up and learning about the world and seeing things getting worse, I was like *Yo, action needs to be taken on such a greater level.*

Part of your philosophy seems to be that youthfulness specifically can be a powerful tool as an activist. Can you explain your thinking around that?

I believe that young people in the world are often seen as the future, like, *Oh, you're going to make a difference in the future; you're going to be a leader in the future*. For me, meeting kids all over the world, there's such an understanding that there is a need for us to take action *now* and to be engaged *today* because our voices are so powerful.

I saw that when I was nine years old and I started taking action in my local community. There were like 12 of us, going up on stage, each delivering a speech about pesticides and how we had to ban them in our parks. The amount of impact that that had on our city council members, that was so huge. We created change. Our voices are incredibly powerful as youth.

More and more we're seeing empowered young people standing up to take action on the frontlines of all these movements. We're going to be inheriting every problem that we see in the world today, and every crisis that is currently happening is going to be so much worse when this world has been passed on to us, so the amount of action we do today will determine the world and how it will be in the future. It's important to start now.

Do you have a sense that youth are becoming more active in the environmental movement than they have been in the recent past?

In the last ten years I've seen an explosion of diversity in the environmental and climate movement. When I first got involved, [the movement was made up of] all of the people that had been involved in the peace and environmental movement in the 1960s, so a lot of older people, and I was that one kid that was at all of the events. Now I see things like the Bioneers Conference, and over 500 young people have come on scholarship, courtesy of Bioneers, and even more young people [have come] independently to participate in this event. It's amazing to see. You know, I just had a jam session with 50 kids, just hanging out, playing music.

So definitely there's a greater sense of awareness, greater sense of necessity to take action, and greater opportunities and tools for young people out there to create change. We are really working as a global community to uplift and empower young people. It's amazing.

You mention new tools, but my understanding is that you have mixed feelings about new technologies, that you think technology can serve as something that disconnects us from each other. Do you also think it can serve as an important tool in the climate movement?

Definitely. The reason I've been able to have such a huge reach with the Earth Guardian movement is because of social media, and the way it connects us all as a global family. We've never been so connected in human history as we are today. It just [depends on] the way social media is used. If it's used in the right way for the right reasons it can work as a catalyst to create a lot of opportunities to share information, to connect people all over the world, to create amazing collaborative projects, to offer new opportunities for solutions that we've never seen before. Every solution that we are seeing is coming from amazing opportunities with new technology, as well as an understanding of these old ways of life that have been passed onto us. So I think that it's a balance, for sure, that is very necessary.

> "Social media can work as a catalyst to connect people all over the world, to create amazing collaborative projects, to offer new opportunities for solutions that we've never seen before."

Your music is obviously a big part of your life, and a lot of your lyrics have pretty powerful messages. Do you see your activism and your music as interconnected?

I feel like my music sprouted from an understanding that speaking to an audience wasn't always gonna reach people. I started writing music as a way to just talk, using hip-hop to talk to young people. [I realized] that maybe they wouldn't listen to an hour-and-a-half speech, but if I performed a song with a message behind it, they would be more keen to listen to that. That's just what it was. I wasn't a talented artist or MC or anything. [But] it's a huge part of my work now. And in just the last year-and-a-half I've fallen in love with hip-hop. The ability to use this music to create change in the world and to inspire people is just off the charts and is so exciting. Now I'm producing a lot, and I'm writing a lot, and I'm performing a lot, and just working on refining my skills. I want to be an artist. That's my passion now.

If you look at the roots of hip-hop, it was created to tell a story. Young people in the Bronx were in the worst conditions that this country had, like ever. Buildings were burning, and drugs were running rampant in the streets, and there was so much hopelessness. Young people used hip-hop to escape that, to tell their stories, to connect to something positive, and to reflect on what was happening in the times.

You know, rap these days is not following what hip-hop was meant to be, and I feel like it is my responsibility as an MC and as an artist to use my voice as a performer to tell the stories of what's happening today, and to reflect on what's happening in the times. And today that's climate change, that's our environmental crisis, that's young people and suicide and drugs, the world that I'm growing up in.

Do you ever get discouraged by the task at hand?
Oh yeah. I mean, it's like hopelessness and apathy are the natural responses to really overwhelming stuff. And I think the most important thing to do is to bounce back from that, and to pick yourself up, even when nothing makes sense in the world. To understand that there is a lot of work to do but there is also a lot of hope, more hope than there are any problems.

You're currently suing the federal government for its inaction on climate change. Why did you decide to join that lawsuit?
I saw the greatest chance for young people to have their voices heard in the legal system. And it was so cool to see that I could connect

with other young leaders who were interested in the same things and wanted to get involved in a deeper, bigger way. You know, community activism is great and it's important, but change has to happen on every level, right? Legal, political, economic, corporate, all these different systems have to change if we want to see a shift in the way that the world is working.

I just thought of it as an opportunity to create really huge, tangible action, to have our voice heard by the world and by a lot more people, and an amazing way to connect with other young people who are passionate about the same thing. It's a unique tactic that I think we haven't seen before in the climate movement.

You mentioned your Aztec background earlier. Could you talk a little bit more about how your indigenous roots impact your worldview, and specifically your outlook on the climate crisis?
I feel like I got a very good sense of the world at a very young age. My dad, being from Mexico City, had a lot to share about his opinions on the world and on this country, and that just opened my eyes. He came from a heavy amount of poverty and [had] very little. But at the same time he learned so much and he traveled a lot. And he would just talk to me about different things like colonization and colonialism, and how we've globalized in such a big way, and how this United States has stolen resources from so many people.

And then being indigenous I connected a lot with the Lakota and Diné traditions in North America, you know, participating in sun dances and sweats, and things like that. My dad was also super involved in ceremony, which really gave me strong roots and spirituality, which helped me understand the world, because the earth is a spiritual being. I was able to understand that through my knowledge of myself, and my cultural identity gave me a greater sense of my place on Earth.

"The earth is a spiritual being."

The indigenous resistance movement goes way back, but seems to be gaining momentum and attention at the moment. Do you have any thoughts on that?

There's such a long line of oppression when it comes to what this country has done to indigenous people. And I feel like there's been a breaking point, like, *we're not going to take no more bullshit*. It's like, *we're done, we're done. We're not going to let you put these pipelines through our land, we're not going to let you frack on our territories, we're not going to let you mine anymore.* It's still happening, the same kind of oppression that happened all those years ago, the stealing of the land, the stealing of resources, the relocating of indigenous populations.

The fossil fuel industry is rooted in the same mentality that created slavery and genocide among indigenous populations. And it's just madness. It's crazy.

I think indigenous people are understanding our place as leaders in the world as well, and we're ready to take that next step and claim our place on this earth as caretakers of this land. Because other people are too afraid to take action, and indigenous people are ready to rise up.

What do you think it's going to take to get more people involved in the climate movement, particularly more young people?

The movement is a little stale in a lot of ways. There are all these figures that people look at, like Al Gore and Bill McKibben, who are [seen as] the environmentalists and as the heads of this movement. I think just changing the conversation a little bit [would help], changing the title, because a lot of kids don't want to be activists. *I don't even want to be a damn activist.* [We need to speak] about it in a way that it's not just about activism.

We don't just need activists. We need artists, we need thinkers, we need poets, we need entrepreneurs. People have to understand that being a part of this movement isn't always just standing with a sign at the front of a march or a rally.

"We need artists, we need thinkers, we need poets, we need entrepreneurs."

[There are] so many different ways to create change and be a part of this. We just have to continue to remind ourselves that there's so much more to this than just the way that we've thought of it traditionally. [We need to change] the traditional conversation and dialogue of what this has been about.

There's also a lot of intersectionality that needs to happen between movements. People have to understand that there's intersectionality between Black Lives Matter, and LGBT, and climate movements. It's incredibly important to see that, to be a part of uplifting and making the world a better place, not just protecting the environment or stopping climate change.

I don't just want there to be, you know, no natural disasters. I don't want to just stop climate change for future generations. There should be less hatred in the world, and less sexism, and racism, and homophobia. Those are all different things we've got to change about the world, and I feel like beginning to build bridges between movements is incredibly important, and having more people want to be interested, so all the Black Lives Matter people are coming to our events, and we're going to all of theirs.

Even just in the environmental movement there is so much finicky competition over trying to be the leaders of the movement. That's not what this is about. This isn't about politics or money or entitlement. It's about the world.

What motivates you to keep fighting the good fight?

When people come up to me, especially young people, and say, *You've inspired me to do these things, and to make these changes*, that's like, *Damn, my voice has that power?* And to see that I'm making that difference inspires me to continue to touch other people's lives and to try to make a difference in even bigger ways.

When I can see the beauty of nature and just be by the ocean or in the rainforest and just lose myself in that, it's like, *This is what the hell I'm fighting for.* I think just those reminders of what it is I'm fighting for, that is what allows me to be like, *It's going to be worth it.* So that 16-year-old kids in the future never have to fight the way that I have today.

There should never be another need for action at the level that I've taken in my life from anyone else ever again after my generation. I'm hoping that it ends with me.

Is there anything else that you want people to hear?
Action to create global change starts small, one lifestyle change at a time. And it goes from your life, to your family, to your community, to the world. It happens in different ways and it's never gonna be the same way for two people. We can create change through our passion. Whatever it is we love to do, we can create change through that, whether it's a woman with Al Jazeera news – I did an interview with them – who told me, *I have a knitting group, and we're going to knit some hats and send them to Standing Rock so they can be warm through the winter*. That's a way to be a part of it. Or riding skateboards and putting together skating events with your homies and raising money for planting trees, or whatever it is.

Change isn't a one-size-fits-all type of thing, and action to make the world a better place isn't one-size-fits-all. We've all got our strengths, we've all got our passions, and we've gotta use that to create change in the world. And we can freakin' do it. There's never been as much hope as there is today. As a kid that's on the front lines of probably one of the most depressing issues that our world has ever faced, I can tell you that there is more hope than there is apathy in the world. And there's so much left to fight for.

© EARTH ISLAND JOURNAL 2016

Chapter 25

SAMSON HART

LET IT BE ALIVE!

'Religion should be a constantly evolving thing.'

Samson is 24 years old and was born in Manchester. From a young age, he spent a lot of time travelling — across South-East Asia, China, Nepal and India, which opened his eyes to Eastern spiritual traditions. He recently completed an MA in Economics for Transition at Schumacher College in Devon. At Schumacher, Sam experienced the richness of living in community. He wrote his thesis on land rights in the UK and their importance for a rural revival and new, more sustainable forms of agriculture. He is currently working on a number of projects in grassroots education, land and political campaigning. His inner journey has drawn him to reconnect with land and with Judaism, and he has lived in Jewish farming communities in Israel and the US.

Sam exudes a great sincerity and openness that really touched me. His story captures a simple but essential characteristic of how the younger generation are expressing their faith. He is a naturally spiritual person, wanting a meaningful daily practice and a way of life consistent with his values. The language and rituals of his family religion don't open the door for him. There is a disconnect. Like many others before him, he travels and, exposed to Eastern traditions, learns to meditate, and continues to meditate with commitment and discipline. But that too leaves him unsatisfied because it remains 'spirituality that happens in private in your bedroom', not linked up with the wider world and the issues of the day.

Sam fits in with the emerging pattern of unbundling the elements of religious tradition and recombining them in new, individually designed ways. He says 'look inside yourself' to find what is meaningful for you, and then 'look outside and find other people who are also doing that'. Find your purpose, find your tribe. As Kingsley Dennis (see Chapter 15) would say, Sam is guided by his own instinctual wisdom, not by ready-made answers. He creates his own spaces; others are nourished by the new rituals he creates (and perhaps also by Sam's own heart-centred warmth) and naturally gather around him.

There is a simplicity in his story that one could easily overlook. He is not gathering thousands of people, like Jesse in Chapter 1, but he is part of the same movement away from the stasis and rigidity of tradition, towards something new, self-made, organic and alive.

Sam's love of land is present behind and between the things he shares. Through Jewish farming movements he is gaining a very hopeful taste of the potential for tradition to evolve and unite with the needs of the time. He navigates through his life by connecting to the many 'small pockets of new ways of living' he sees bubbling up around him. Guided by his heart, and by his faith in what is possible, he moves from one to the next, following the invisible thread of the new.

Motifs in this chapter:

- Protecting Earth
- New spaces
- Challenging orthodoxy
- Evolving traditions

JH: So, Sam, tell me a little about your own journey with faith and spirituality.

Sam: I grew up in a really traditional Jewish background. Both parents have Lithuanian roots – five generations on one side, four generations on the other. We were traditional, celebrated Shabbat and all the festivals. I went to a Jewish primary school and so obviously all my friends were Jewish up until the age of maybe 11 or 12. I went to synagogue fairly often (but didn't understand Hebrew so I found myself sitting there, sulking), took my Bar Mitzvah when I was 13, spent time with my Rabbi learning my piece. But it was never meaningful. And at a certain point in my life I started questioning it. There was never any understanding of a way to engage in daily practice. It was very static, very old, very male, and not very inviting as a young person. When I was about 15 I completely rejected it, put it to one side and defined myself as atheist.

JH: Is that a fairly common experience?

Sam: Fairly common. But the norm is not to reject it, to keep to some traditions like eating in a particular way, making sure you have lots of Jewish friends, marrying someone Jewish. I experienced a lot of new things by spreading my wings a bit.

When I was 18 I started practising meditation, Tibetan Buddhism, which is Mahayana Buddhism. I found something in that, something more meaningful in the philosophy as well as in the practice. For about five years I had a good meditation practice. That was spirituality, but spirituality that happens in private in your bedroom. Recently I came to thinking, okay there must be such a thing as spirituality that happens on a day-to-day basis, which is lived. Not necessarily about practice but about how we see things and act on a daily basis.

JH: So what does that mean for you?
Sam: At my college, we were three Jewish people – two Israelis and myself. We decided to celebrate Shabbat in a way that spoke to us. So on a Friday at six o'clock we would get together, and my friend makes *challah*, which is a traditional Jewish bread. We did the normal kind of blessings on the wine, and on the bread, and do the blessings to the candles. But we would also say something a bit more meaningful for us. When we ate the bread, we'd sit and contemplate all the beings that helped put the bread in our hand and connect to that on a deeper level. So we made it into something that we could really connect to.

What was amazing was how popular it became in the college. At six o'clock I'd feel the same rush – the feeling of Shabbat coming I had as a child was there again. One person would be running to get the bread out of the oven, one person would be getting the salt, somebody would be getting the candles. Only three of us there were Jewish. The rest were all sorts of faith backgrounds. So we'd sing songs from different faiths. So this was a really beautiful thing. At one point it got so big, we had over 30 people in the room, all singing together.

It became quite an emotional thing for me. I told my grandma on the phone and she cried. As someone who comes from the diaspora, from the experience of persecution, she has the mindset that you need to stay separate – look after your own people because no one is going to look after you. So that was a big deal for her. She ended up visiting and staying with me because she wanted to see it. And she was incredibly emotional.

JH: Because people were there from different backgrounds?
Sam: Yeah, we wanted her to have a part. So she did her prayer. It was not like any Shabbat service she'd seen before, but she was completely mesmerised. We also celebrated once in the forest outside the college.

I can really feel it in my heart when I talk about it. There was something special in it. Everyone was connecting to this idea that we were together and welcoming in the weekend, a period of rest after working all week. We were seeing it as welcoming in a time for reflection, contemplation and regeneration. There

"It was not like any Shabbat service she'd seen before, but she was completely mesmerised."

was just something incredibly beautiful about it. That was the first time I had connected to anything Jewish for a long time.

From there I started to look for other things I might connect to also. And I started this process of reconnecting to land, wanting to grow food. I heard about the Jewish renewal movement in the US. It's a movement that is trying to look at Judaism in a new light – the kind of Judaism that works for the problems of our time. Places like Adamah, the Jewish Farming Fellowship. *Adamah* is the Hebrew word for land. It gives people a taste of a different way to live, a new way of being Jewish.

I went to visit The Sadeh, a farm in Kent, started by a few Adamah alumni. They are just starting to grow food there and put on courses. I went to their opening event for the festival of Tu B'Shevat, at the time of year when the sap is rising, and people are encouraged to plant

"It was an incredibly powerful experience for me, blessing the land and the trees, singing."

trees. It was an incredibly powerful experience for me, blessing the land and the trees, singing. We were thanking the ancestors and everything we were doing was very Jewish, but it really spoke to me. I think that was because it was about being Jewish but also connected to being human, to being really part of the land.

Rabbi Abraham Joshua Heschel said, 'The primary purpose of prayer is not to make requests. The primary purpose of prayer is to praise, to sing, to chant. Because the essence of prayer is song and man cannot live without song.'[1] I felt like I was singing my songs, songs that had been sung by my ancestors. There was something particularly beautiful about it that I had never experienced before.

JH: Tell me more about why land is important for you.
Sam: It's interesting because Judaism has tried not to tie itself to land in the last few hundred years because it is a diaspora religion. To survive it has to be able to be practised anywhere. But I think for me there is something incredibly beautiful about knowing a place, about really feeling that place, understanding it. Because once you understand it, you know a place, then you can love it, and once you love it, you will protect it.

It's also about power. In our current system, land is commodified, which means essentially it puts some people in power and others in a position of oppression. One of the biggest problems of today is land ownership, land being owned by very small sections of society. In England land costs £25,000 a hectare. One of the highest in the world. So land has both spiritual and politico-economic connotations.

JH: You're doing an MA in Economics for Transition. Is there a link between spirituality and that dimension of life for you?
Sam: Try and talk about spirituality in any political and economic context, you will get shut down. But to really live in a new economy, a new society, you need to be that new society. Which requires a complete shift in ourselves. I guess for me, the relationship to spirituality is about changing ourselves, trying to transition in ourselves, into a way of life that is connected to others and to nature.

JH: You talked about a 'new way of being Jewish'. What does that mean for you?
Sam: Religion should be a constantly evolving thing. The problem is, we're still reading the same book that was written a long time

---

1   *Moral Grandeur and Spiritual Audacity: Essays*, Abraham Joshua Heschel (Farrar, Straus and Giroux, 1997), p.397.

ago. When you get bogged down in the semantics and the specifics of old texts, you're going to lose that essence. It has a lot of beautiful meaning, but if it doesn't engage with the critical issues of the day then it's not enough for me. It needs to be engaging with that. Religion is also powerful. If it was able to engage in some way, a lot of people would be influenced, a lot of people could shift their views. We are facing real crisis now, particularly the climate crisis. It's crazy that those things aren't taken into account more. A new way to be Jewish allows for individuality, for different viewpoints. It needs to be something more malleable, for example around gender equality. Why can't we talk about these questions? It's not even allowed in the room for discussion in Orthodox communities.

JH: Given all that, what would you say to the Chief Rabbi of this country?

Sam: I guess I would tell him to listen to the youth. Let it be a discussion. Let it be alive. I can't see it coming from within Orthodox communities or from within the mainstream, but I do see it springing up elsewhere. Small pockets of things are happening already. It's the same thing with political movements. We're not going to change the system overnight, but small pockets of new ways of living are always going to be bubbling up. And the status quo can sometimes follow that. So you know, I have faith! If you'll excuse the pun.

> "Let it be a discussion."

JH: What is your message to other young people?

Sam: Look at the traditions you follow and ask if it's really meaningful. I find a lot of young people do keep their Judaism. They'll keep kosher but do it out of routine and habit rather than a genuine belief about how life should be lived. So I just say, look inside yourself, and once you've looked inside yourself look outside and find other people who are also doing that. I guess small, small changes.

JH: Like your Shabbat celebrations at college. You were using a traditional pattern but you were, in a small way, recreating it from within yourselves, rather than following somebody else's way of doing it. Something in that came alive and suddenly everyone wanted to be a part of it. That was something that came from the heart, and everyone was nourished by it.

Sam: I'm with you on that. Something really happened there. It touched people.

Chapter 26

DEKILA CHUNGYALPA

THE INFINITE CHORUS

'Evolution is a combination of glacial generational changes and sudden wildfire sparks.'

Dekila Chungyalpa was born in Tibet into a Buddhist family and moved to New York in her teens. She is an associate research scientist at the Yale School of Forestry & Environmental Studies and is currently designing a new programme that provides environmental training to religious leaders from around the world. Dekila also serves as the environmental adviser for His Holiness the 17th Karmapa, head of the Karma Kagyu School of Tibetan Buddhism. Under his auspices, she coordinates over 50 monasteries and nunneries in the Himalayas carrying out environmental projects in reforestation, climate mitigation and freshwater conservation. She has a Bachelor's degree in International Environmental Studies and a Master's degree in Sustainable

Development. In recognition of her innovative work, she received the prestigious McCluskey Award at Yale University in 2014. Dekila speaks Sikkimese, Tibetan, Hindi, and Nepali and describes herself as 'thriving on new challenges'.

Although not a millennial, Dekila is a young leader who embodies a deep love for Earth. Like many migrants and indigenous peoples, Dekila has known the suffering of disconnection – struggling to be true to her faith in a secular culture that has conditioned Westerners to think the unseen worlds are superstition and has alienated us from the magic of nature. Working with the 17th Karmapa, the head of the Karma Kagyu lineage of Buddhism, who is himself a millennial, she has had a unique opportunity to reunite those worlds, bringing together the wisdom of Buddhism with practical ecological action. Dekila is someone who is walking the inwardly demanding journey of bringing together spirit and matter, science and belief, inside herself – and she shares that message with the young people she meets.

Dekila is embedded in a religious system with a long history, and one that has a growing influence in the West and much to offer our current predicament. From that vantage point of tradition, she has unequivocal views on the 'cherry-picking' of different spiritual ideas and practices. She names the risk of cultural appropriation and the danger inherent in the commodification of religious practices sold in the marketplace of Western consumerism. But, she still shares with others the instinct to 'go inwards for answers' and then outwards to seek the 'brothers and sisters we trust to walk next to us'.

I love Dekila's description of 'glacial generational changes and sudden wildfire sparks'. Those wildfire sparks are burning brightly in young people striving to live in harmony with our Earth. May the door be opened for these courageous pioneers of a more beautiful world!

Motifs in this chapter:

- Protecting Earth

- Evolving traditions

- Complex identities

Dekila Chungyalpa writes:

At the age of 15, I moved from a remote area in the Himalayas to New York City. My mother had recently taken vows to become a Tibetan Buddhist nun and entered a three-year solitary retreat, and my youngest aunt took over my upbringing and brought me to the United States. As you can imagine, it was a bewildering shift. I grew up in Sikkim, a tiny Himalayan-kingdom-turned-Indian-state, often living in remote wilderness areas with my mother, who was a fiercely unorthodox woman. Homesick and stranded among tall, shining buildings that imprisoned the sky, I branded myself as an environmentalist and Buddhist almost at once. Looking back, I realise it was the only way I knew how to be loyal to the land, the elements and the Himalayan wilderness that I loved so deeply, and to my mother who had chosen a gruelling and lonely path to Buddhahood.

Buddhism is often described as the most scientific and secular world religion; however, as time went on, these two halves of me – the environmentalist and the Buddhist – gradually progressed onto parallel tracks and I found myself straddling two very different worlds. Like so many immigrants before me, I was an uneasy union of two cultures: a secular professional at work and a Tibetan Buddhist at home.

> "Like so many immigrants before me, I was an uneasy union of two cultures: a secular professional at work and a Tibetan Buddhist at home."

And that was how things went for the next 15 years as I completed my education and began working in the field of biodiversity conservation.

I found myself managing the World Wildlife Fund's US portfolio for the Greater Mekong region. I was ostensibly a success: one of the youngest directors in the organisation, an indigenous woman that had crossed the invisible boundary and worked in other parts of the world, a brown woman without a PhD who could represent the world's largest environmental organisation to the media. I loved my job. My world had expanded beyond any ambitions I had, and yet I was deeply fractured and unable to stabilise myself emotionally. My mother and grandmother had passed away when I was in my early twenties, leaving me so raw that I could not gather my inner spiritual resilience. A decade punctuated by several deaths of loved ones followed, including those of close friends and my mentor at WWF, who died in a helicopter crash in the mountains of Nepal. The only way I could process these losses was to move from one place to another, grateful that my work encouraged a nomadic lifestyle and allowed me to ignore how ungrounded I really was.

That year, I joined my family on annual pilgrimage to Bodh Gaya to attend Kagyu Monlam, the largest gathering of Karma Kagyu Buddhists, led by His Holiness the 17th Karmapa. His Holiness, the head of the oldest Tibetan Buddhist reincarnation lineage, gave a talk one afternoon about the importance of the environment and how much it mattered to him as a Tibetan Buddhist. It was a life-altering moment. As he spoke, it slowly dawned on me that my drive and passion to protect the environment was a manifestation of my Buddhist faith and commitment to benefit all sentient beings. It seems so obvious now; however, it was an epiphany at that time and brought the first measure of stillness I had felt in years. As *karma* would have it, I ended up having a meeting with His Holiness soon after, where he directed me to create environmental guidelines for Karma Kagyu monks and nuns so that they could better understand environmental problems plaguing the Himalayas and Tibet. Of course, I agreed to help, thinking that it would take me a few weeks to write it! Ten years later, I am still serving his vision and continue to work with monasteries and nunneries on implementing environmental projects across the Himalayan region.

My mother used to say that there is no path except where your foot falls next and that the greatest lesson in life is to know how to get out of your own way. I am so grateful that I listened. From that one initial commitment to His Holiness came a natural unfolding of events that took me from

"There is no path except where your foot falls next."

one career trajectory to a scarier unknown one and, in the process, united my two halves into a whole.

I did not anticipate the hunger that monks and nuns felt for science education and their desire to become problem solvers for their communities. In response to their requests, we held a training workshop for senior monks and nuns out of which emerged Khoryug, an association of eco-Buddhist monasteries and nunneries led by His Holiness. Today, there are over 50 Tibetan Buddhist monasteries and nunneries, ranging from Ladakh in northwest India, across Nepal, to Bhutan, that run their own projects on climate change adaption, disaster management, organic farming, reforestation, river clean-ups, and so on. Khoryug was a wake-up call for many conservationists inside and outside the WWF network, and continues to exemplify what faith-based conservation could look like. On a personal level, it became the anchor that grounded me and brought me home.

I find myself telling young people this story again and again – especially those who come from indigenous backgrounds. It is possible to hold our personal faith, our origin stories, our cosmological views in one hand and scientific training and practice in the other. The need for logical consistency is a legacy of Western education that emphasises deconstruction over mystery and a bias towards rationalism. We may find ourselves surrounded by professors and colleagues who conflate rationalism with secularism, but that does not mean that deductive reasoning is the only path to wisdom. Our heritage, our spiritual practice and our life experiences are all sources of knowledge we can rely upon. We do not owe anyone an explanation for our spiritual beliefs and we need not give up our scientific mindset to follow our faith. The meaning of spiritual ecology is to heal the rift between the two worlds of spirit and matter and to bring the sacred back into science.

"The meaning of spiritual ecology is to heal the rift between the two worlds of spirit and matter and to bring the sacred back into science."

At the same time, it is critical to avoid cherry-picking rituals and practices from different faith traditions without delving into the deeper philosophy and historical context. While yoga does not have to be religious, it is not secular. It is based on an ancient cosmology and religious worldview that requires thoughtfulness on the part of the yogi student. Similarly, mindfulness is not a quick fix to enlightenment and the cessation of suffering. It is one Tibetan Buddhist technique among thousands to train your mind. We are free to try and discard as many spiritual or secular identities as we want in an authentic search to find what gives the most meaning to our lives. However, when we shop for these spiritual identities without respecting the traditions these practices are rooted in, we are behaving as mindless consumers, there to extract and exploit without compunction.

So much of the knowledge and wisdom from indigenous groups, from people of colour, from spiritual traditions have been stripped off, repackaged and commodified in such a way that the knowledge appears to be alien when presented back to us. Examples abound, from turmeric to quinoa, from acupuncture to ayahuasca. These are examples of traditional knowledge scoffed at until they were repackaged as commodities and inserted into today's consumer psyche. Suddenly, they are palatable to the worlds of Western science and medicine. Imagine the confusion in our collective identity as we are told something we value is worthless, and then worthy, and then unaffordable to us and out of reach. Now imagine that this happens again and again to our values, our spiritual knowledge, our foods, our clothes and our customs, and that it never stops. The legacy of colonialism is unfortunately still alive, if mutated. In that grey area between cultural appreciation and cultural appropriation lies one difference, and that is of citation. It is crucial that we cite our sources, cite our inspirations, and cite those who have done the hard work of paving the road before us.

Young people today have an incredible level of intellectual freedom and understanding of that intersectionality. Kimberlé Crenshaw's theory that there are overlapping systems of oppression and discrimination based on race, gender, age, health and other characteristics[1] is the right lens to work through social and environmental issues. It gives me great hope to see them form intersectional partnerships and build movements from the bottom up and around the globe with such directness and clarity of motivation. Working with them has taught me that evolution is a combination of glacial generational changes and sudden wildfire sparks, and that we need the wisdom and strength of all ages to get it right.

Glenn Albrecht, the philosopher, coined the concept of solastalgia, which refers to the acute emotional distress experienced by environmentalists when they see damage done to the environment. It happens because environmentalists have bonded with and expanded their sense of self to include the Earth's habitats, wildlife or processes. Whatever the issue we gravitate to becomes our mission for living and, at the same time, the reason for our sorrow. We are re-wounded again and again in the process of trying to save what we love while failing to do so. Therefore, it is important that we learn to heal ourselves and that we give ourselves permission to rest when we are tired, to be held when we are lonely, to grieve when we are heart sick, and to celebrate always. Whether we are trying to protect our human communities or the Earth, building our personal resilience must also be a priority.

How do we protect ourselves from despair while keeping our hearts as wide open as possible? How do we match our spiritual courage with practical action, knowing that the effort is both Herculean and uncelebrated? I do not have all the answers, but I know this much. It requires tenacity, courage and learning to pace ourselves. It requires humour to put our frustrations in perspective. It requires faith in ourselves, in humanity and in the order of the universe. To have all these things, we must first locate our community: those sisters and brothers that we can trust to walk next to us through our lifetimes. It may not be easy, and it may take decades to find, but we

---

[1]   See, for example, her 1989 paper published in *The University of Chicago Legal Forum*: https://philpapers.org/archive/CREDTI.pdf

will know them – they will be the ones lighting up our path even in the darkest forests. And we must learn to go inwards for our answers and find the strand that connects us to everything else.

For me, building my inner resilience has always come back to breathing; inhaling and exhaling along with nature, with all the living beings on this planet, and the sentience of the Earth. I remember that I am here for a flicker of a moment and part of an infinite chorus. I remember that we sing the great long song, and we hold each other up.

Chapter 27

TIOKASIN GHOSTHORSE

EVERY GENERATION IS THE SEVENTH GENERATION

'We're all needed in this.'

Tiokasin Ghosthorse is from the Cheyenne River Lakota (Sioux) Nation of South Dakota and is the host of First Voices Indigenous Radio. He is a survivor of the 'Reign of Terror' from 1972 to 1976 on the Pine Ridge, Rosebud and Cheyenne River Lakota Reservations, and also lived through the US Bureau of Indian Affairs Boarding and Church Missionary School systems, which were designed to 'kill the Indian and save the man'.

Tiokasin has had a long history in indigenous rights activism and advocacy. As a teenager, he spoke at the United Nations in Geneva and since then has been actively educating people who live on Turtle Island (North America) and around the world about the importance of living with each other and with Mother Earth. He is a guest faculty member at Yale University's School of Divinity, Ecology and Forestry, focusing on the relational/egalitarian philosophy and cosmology of indigenous peoples vs. the rational/hierarchical thinking processes of Western society.

Tiokasin is also a master musician of both traditional and contemporary music and has been a major figure in reviving the tradition of the ancient red cedar Lakota flute. He has performed in many locations around the world, including in New York City at the Cathedral of Saint John the Divine and Madison Square Garden.

JH: Watching you work with young adults, I've had the feeling you love to work with the younger generation. I wondered what qualities you see in young people today that you feel are important?

Tiokasin: We are classifying the generations with historical labels. So there's a Generation X, and a Generation Z, and then there's no more generations after that because we've run out of alphabet so what are we going to do? We're putting millennials in a special place – which is a lonely place, an isolated place. We're basically severing them from the relationship to their elders. Because they're 'special'.

I just read about how the Merriam-Webster dictionary has put out a new edition and they had to take out words that were natural, like *sunflower*, like *dandelion*, all these words were being taken out of the dictionary and replaced with technical, digital, computer terminology. They're actually removing natural words that describe a type of flower, taking them away from that generation, and teaching them something else. These are the instructions for how you're going to forget about nature, because it's not gonna exist anyway. So this is how they're really preparing young people for the future, everything is going to be technological.

I want to make sure that children and young people know that the other world is still available, beyond the human, anthropocentric mind. Because it's going to exist no matter what. As long as we breathe, Earth has to exist.

JH: So what advice would you have for the younger generation in terms of how they come into right relationship with Mother Earth?

Tiokasin: They've been told to look for new ways, but that's a Western thing, that's a Columbus thing – the New World, the New Way. As an indigenous person, there's no new way, there is only a continuum of the 'old way'. We've been told it's a new way – and we don't want to be outdated or dated and go back – but you really can't do that with an indigenous mindset. The consciousness has always been here. It hasn't become new and it hasn't become old, it has just been here all along.

When we say 'Let's go back to the old way' or 'Let's think of new ideas', these are words of neglect. We don't see it, but we never want to be conscious of what's going on right now. We are neglecting what's going on right now this moment. So I think that would be some good advice.

We've divided up young people and old people. What were we before you were English, before I was Lakota, before you were Justine, before I was Tiokasin? What were we before those labels, like 'millennials'? We were all human beings. Maybe we need to see that in order to do what's really required. It doesn't matter what age you are, the spirit is ageless. We need to intuit that. We left our hearts behind. The heart has never lost its ability to feel or to be intuitive.

One thing I know as a native person is that the West seeks and searches to solve the Mystery. I don't want to put up any dividing walls there, but native people aren't trying to solve the Mystery. They've accepted the Mystery. In the West, we've been kept away from that idea – that there is Mystery and that we can accept it. Rather than putting the world behind us, we should put the world in front of us – the Earth, the planet, the knowledge, the intelligence, the spirit – it's all in front of us – that world of non-greedy opportunity. And that is ageless.

We say the whole world, your whole future, is in front of you. But we never define what that future is, because we don't know it. If we think of it that way, if the whole world is in front of you and has no labels on it, whether you're a millennial or Geritol generation[1] or whatever, it doesn't matter any more. We're all needed in this.

> "Whether you're a millennial or Geritol generation or whatever, it doesn't matter any more. We're all needed in this."

And if we can get away from the human, thinking that we're important – more so than the tree. For the youth, an advisable way to think is beyond the anthropocentric way.

---

1   US term for the older generation who rely on vitamin supplements to stay healthy. Geritol is a well-known brand of supplements.

JH: What advice do you have for young people in terms of how they stay resilient or how they face the challenges of the times that may be ahead of us?

Tiokasin: Understand what creates a resourceful spirit within themselves. It's not that necessity is the mother of all creation, that's too easy, that's too noun-filled. They will all have to understand things that are non-technological. There is a generation, and generations, that will be able to do this. Because the uploading has begun. We are done downloading. When they understand this, when ancient traditions have become the future, then they will understand the continuum. The key is the continuum. Life is always going to continue.

> "They will all have to understand things that are non-technological. There is a generation, and generations, that will be able to do this."

And young people shouldn't put their eggs in one basket, because they too will become old.

JH: All over America, and in the UK, young adults are dis-affiliating from religious institutions and not identifying with organised religion. What's your sense of how the spirituality of the future will look? Do you have any sense of what's unfolding?

Tiokasin: There is a Hopi prophecy, the Prophecy Rock,[2] which shows two potential roads humanity can take. There is the road of technology, which many take, and ultimately disintegrates and goes nowhere, and the road where people stay with the Earth, in harmony with nature. Very few continue to recognise the ancient traditions and stay with this continuous Path of Life.

I don't want to point fingers, but religion plays a part in that. I went to boarding school, and my experience of religions was that they tried to take me away from a native way of thinking and being and feeling, away from who I am, and tried to make me a member

---

2   Near Oraibi, Arizona, a petroglyph known as Prophecy Rock.

of a 'salvation-point mentality' – teaching me that everything else was going to save me except myself. So I forgot personal sovereignty, wasn't taught what freedom is about. One of my elders said that all freedom means is to be responsible. Religion taught me to follow the rules and regulations of an institution. From a native point of view, I could see that chopping down a tree and making a book was not the right thing. I didn't understand it when I was young. Why are you chopping that tree down to make a book – when the tree *is* the book? Is the purpose of that book to lead someone away from nature – or lead them back to the continuum of nature?

Is there room enough in religion to allow other people's ways? Because, of the 220,000 organised religions in the world, all of those are dogmatic. But there's only *one* spirituality. And I think that's what we're seeking in America.

There's another prophecy that says the new people that came here begin to understand that the DNA within the land is filled with native people's bones and ashes and prayers and contemplations. And now the plants, and the animals who eat the plants here on this side of the world, are full of those aspirations, those prayers. The DNA of our people has become a part of the Americans that are here. And the younger people are waking up with the consciousness of the native people. I think that's what the young people are finding out – that there is not *religion*. In our languages, in our cultures, we don't even have a word for religion.

> "Of the 220,000 organised religions in the world, all of those are dogmatic. But there's only *one* spirituality. And I think that's what we're seeking in America."

I think that's the ultimate consciousness to have. Does it really matter what we as human beings are doing? Or do we just matter to ourselves? I think that's the backbone of that whole separation from religious institutions. I can't say it's a good thing or a bad thing – that will put me in a mind of discrimination and I'm trying not to come from that mind of judgemental processes.

AFTERWORD

Whatever your age, the central message of this book is the same.

Our world is in crisis. We cannot pursue a meaningful spiritual life except in full relationship with that knowledge. Similarly, our social action will have little impact unless it emerges from a deeper, more transformative place.

Between the lines of this story about Generation Y is another story of what went wrong further upstream, about how so much of our spirituality has been colonised, corrupted, commodified or stagnated. But it is not too late. Every crisis contains an opportunity. The opportunity before us now is to put our egos aside and to rediscover the joy of service – to feel the expanded sense of energy and purpose that comes from knowing ourselves to be part of a vast interconnected universe. To live the lightness and inner strength that comes from surrendering to something beyond ourselves. The freedom that comes from knowing it's not about us.

There is much work to be done embedding an interdependent worldview into how we work and organise and live on this Earth, and in relation with Earth. Soulful, experimental, profoundly fulfilling work. There is work to be done protecting what is sacred, carving out spaces where the tentacles of consumerism cannot reach. Where prayer, silence, ceremony and connection with nature keep us aligned with what is real and true. Where our souls are nourished, and our prayers can nourish the Earth and the inner worlds in reciprocity. This is deep, beautiful, humble work, which needs no special tools or job titles, just simplicity and intention. Lastly, there is work to be done shaping communities, gathering ourselves in living networks, honouring relationship, building bridges, growing in empathy, learning to walk in each other's shoes and love across differences of all kinds. This is heartfelt work that reminds us what it is to be human.

Generation Y are the innovators. They are joining up the dots with a new congruence, synthesising a deeper wholeness than most of us have managed in the past. But there is not one of us who isn't needed in this great work.

Elders – listen to the young people in your communities. Learn from them. Make space for them. They need your support. They also need practical resources, land, funding, mentoring and opportunities to influence.

Young people – know you are seen and valued. Inside you is a blueprint for where and how to live the gifts that are within you. Trust yourself and follow your heart. You are life re-creating itself. You are not alone.

Together we are stepping into the new, responding to a call from within us and beyond us to live our deepest sense of meaning in a new way. As American poet and Jungian psychoanalyst Clarissa Pinkola Estés said, if we are here on the planet today, 'we were made for these times'.[1]

The path ahead will be full of tremendous challenges, but if we approach it asking what we can give, not what we can get, it will bring us fully alive.

You are a part of that story.

---

[1]   From 'A Letter to a Young Activist During Troubled Times': www.mavenproductions. com/letter-to-a-young-activist

ST ETHELBURGA'S CENTRE FOR RECONCILIATION AND PEACE

The tiny medieval church of St Ethelburga sits in the heart of the financial district of London. Originally built in the 15th century, it was destroyed by an IRA bomb that tore the City apart on a Sunday morning in 1993. The church was restored and dedicated to peacemaking and reconciliation through the lens of faith and spirituality. Today the centre is a 'maker of peacemakers', a vibrant hub of change-makers from diverse backgrounds, working in service to a better world.

St Ethelburga's values are embedded in the fabric of the building and its unique history. The destruction and rebirth of the church reminds us of the opportunities for positive change and evolution that lie at the heart of conflict. The life of Ethelburga, a sixth-century abbess and a healer who nursed plague victims, calls us to put our spiritual values into action in times of crisis. A Christian space sitting alongside a Bedouin tent and Islamic-style peace garden demonstrates the power of collaboration across faiths and cultures. And a tiny patch of land that has remained consecrated ground for hundreds of years while the commercial world has grown up around it – this speaks of the urgent need to protect what is sacred – our places of worship, our deepest human values, and also the natural world, which is surely our most endangered sacred space.

Much of St Ethelburga's work focuses on empowering young adults to lead in times of transition. Our programmes include:

- **Dynamic Social Witnessing** – Young people volunteer in refugee camps in Europe and return home to share their story, building empathy for the plight of displaced people, and galvanising others into action.

- **Spiritual Ecology** – Based on the principles of inter-connectedness, reverence for nature, service, stewardship and compassion, this programme works with young leaders from diverse backgrounds to help them inspire their own communities to reawaken a sense of Earth as sacred and bring that together with practical action.

- **Sacred Activists** – Young adults build bridges between faith traditions and cultures, learn from innovative youth-led spaces, share powerful stories of spirituality and social change, and take action together.

- **Reconcilers Together** – Calls emerging Christian leaders to turn their churches into hubs of reconciliation expertise, change the way congregations deal with conflict, and offer a peace-making function for their wider local communities.

For more information see https://stethelburgas.org

YOUNG SACRED ACTIVIST OF THE YEAR AWARD

Which young leader in your networks deserves recognition? Who inspires you or is doing something a bit special that you think more people should know about?

If someone you know aged 18–35 is making an unusual contribution in the area of social justice, environmental action, peacemaking or community building, and grounds their social action in spirituality, we can give them a boost.

You can nominate them for the Young Sacred Activist of the Year Award, which comes with a cash prize equivalent to 15–20 per cent of the annual income generated by this book.

Visit https://stethelburgas.org/projects/young-sacred-activist-of-the-year-award/ to find out how to nominate (and yes, you can nominate yourself!).

RESOURCES

Reading list

Becoming Wise: An Inquiry into the Mystery and the Art of Living, Krista Tippett (Corsair, 2016)

Do It Anyway: The New Generation of Activists, Courtney E. Martin (Beacon Press, 2010)

Occupy Spirituality: A Radical Vision for a New Generation, Adam Bucko and Matthew Fox (North Atlantic Books, 2013)

On the Brink of Everything: Grace, Gravity, and Getting Old, Parker J. Palmer (Berrett-Koehler Publishers, 2018)

Speaking of Faith: Why Religion Matters — and How to Talk About It, Krista Tippett (Penguin Books, Reprint 2008)

Spiritual Activism: Leadership As Service, Alastair McIntosh and Matt Carmichael (Green Books, 2015)

Spiritual Ecology: The Cry of the Earth, a Collection of Essays, Llewellyn Vaughan-Lee (Golden Sufi Center, 2013)

The New Monasticism: An Interspiritual Manifesto for Contemplative Living, Adam Bucko and Rory McEntee (Orbis, 2015)

We Rise: The Earth Guardians Guide to Building a Movement That Restores the Planet, Xiuhtezcatl Martinez and Justin Spizman (Rodale Books, 2017)

The following reports from a project at Harvard Divinity School initiated in 2015 were published jointly by Harvard Divinity School, Fetzer Institute and On Being with Krista Tippett under the label 'How We Gather' and can be found at www.howwegather.org/reports

Care of Souls, Casper ter Kuile, Angie Thurston and Sue Phillips

December Gathering, Casper ter Kuile, Angie Thurston and Sue Phillips

Faithful, Casper ter Kuile, Angie Thurston, Sue Phillips, Lisa Greenwood and Gil Rendle

How We Gather, Angie Thurston and Casper ter Kuile

Something More, Angie Thurston and Casper ter Kuile